Great Stories from Westerly's Past

The A.F. Kinney and Son Grocery Store on Beach Street, June 1910
(Photo: Westerly Historical Society)

Great Stories from Westerly's Past

Zachary J. Garceau

Westerly Historical Society
2021

First Printing: 2021

ISBN 978-1-312-38407-1

Westerly Historical Society
P.O. Box 91
Westerly, RI, 02891

www.westerlyhistoricalsociety.org

To Anna,
Thank you for always supporting my crazy endeavors and helping me do what I love.

To Mom and Dad,
Thank you for helping me to get where I am today and for always being there when I need you most.

Contents

Acknowledgements

I would like to thank the following people who helped to bring this book to fruition:

Nina Wright of the Westerly Public Library: Thank you for all your assistance in my research efforts and for always helping me to find exactly what I am looking for.

Ed Liguori: Thank you for all the ideas you provided and for spending time talking about the history of our town with me.

The Westerly Historical Society: Thank you for making the publication of this book possible and for providing me with the resources to bring these stories to life.

Ann Smith: Thank you for your invaluable help with reviewing and editing this _entire_ book for me.

Preface

All the articles contained in this book possess two common threads. The first is that they analyze monumental facets of the history of Westerly. Although I was born and raised in Westerly, I can readily admit that it was not until I was in college at the University of Rhode Island that I first realized my love of history, and it was shortly after that discovery that I also found a passion for local history. Through a chance meeting between my wife, Anna, and Maria Bernier, the Secretary of the Westerly Historical Society, I became the Society's archivist in 2016. Ever since that time, I have been fascinated by the stories of Westerly's past, many of which I had been unaware until recently. Many of the narratives that are presented in this volume were discovered often by accident. As is often the case, when reading about one topic, I would inevitably come across a name of a person or place that piqued my interest and I was off to find out more. I hope that the stories you are about to read will produce similar results.

The second common thread in all of the stories in the pages that follow is that they are as much about the people as they are about the places, events, and environment. Without the people in these stories, Westerly, quite simply, would not be the place that it is today. While these figures from the past cannot tell their tales to today's audience, it is my goal through this book to make their stories known. All of the pieces found in this work were made possible because someone, at some time, left behind records, firsthand accounts, and personal documents which were used as the basis of my research.

While there are more than sixty individual vignettes across the chapters of this book, there are also several stories which, although fascinating, were simply not able to be presented in this book. Many potential stories had to be shelved either due to the absence of credible evidence to warrant their inclusion, a lack of time to fully research their background, or in some cases, both. Still, these topics are of great interest and, for this reas--on, they deserve a brief mention.

The first concerns a guitar played by the famed singer-songwriter Richie Havens. It is a well-known fact that Havens played guitars made by the Guild Company throughout his career including the guitar he played during his set which opened Woodstock in August 1969. For many years, I have found myself wondering if the guitar Richie Havens played at Woodstock was built in Guild's factory in Westerly, where they made their home for more than three decades. Unfortunately, verifying this possibility has proven quite challenging. Although I have reached out to a man who claims to know the person who later owned the guitar, all attempts to reach them as of the time of this writing have been unsuccessful. While it is quite possible the first guitar to be played onstage at Woodstock was handcrafted in Westerly, this is sadly an unconfirmed theory until further research can be conducted.

In the first half of the nineteenth century, there was a man who resided in Westerly by the name of David Wilbur. In *Westerly and Its Witnesses*, Reverend Frederic Denison claims that Wilbur was a recluse who resided in forests of the town and was known for being eccentric, having earned the nickname of "the wild man." Wilbur supposedly died in the late 1840's at about seventy years of age and although Denison does recount several notable aspects of Wilbur's personality and demeanor, there is no mention of where this information was derived and records of the life of David Wilbur are virtually nonexistent.

Perhaps, one day, time and the discovery of new source material may allow for a worthwhile analysis of these stories, but until then....

Introduction

Over the past three and a half centuries, the town of Westerly, Rhode Island has developed many stories that have been passed down through generations. The accounts published in this collection tell the stories of people who lived remarkable lives as well as those whose times were fairly ordinary aside from a particularly remarkable event. Also found among the pieces collected in this volume are tales of places in Westerly both past and present that have played a substantial role in shaping the town's history.

This collection starts with a series of pieces documenting the early history of Westerly, including the earliest known account of European exploration of Rhode Island, a comprehensive history of Misquamicut across the years, and the possible origins of Westerly's name.

The second chapter is a series documenting the history behind the murals painted on walls throughout downtown Westerly. These stories provide context for understanding the scenes depicted in the fantastically designed murals.

Following that series, there are accounts of several historic events that took place in Westerly as well as descriptions of several worldwide events and how they were celebrated within the town. The latter group includes Westerly's commemoration of the American Centennial in 1876, the observance of the Christmas season across the years, and New Year's celebrations in 1900 and 2000.

As previously noted, there are also multiple profiles of notable people who were born in or spent a part of their life in Westerly. Many of these individuals may not be known outside of southwestern Rhode Island, but they are remembered fondly by locals who knew them. There are tales of survivors of major disasters including the sinking of the *Titanic* and the Hurricane of 1938 as well as champions of the important cause of the abolition of slavery.

While a legacy of success in sports may not be the first thing that comes to mind when anyone thinks of Westerly, there are multitudes of stories worthy of attention that are highlighted within Chapter V. Whether one prefers baseball, football, or even professional wrestling, there is a story for everyone.

For those seeking a record of one of Westerly's more salacious incidents, the accounts in Chapter VI are highly recommended. There, readers will find stories of murder and arson alongside depictions of prominent Rhode Island politicians and important presidential elections.

Businesses and organizations form the cornerstone of the community in Westerly, which is exactly why one will find a plethora of detailed stories recounting the history of many of the town's most prominent institutions. No discussion of Westerly's past would be complete without a series on the various entertainment venues and the people who performed in their hallowed halls, and for this reason, these same discussions conclude this work.

With this, I hope you enjoy these great stories from Westerly's past.

- Zachary J. Garceau
  August 2021

Chapter I
The First Two Centuries, 1524 to 1700

Due in large part to the absence of a written record of the period prior to European colonization of the land that is now Westerly, much of what is known about this area begins at the time of the Misquamicut Purchase on 29 June 1660. This is not to say, however, that there were not any events worth noting that occurred on this land before 1660. Quite the opposite is true, in fact. This area was almost certainly home to Indigenous Peoples for many centuries before the agreement between Chief Sosoa and the cohort of white men from Newport. The story of these Peoples, both before the Misquamicut Purchase and in the three and a half centuries since then, could likely fill an entire volume on its own.

The following chapter is a series of stories documenting the history of the town of Westerly (and in some cases, the State of Rhode Island) leading up to the year 1700.

The first story presented is an account of the visit of Giovanni da Verrazzano to Rhode Island in 1524. While Verrazzano is not thought to have set foot on any land that is now Westerly, his voyage is a key starting point as it presents what may be the first encounter between Indigenous Peoples of Rhode Island and European explorers.

Also in this chapter is an abridged version of the history of Misquamicut over the last three centuries. This account spans from the Misquamicut Purchase in 1660 up to the present time and chronicles three distinct eras.

Another piece found in this chapter challenges the commonly held beliefs about the origins of Westerly's name. While it is almost certain that the common-sense explanation that the town's name is based on its geographical position is accurate, there may have been another factor that was considered.

These accounts and the others within this chapter form just a small portion of the larger history of Westerly before the year 1700.

The Various Names of Westerly's Past

Over the last four centuries, the town of Westerly has been known by a number of different names. Below are just some of the names the used to identify the community.

Ascoamacot- One of the many variations of the spelling of Misquamicut that has been used over time.

Ascomicutt- first seen in a petition to the Rhode Island General Assembly on 27 August 1661. The variation, **Ascomacut**, was also used on occasion.

Haversham- the name of the town was very briefly changed to Haversham in 1685.

Misquamicut- the most common modern spelling of the beach community, this name was used for the entire tract of land that included Westerly as well as several other towns.

Mishquomacuk- a spelling used by Roger Williams in a testimony dated 18 June 1682.

Michquamicuk

Mishquamicuk- found in the affirmation of the ownership of land by Wawaloam, wife of Miatonomy, dated 25 June 1661.

Musquamacuk- A variation of the name listed above.

Squomacuk, Squamicut, Squammicott- These three names were variations of Misquamicut that were used at times.

Westerly, Westerle- The spelling 'Westerle' appears in modern accounts, but has not been found in seventeenth century documents.

Giovanni da Verrazzano, *La Dauphine*, and the Discovery of Narragansett Bay

"Found it as pleasant as I can possibly describe, and suitable for every kind of cultivation…"

The land that is now the State of Rhode Island was first settled by Europeans in July 1621, however, this was not the first time that non-indigenous groups had visited and spent time in the area. That distinction belongs to Giovanni da Verrazzano and the crew of *La Dauphine* who explored the area in 1524 and spent fifteen days with members of the Narragansett and Wampanoag Tribes, leaving behind a detailed account of their journey for future generations.

While no official record of his birth has been found, the consensus among scholars and historians is that Giovanni da Verrazzano was born in Val di Greve in the Republic of Florence c. 1485.[1] Although much is known about his travels due in large part to the extensive and highly detailed logs of his journeys, relatively little is known about Verrazzano's life. Around the age of twenty-one, Verrazzano settled in the French port of Dieppe and began his career as an explorer.[2] In 1523, upon the request of Francis I, King of France, and with the financial support of banks in Lyons and Rouen, Verrazzano set sail for the New World with a fleet of four ships.[3]

After violent weather caused the loss of two ships, the two that remained, *La Dauphine* and *La Normande* were forced to return to France. The ships launched once again in the final weeks of 1523, however, further issues forced *La Normande* to return to France once more and *La Dauphine* finally departed from Portugal on 17 January 1524.[4]

The one ship which survived the journey to North America, *La Dauphine*, was built at the Royal Dockyard in Le Havre, Normandy, France in 1518. The vessel could hold fifty men and was named after the Dauphin of France, Francis III, Duke of Brittany, heir to the French throne.[5] During the 1524 expedition, *La Dauphine* was piloted by Antoine de Conflans.[6]

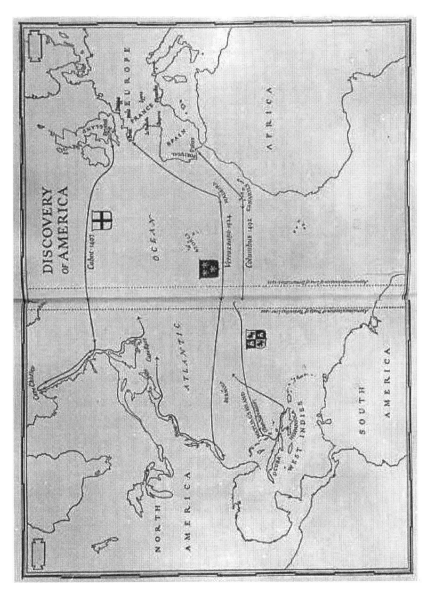

A Map of Verrazzano's Voyage, 1524.
(Photo: Library of Congress, Anthony Angel Collection)

La Dauphine first encountered North America when it reached Cape Fear in modern-day North Carolina at the beginning of March. In a letter to the King of France, Verrazzano stated that he believed Pamlico Sound on the Carolina coast was the beginning of the Pacific Ocean.[7] That the landscape of the continent was unknown is apparent, given that Verrazzano did not notice the entrances to the Chesapeake Bay or the mouth of the Delaware River, and he mistakenly believed the entrance to the Hudson River was a large lake.[8] After moving up the Atlantic coast and sailing along Long Island, *La Dauphine* ventured past a triangular island, now known as Block Island, which reminded him of the Isle of Rhodes in Greece.[9] In his letter to Francis I, the explorer wrote:

"We discovered a triangular-shaped island, ten leagues from the mainland, similar in size to the island of Rhodes; it was full of hills, covered in trees, and highly populated to judge by the fires we saw burning continually along the shore."[10]

It has since been speculated that Roger Williams, a well-read scholar, was aware of Verrazzano's journey and may have interpreted the account as Verrazzano naming Aquidneck Island instead of Block Island and hence, Aquidneck Island became "Rode Island."[11] Despite describing Block Island as similar to Rhodes, Verrazzano actually named the island in honor of the King's mother, Aloysia.[12]

After passing Block Island, where *La Dauphine* encountered unfavorable weather, they entered Narragansett Bay where they were greeted by a gathering of Wampanoag and Narragansett people. Once the ship crossed into the bay, it was surrounded by nearly twenty canoes holding Native Americans "uttering various cries of wonderment" who guided the ship to land.[13] Verrazzano anchored *La Dauphine* in present-day Newport Harbor (much debate has been brought about regarding the exact location of the ship's landing) and the crew stayed among the Wampanoag People for fifteen days.[14] During this extended stay, the crew explored the land at length, venturing as far as thirty miles and reaching plains in what is now Pawtucket, Rhode Island.[15]

Giovanni da Verrazzano left lengthy and comprehensive depictions of the Native Americans who welcomed him in Rhode Island, providing historians with a plethora of information. It must be noted, however, that the available information regarding this encounter is available entirely from only one side. While it is known how Verrazzano regarded the Indigenous

Peoples he interacted with, it is not known how those same Peoples felt about the visiting Europeans.

According to his depiction of the first encounter, those he encountered stared at the ship in wonder and "all together they raised a loud cry which meant that they were joyful." In comparing the various Tribes he encountered on his journey, Verrazzano claimed "these people are the most beautiful and have the most civil customs that we have found on this voyage."[16]

Verrazzano also noted that the Wampanoags were generally uninterested in the items which were highly prized by the Europeans, writing: "They did not appreciate cloth of silk and gold, nor even of any other kind, nor did they care to have them; the same was true for metals like steel and iron, for many times when we showed them some of our arms, they did not admire them, nor ask for them, but merely examined the workmanship." The explorer often spoke highly of the individuals he came across in Rhode Island, proclaiming that "they are very generous and give away all they have." Perhaps most interestingly, he also noted that "they live a long time, and rarely fall sick; if they are wounded, they cure themselves with fire without medicine; their end comes with old age."[17]

Giovanni da Verrazzano's descriptions of the interior land which would later be known as Rhode Island also provided the earliest recorded glimpse of the future state's landscape. According to his retelling of their explorations, the crew often traveled five to six leagues inland (fifteen to eighteen miles) and "found it as pleasant as I can possibly describe, and suitable for every kind of cultivation grain, wine, or oil. For there the fields extend for twenty-five to thirty leagues (seventy-five to ninety miles); they are open and free of any obstacles or trees, and so fertile that any kind of seed would produce excellent crops."[18] Perhaps Verrazzano's favorable depiction of the topography of the land inspired future explorations.

After *La Dauphine*'s fifteen day stay in Rhode Island, the ship continued its trip up the North American coast where Verrazzano traveled along Cape Cod Bay, a fact which was proven in the form of a map from 1529 which clearly shows the outline of Cape Cod.[19] The crew then continued their journey northward along the coast of modern-day Maine, Nova Scotia, and Newfoundland, at which time they began the long expedition back to Europe. *La Dauphine* returned to France by 8 July 1524.

Despite his achievements and the notoriety they brought Verrazzano, the explorer's fate after 1524 is ultimately unknown. In fact, there are several conflicting accounts of how his life came to an end. One version suggests that during a subsequent visit to North America in 1528, Verrazzano made stops on several islands, including, perhaps Guadeloupe, where he anchored and rowed ashore. It is said that Verrazzano was killed and eaten by the native Caribs while his fleet, who were anchored out of gunshot range, could not prevent his death.[20] Older historical accounts, however, speculate that Verrazzano was actually the same person as Jean Fleury who was executed for Piracy in Puerto del Pico, Spain.[21] Although the details of his life and death after 1524 are not entirely clear, it is largely believed that Giovanni da Verrazzano was the first European to have explored Rhode Island.

In 1975, the Rhode Island Legislature acknowledged Verrazzano's voyage, passing a law to proclaim April 21 as Dauphine Day, "in honor of the arrival of the "Dauphine" to Rhode Island in 1524."[22]

A statue of Giovanni da Verrazzano in Battery Park, New York City
(Photo: Library of Congress, Anthony Angel Collection)

The Three Histories of Misquamicut, 1632 - Present

"The purchasers of this land are said to have settled on it starting in 1661. The entirety of the purchase included much of what is today Westerly, Richmond, Hopkinton, and Charlestown."

In any discussion about the history and settlement of Westerly, the most evident starting point is the Misquamicut Purchase of 1660. With the purchase of a large tract of land known as Ascomacut or Mishquamicuk, the groundwork was laid for the founding of Westerly.[23]

The Pioneer Era, 1632-1894

While the earliest history of Misquamicut is largely uncertain due in large part to the absence of written records, it is believed that prior to the year 1632, the land was settled by the Pequot Tribe. Between 1632 and 1635, a war was waged between the Pequots and the Narragansett Tribe led by Canonicus, his nephew Miantonomoh, and Chief Sosoa. In victory, the Narragansetts took control of the land which was eventually known as Misquamicut.[24] As a token of appreciation for Sosoa's service in the Tribal War, he was granted land totaling more than 20,000 acres.

On 26 August 1635 a devastating hurricane, perhaps even more destructive than the famed Hurricane of 1938, struck New England. There are no known written accounts of this storm in southern Rhode Island, but it almost certainly ravaged what little existed in Misquamicut. Modern data suggests the storm made landfall near Westerly around 5 a.m. on the 26th. According to an account of the storm in the Massachusetts Bay Colony by John Winthrop, waves more than fourteen feet higher than usual struck the shores of Providence, and therefore, it is likely that Westerly was hit hard as well.[25]

On 29 June 1660, Chief Sosoa sold the land comprising Misquamicut and its environs to a company of men from Newport who intended to settle upon the land. The deed was signed by five white men, Jeremy, Latham, and

Henry Clarke, George Webb, and George Gardiner.[26] On 25 June 1661, Miantonomoh's wife, Wawaloam, provided a deposition affirming that Sosoa was granted the land, confirming his right to sell the land. The purchase, which covered a span roughly ten miles wide by twenty miles long, was then divided into eighteen shares. The purchasers of this land began settling in Westerly on 1 September 1661 when the first of the purchasers is believed to have arrived.[27] The entirety of the purchase included much of what is today Westerly, Richmond, Hopkinton, and Charlestown.

The land that is today known as Misquamicut had a fairly unremarkable history over the next two centuries. According to one history of that area, from 1661 to 1894: "whites cultivated the land in the rear of the shore and prospered."[28] Virtually nothing else is known about Misquamicut during the eighteenth and most of the nineteenth centuries.

The Pleasant View Era, 1894-1928

By the late nineteenth century, Misquamicut was little more than land for cultivation and home to few permanent residents. That all changed in 1894, when a prominent local man named Courtland B. Bliven realized the natural beauty of Misquamicut and foresaw its potential as a summer resort. That same year, Bliven constructed the first cottage in the area and named it 'Pioneer.'[29] Bliven's wife, Eugenia (Lamphere) Bliven, also contributed to the area's history by giving it the name Pleasant View, a moniker it would retain for the next thirty-four years.[30]

The construction of homes in the area was initially somewhat slow. According to a map dated 1895, there were only seven cottages on Atlantic Avenue in Pleasant View. At that time, it appears that the road was a relatively short one, extending between the intersection of Crandall Avenue and Narragansett Beach (later Misquamicut State Beach) before ending abruptly.[31] Between 1894 and 1903, twenty-eight cottages were built in the area, an average of more than three per year.[32]

The Pleasant View Post Office, Early Twentieth Century
(Photo: Westerly Historical Society)

In 1903, Pleasant View saw the completion of its first hotel, the Pleasant View House, which was built by James Collins.[33] The hotel was initially torn down in 1917 and rebuilt shortly thereafter. This second building survived for over two decades until it was irreparably damaged by the Hurricane of 1938. A third version of the hotel eventually opened once again in 1940.[34] In 1904, C. B. Bliven, the man who started the migration to Pleasant View in 1894, opened Pleasant View's second hotel, the Wigwam. This hotel also suffered extensive damage in the Hurricane of 1938. The site later became Paddy's Wigwam and is where Paddy's Beach Club stands today.

Another enduring hotel in Pleasant View is the Andrea, which opened as a guest house named "Hate to Quit It" in 1912 before taking on its current name in 1919. Before St. Clare's Chapel opened, church services were held in the dining room of the Andrea which also contained a library operated by local nuns.[35]

In the days before automobiles were in every driveway, getting to and from Pleasant View could be quite a struggle. That was until December 1911, when the Westerly and Norwich Traction Company extended their trolley line to Pleasant View, giving residents and visitors a direct line from downtown Westerly.[36] In 1922, during the peak season, the Shore Line Electric Railway Company ran hourly from 6:45 a.m. to 10:45 p.m., allowing visitors to spend a full day enjoying all the beach had to offer.[37]

The Wigwam Cottage, Early Twentieth Century
(Photo: Westerly Historical Society)

In 1903, a fifty-foot lot could be purchased for just fifty dollars (approximately $1,450 dollars in 2021).[37] In 1915, the same size lot would cost about $1,000 (approximately $26,000 in 2021). As the area became more developed, the need for public services and utilities grew. In 1908, the United States Post Office Department opened a post office in W.D. Main's grocery store, where it remained until 1914 when it was moved to Winnapaug Grocery.[38] In 1910, Westerly Water Works installed city water in Pleasant View and the following year, Westerly Light and Power Company installed electric street lights.[39] As the summer population of Pleasant View increased with each passing season, so did the variety of local entertainment. In 1911, Atlantic Beach Casino, a roller-skating rink, opened, and it still exists today as the Windjammer.[40]

Growth in the area continued at an exponential rate over the next several years. In 1913, there were 129 buildings listed in the area directory and two years later, that number increased to 145.[41] While the total number of buildings grew by sixteen between 1913 and 1915, this does not account for the several that were damaged in a storm on 2 March 1914, including five cottages that washed up on the beach.[42] By the 1920's, Pleasant View had nearly every type of business that one could ever need including grocers, barbers, bakers, automobile repair, and even an attorney.[43] In 1915, the Pleasant View Fire District was established and in 1926, the company constructed a new firehouse in Post Office Square at the intersection of Atlantic Avenue and Winnapaug Road.[44]

The Misquamicut Era, 1928-Present

On 1 October 1928, at the request of the United States Post Office Department and with a great deal of local support, Pleasant View's name was changed back to the area's original name, Misquamicut.[45] In many ways, this was more than just a name change, but also a sign of a new era. By the end of the 1920's, automobiles were becoming more popular and as a result, Westerly residents could more easily spend a day at the beach without having to invest a great deal of time in travel.

In 1929, another hotel, the Misquamicut House, opened, however, its tenure was relatively short, as the building was one of the many destroyed in the Hurricane of 1938.[46] Throughout the 1930's, Misquamicut persisted as a popular resort destination for visitors and locals alike.

Catastrophe struck in September 1938 when a devastating hurricane ravaged the area. Homes and businesses were destroyed in the storm and a great deal of rebuilding was required. [For a detailed account of this storm, see page 70 in the following chapter.]

Within two years, some of the buildings which were affected by the hurricane including the aforementioned Pleasant View House and St. Clare's Chapel were reopened.[47] Tourism to the beach, like many industries, was curtailed by the onset of World War II. In the post-war era, much remained the same as before the war, with many visitors to the area arriving each summer. Another storm wreaked havoc in 1944, and just sixteen years after the Hurricane of 1938 decimated Misquamicut, a third powerful storm struck. In 1954, Hurricane Carol wiped out nearly all of Misquamicut.

According to one account, more than two hundred cottages were washed away and only two buildings were standing when the storm was over.[48] Another description indicated that Atlantic Avenue was buried in more than one foot of sand.[49] According to some, the damage leveled by Carol exceeded that which was seen in 1938.[50] It would be several years before the area recovered from the storm's violent impact.

(Photo: Westerly Historical Society)

Although Carol's effects were severe, the late 1950's marked the start of positive changes for Misquamicut. In the second half of the decade, efforts to secure a State Beach for Misquamicut were successful. In December 1958, estimates for the cost of the project were given at $600,000 with $112,000 to be contributed by the town of Westerly.[51] In May 1959, ground was broken for the project and the following month, Misquamicut State Beach was officially opened.[52] Now, for the first time, visitors from other states were able to take full advantage of the area's beaches.

The 1960's was a decade of ups and downs for the area. In May 1960, sand fences were constructed in Misquamicut, allowing for the preservation of dunes at the State Beach where many critical species reside.[53] That same year, Misquamicut also suffered a potential environmental disaster when the tanker *P.W. Thirtle* of the Sinclair Refining Company ran aground in Jamestown, Rhode Island, and spilled 339,000 gallons of oil into Narragansett Bay.[54] Within days, reports came in stating that a "thick black scum" was visible as far away as the Pawcatuck River.[55] Eventually, the oil was cleaned up and by the next season, Misquamicut returned to its status as a premier tourist destination. By 1971, a study reported that Rhode Island State Beaches, including Misquamicut, were visited by over one million people each year.[56]

(Photo: Westerly Public Library)

Over the next several decades, Misquamicut continued to be a popular summer destination. In the 1980's and 1990's, Peter Pan Bus Line advertised direct trips to Misquamicut from Western Connecticut and Massachusetts, permitting people throughout the tristate area an opportunity to visit Westerly's beaches.[57] In addition to sun, sand, and surf, the 80's and 90's brought consistent popular entertainment to Misquamicut every summer. During this time, seaside venues featured acts such as Sawyer Brown and John Cafferty and the Beaver Brown Band.[58]

In 2000, the Misquamicut Business Association was formed, and in the years since their founding, they have made Misquamicut an ideal destination for the whole family. Over the last two decades, the MBA has hosted a series of successful events which have drawn a large number of visitors to the area, including Spring Fest, which has been held nearly every year since 2010. In 2012, Misquamicut was struck by Superstorm Sandy, resulting in destruction and devastation to the community. Through the perseverance and dedication of the residents and business owners, Misquamicut has successfully rebounded to return to a wonderful place to visit. Over the last 125 years, Misquamicut has remained a destination for all who seek fun and sun on the Rhode Island shore.

Westerleigh: John Crandall and the Origins of Westerly's Name

"The roots of our town's name can be traced to South Gloucestershire, England, to a village of just four thousand residents by the name of Westerleigh."

How did Westerly get its name? Popular wisdom and common sense both suggest that the name was derived from the town's position as the westernmost point in Rhode Island. Westerly's geographic position almost certainly was the main reason the name was chosen. There is, however, another possible, albeit lesser-known source. The roots of the town's name can be traced to South Gloucestershire, England, to a village of just four thousand residents by the name of Westerleigh.

On 18 May 1669, "a list of the free inhabitants of the towne of westerle" was drafted, and the very first name of the list was John Crandall, an important figure in the early history of Westerly and the first elder of the town's Baptist Society.[59] It has long been known that the first confirmed appearance of John Crandall in Rhode Island was on 8 September 1643 when he served as a grand juror in Newport. On 27 August 1661, Crandall, along with William Vaughan and Hugh Mosher, petitioned the Rhode Island Assembly for support when attempting to settle in the area then known as Misquamicuck. The petition was granted and Crandall remained on the land until he returned to Newport where he died c. 1676.[60]

For nearly sixty years, it was largely believed that John Crandall was from the town of Chepstow, Monmouthshire, Wales, although the support for this theory was considered tenuous. It was not until the mid-1990's when a record for the baptism of John Crandall, son of James Crandall, was found in the village of Westerleigh, just fifteen miles from Chepstow. The surname Crandall is relatively rare in England, and the first known mention is found in the county of Worcestershire. There, a man named Hugh de Crundel was mentioned in a court case dated 8 June 1230. Over time, branches of the family migrated into the counties of Shropshire, Warwickshire, and Gloucestershire, where the surname was recorded variously as Crandell, Crondell, and Crendell.[61]

A Map of Gloucestershire from the Seventeenth Century
(Photo: Library of Congress)

John Crandall's earliest proven ancestor was a man named Edward Crondall who was enumerated on a list of free tenants in the town of Tewkesbury, Gloucestershire in 1539 and 1540. [62] Edward is believed to have had a son, Nicholas Crundall (born c. 1525), who served as the parish clerk of Tewkesbury. This Nicholas Crundall had a son, Nicholas (born c. 1555) who married a woman named Elizabeth. Nicholas and Elizabeth had a son, James (1589-1662), who had a wife named Eleanor. James Crundall was recorded among Westerleigh residents in manorial books as early as 1624, although he likely was living there by 1617, when his son, John, was born there. James' son, John Crandall, was almost certainly the same man who was later a founder of Westerly, Rhode Island. [63]

The hometown of John Crandall has a history which extends back more than eleven centuries. The village of Westerleigh was first mentioned in Anglo-Saxon documents in 887 BCE. By the year 1086, several of the surrounding communities were recorded in the Domesday Book, a survey of England ordered by William the Conqueror. The largest nearby community at the time was Pucklechurch, which contained fifty-three households and was considered "very large."[64] It was Westerleigh's relationship to Pucklechurch which inspired its name, as 'ley' or 'leigh' signifies the 'up-hill pasture' which was west of the main settlement.[65] The church of St. James the Great in Westerleigh village was consecrated on 16 April 1304 and celebrated its seven hundredth anniversary in 2004.[66]

At the start of the seventeenth century, the village was thriving, as it was home to numerous businesses including "a shoemaker, a blacksmith, a sawyer, a flour mill, a malt house and two public houses, both brewing their own beer."[67] In 1660, coal was discovered in Westerleigh and the surrounding communities. For the next several centuries, coal mining was the most common source of employment for residents. This continued until the 1930's when the local supply of coal was exhausted and many of the mines were closed. Although it remained relatively small throughout the nineteenth century, Westerleigh was often featured in railroad atlases, as it served as a junction where the Great Western Railroad (which ran east to west) and the Midlands Railroad (which ran north to south) met.[68] Tragedy befell the church of St. James the Great in 1863, when the building was struck by lightning and caught fire destroying much of the original architecture, which was subsequently rebuilt.

In 1876, there were still numerous businesses and professions in the village including: "farmers, a bootmaker, shopkeepers, innkeepers, butchers, a plasterer, a blacksmith, a wheelwright, a market gardener and a carrier."[69] By the turn of the century, many of these trades began to die out and a number of the old houses in Westerleigh were demolished. Early in the twentieth century, the railroad and coal mining provided much of the work for locals, but in recent years, residents have found employment in the nearby communities of Yate and Bristol.[70] While few know of the connections between Westerly, Rhode Island and the village of Westerleigh, the historic English village likely provided our town with not only its name, but also one of its founding fathers.

The Lewis-Card-Perry House: An 18th-Century Home and a 21st-Century Treasure

"The use of building materials contemporaneous to the house's origins from these local historic homes allowed the Perrys to create a historically accurate eighteenth-century home in the twentieth century."

Of all the streets in Westerly, perhaps none represents the town's history and beauty quite like Margin Street. Directly across from the Pawcatuck River lies the Perry Homestead District, a stretch of seven lots between Margin and Beach Streets containing some of Westerly's most iconic houses. Within the district sits the Lewis-Card-Perry House, a home that has been standing for more than three hundred years with a truly fascinating history.

The exact year that the Lewis-Card-Perry House was built is unknown, although it may have been built as early as 1700.[71] The house was originally constructed for John Lewis (1658-1735), one of Westerly's earliest settlers.[72] What is certain, however, is that the home was built at some point during the early eighteenth century, and around 1730, an addition on the house's north end (the parlor) was erected.[73]

The provenance of the house during the eighteenth century is largely unknown. It is known, however, that in 1805, Asa Nash purchased the property from Samuel Brown. At that time, there was both a dwelling and a store on the property. A man named Clark Edwards then purchased the property at a sheriff's sale in 1818. After that time, the house was also owned by Jonathan Nash, William Peckham, Samuel A. Coy, Ray G. Burlingame, Silas Greenman, Captain Oliver Gavitt, and eventually his daughter, Mary A. Gavitt.[74] In 1868, Captain William Card purchased the home from Mary A. Gavitt.[75] At some time during the nineteenth century, the house was believed to have been expanded to two rooms, with space added behind the chimney along the rear. Unfortunately, by the turn of the next century, the house had fallen into disrepair. In 1905, the south end of the home was demolished.[76]

As a result, the chimney, which was once in the center of the house, came to form the rear wall.

In 1919, the house was purchased by Charles Perry from the heirs of Captain Card. The following year, Perry began a series of renovations to the home that included adding a bathroom, a closet, and repairing the floors and walls.[77] In 1929, the house passed by bequest to Charles' son, Harvey Chace Perry (1881-1978). Harvey C. Perry was a well-known man in Westerly, serving as director of the Washington Trust Company, while also remaining active in the Westerly Historical Society, the Westerly Public Library, the Westerly Hospital, and the YMCA, among other institutions.[78] [For more on Harvey C. Perry's role in Washington Trust, see page 293.]

The Lewis-Card-Perry House
(Photo by Author)

That year was a pivotal year in the house's history, as it was the year in which major restorations began. The work was largely undertaken by noted architect and scholar Norman Morrison Isham (1864-1943), who was responsible for various remarkable renovations on historic structures in Rhode Island including the Babcock Smith House in Westerly, Old

Narragansett Church and Smith's Castle in Wickford, Trinity Church and the Colony House in Newport, and the Eleazer Arnold House in Lincoln.[79]

Norman M. Isham was a proponent of the Colonial Revival movement which originated in the mid-nineteenth century. The movement became more popular as the American Centennial of 1876 [For more on the American Centennial, see page 99.] approached, as there was an eagerness to celebrate the homes and workplaces of America's earliest settlers. For this reason, Isham was considered the ideal candidate for this project. Isham authored the work *Early Rhode Island Houses*, considered a groundbreaking source for understanding colonial homes in the state. Isham personally examined and surveyed every house cataloged in his tome which put emphasis on scientific and historically accurate data.[80]

Isham's work on the Lewis-Card-Perry House produced an artfully restored five-room home. The most intriguing features of the residence are its materials which were acquired from a variety of historic houses in the local area.

One of the local homes which contributed materials to the restoration was the Kenyon House, an early eighteenth-century home in Hopkinton, which was the source of the wide, beveled wall and floor boards for the revamped front hall. Additional wallboards were also procured from the Swan House in North Stonington. Wood paneling and framing elements were obtained from the Copp Mansion of Stonington, believed to have been built before 1720 and those which could not be taken from the Copp Mansion were reproduced to match. Floor joists were procured from the Minor House in North Stonington. By the time the restoration was complete, materials had been obtained from thirteen different homes.[81] The use of building materials contemporaneous to the house's origins from these local historic homes allowed the Perrys to create a historically accurate eighteenth-century home in the twentieth century.

Today, the house is a one-and-a-half story Cape style home with a center chimney and contains two-panel doors, historic iron hardware and wide floorboards which are contemporary to the house's initial construction. The home sits on a granite foundation and is covered by a wood-shingled roof centered around the original stone chimney. Isham's work was a contributing factor in the home being added to the National Register of Historic Places, signifying its historical merit, in 2005.[82] Today, the Lewis-

Card-Perry House stands as a representation of both an eighteenth-century home and the ability of restoration architects to recreate and restore a more than two-century-old home in the early twentieth century.

Chapter II
The Bricks and Murals Series

In 2017, several local groups came together in collaboration with the nationally-known organization, Bricks and Murals, to develop the Bricks and Murals project. This ambitious venture resulted in the creation of seventeen murals throughout downtown Westerly.

The murals that were created tell the stories of some of Westerly's most momentous events, important citizens, and valuable ideas. The series that follows is a collection of twelve articles providing context for the history behind several of the murals.

Some of the articles in the following chapter offer unique takes on the stories behind these murals as a way to shine a light on otherwise little-known tales. One such offering is the analysis of how the Pawcatuck River came to serve as the border between Rhode Island and Connecticut. While this is not the story explicitly told in the Pawcatuck River mural, it is one that focuses on the river as a catalyst for a key episode in local history.

Another piece in the following chapter is rather unique for this collection as it is a list of the top ten Thanksgiving Day football games between Westerly and Stonington. Once again, this is not the specific focus of the mural highlighting the Westerly-Stonington rivalry, but anyone who attended either school will tell you that the Turkey Day games are the premiere event of each football season for the two towns.

One other narrative which differs in some ways from the image depicted on the mural is the story of the former village of Stillmanville. The mural celebrating Westerly and Pawcatuck's industrial history does not single out a particular mill or area within either town, however, Stillmanville was such an inextricable part of the industrial story that it is certainly worthy of being highlighted.

The memories that inspired each mural are, at their core, significant portions of the larger history of the town of Westerly. Many of these accounts offer a detailed look into the very heart of Westerly.

A final note to the reader, in some of the articles that follow, a description of the location of the murals in question is given. These descriptions are based on businesses and buildings which were present at the time of this writing in 2021. In true Rhode Island fashion, the landmarks cited in this chapter may change over time.

The Train Kept A Rollin': Westerly, Railroads, and the Blues

"Westerly's first train station opened for business on 10 November 1837, and ever since the first train pulled into the station, they've continued to run through the town for the more than 180 years."

The following story will discuss two murals, the first is dedicated to the New York, New Haven and Hartford Railroad and can be seen from the Amtrak station in Westerly and the second mural celebrates the history of the Knickerbocker Music Center and can be found on the side of the Knickerbocker building.

The railroad revolutionized transportation in the United States and when one considers the impact that trains have had on Westerly, this statement certainly appears to be true. Westerly's first train station opened for business on 10 November 1837, and ever since the first train pulled into the station, they've continued to run through the town for the more than 180 years.[1]

When the first Westerly station opened in 1837, it was incorporated as part of the newly built Stonington and Providence Railroad which ran between Hill's Wharf in Providence and Stonington Village.[2] In 1892, the Stonington and Providence Company was purchased by the New York, New Haven, and Hartford Railroad Company, the operator of the train depicted in the mural.

For the first time, citizens of Westerly could easily travel to and from Providence with relative ease. In 1846, a direct line was established between Providence and Boston, allowing Westerly residents to travel to Boston faster than ever before.[3] Despite the convenience these trains provided, they had a severely limited schedule, with only three passenger trains, one mail train, and one freight train leaving Westerly daily in 1857 (as compared to the twenty-one that stopped in Westerly in 1890 or the thirty-three that made stops daily by 1904).[4]

A Train in Westerly
(Photo: Westerly Historical Society)

After thirty-five years of service, the original Westerly train station was closed, and a new station was opened in 1872. The original station building was relocated and used as a freight facility.[5] The year 1889 was crucial for the railroad in Westerly, as the Thames River Railroad Bridge was completed, and thus, an all-rail link between Boston and New York City was completed.[6] This allowed Westerly residents to travel between the two cities and made Westerly a hub for urban travelers.

In 1892, the Stonington and Providence Railroad was acquired by the New York, New Haven and Hartford Railroad.[7] The Railroad, commonly known as 'the Consolidated' or 'the New Haven,' was the dominant force in transportation through southern New England by the turn of the twentieth century.[8] In addition to controlling train travel between Boston and New York, the company also controlled most of the area's steamships and streetcars.[9] The railroad's ability to overtake its competition was due in large part to the financial support of one of its chief investors, J.P. Morgan.[10]

The Westerly station continued to serve as a crucial stop along the line between the area's two largest metropolises, and for this reason, a new station was proposed for Westerly as early as 1899. It was not until 1911, however, that these plans came to fruition. The development of a new station on Railroad Avenue required several crucial steps which shaped the physical landscape of the town.

Railroad Avenue
(Photo: Westerly Historical Society)

The 1911 plan proposed purchasing and removing all of the houses on Dixon Hill, reshaping the hill to the railroad grade, tearing down the Armour and Company Meat Packing building and constructing a new site on Canal Street, realigning Friendship Street further to the north, and doubling the size of the West and High Street bridges.[11] These proposals were accepted, and the station opened in 1913. When the station opened, the first customer was Col. A.E. Dick, a summer resident, and the manager of the Watch Hill House.[12]

The 1913 train station still stands on Railroad Avenue today, with relatively few changes over the last century. In 1950, the Leatherbee Company of Brookline, Massachusetts made an offer to purchase the station and transform it into retail space, but public outcry resulted in the railroad rejecting the offer in 1952.[13] In 1969, the Penn Central Railroad assumed ownership of the New Haven company and maintained the line through Westerly until 1976, when the United States Congress created Amtrak, which assumed ownership of all of Penn Central's assets.[14] To this day, Amtrak holds ownership of the Westerly railroad station and operates several trains which run through the town every day.

Directly across from the railroad tracks, you'll find the Knickerbocker Music Center, known locally as 'The Knick.' The music club, which opened in 1933, is said to be named for the Knickerbocker train, that ran through Westerly, right outside the club's doors.[15] The only known train named the Knickerbocker which was operating in 1933 ran between New York City and Boston via Albany, and therefore, would not have passed through Westerly.[16] There was a train which ran from New York City to Boston via Providence in 1933 on the New Haven Railroad, however, this train was named the Merchants Limited.[17]

Despite this, it is clear that the railroad had a big impact on the club, as train passengers disembarked on Railroad Avenue, with the club only yards away, making it a popular stop for visitors and locals alike. Over the years, the venue has hosted a number of popular Blues and Jazz musicians, including "Big Joe Turner, Albert Collins, Johnny Copeland, Johnny Nicholas, Leon Russell, Eric Burdon and Stevie Ray Vaughan."[18] [For an account of Stevie Ray Vaughan's 1979 concert at the Knickerbocker, see page 342.]

Perhaps the most well-known band to play the Knick on a regular basis is Westerly's own Roomful of Blues. Since forming in 1967, Roomful of Blues has experienced a great deal of success, garnering five Grammy nominations and seven Blues Music Awards, including a victory in the Blues Band of the Year Category in 2005.[19]

The band maintained a consistent Sunday night gig at the Knickerbocker for many years, continuing to build their local and national fanbase.[20] Over the last five decades, the band has featured more than fifty different musicians and continues to bring new musicians into the fold, while earning praise on the national blues scene.

According to Roomful of Blues founder Duke Robillard, the Knickerbocker was "the hip, trendy place to be."[21] Duke also noted that because the club was close to both Watch Hill and Newport and that affluent visitors would hear about the club and make their way down to Westerly to catch a show.[22]

More recently, the Knickerbocker has shifted its focus, transforming into the Knickerbocker Music Center, partnering with the Rhode Island Philharmonic and Music School. In doing so, they have developed a mission to "preserve, cultivate and grow the "Knick's" unique brand of blues, as well as expanding access to music of all genres, by transforming the Knick into both an exciting performance venue and an exceptional center for music education."[23], [24] Doing so allows the club to continue its tradition of outstanding music, while also helping to develop the musicians of tomorrow.

"Gallant and Meritorious Conduct in Action": James Albert Barber and David Naylor Johnson's Civil War Valor

"Corporal Barber was presented with a Congressional Medal of Honor, the highest possible award for bravery given by the United States Government, as a result of his "gallant and meritorious conduct in action at Petersburg."

On 2 April 1865, twenty soldiers from the 1st Rhode Island Light Artillery Regiment, Company G voluntarily joined in an assaulting party against a troop of Confederate soldiers in Petersburg, Virginia. When all was said and done, the assaulting party had turned the enemy's own guns upon them, neutralizing the threat they posed. Among those Rhode Island Artillerymen was Corporal James Albert Barber, a lifelong Westerly resident.[25] Barber's bravery and valor in this mission did not go unnoticed, as he was awarded a Congressional Medal of Honor on 16 June 1866.[26] Barber's legacy led to the creation of a mural in his honor, allowing his story to be forever preserved in the public consciousness.

James Albert Barber was born in Westerly on 11 July 1841 to Matthew Stillman Barber and his wife, Phoebe Elizabeth (Hall) Barber.[27] On 11 November 1861, at the age of twenty, Barber enlisted in the army seven months after the outbreak of the Civil War and he was assigned to the 1st Rhode Island Light Artillery Regiment, Company G.[28] He saw action at Yorktown, Antietam, Fredericksburg, and the second battle at Gettysburg. Barber's first enlistment was for a three year term and after his first enlistment ended, he reenlisted as a veteran volunteer for another three years, serving until the war's end. On 15 July 1864, Barber was wounded at Petersburg, Virginia and was taken to the General Hospital in Philadelphia until he was able to return to the battlefield on 25 September 1864.[28,29]

On 24 June 1865, after more than three years of service, during which time he attained the rank of Corporal, Barber was mustered out and discharged from his battery.[30] Corporal Barber was presented with a Congressional Medal of Honor, the highest possible award for bravery given by the United States Government, as a result of his "gallant and meritorious conduct in action at Petersburg."[31] After his discharge, Corporal Barber returned to Westerly, where he married his wife, Hannah Josephine Tourgee, on 14 March 1865 and the couple were parents to seven sons.[32]

Known locally as 'Captain Jim Barber,' the Corporal spent his post-service life as a fisherman, a career he had begun before the War. At one time, he served as the captain of the Watch Hill Life Saving Station. Barber worked as fisherman from the end of the Civil War until 1913, at which point he abandoned his chosen profession due to "a scarcity of fish and consequent unprofitableness of the business." For more than fifty years, Captain Jim utilized the same boat that he built by hand at the close of the Civil War. In his obituary, it was said that "he loved the sea and for years made his home on a sloop, the *Triumph*, anchored in Thompson's Cove."[33] Sadly, in 1881, James Barber's wife, Hannah, died at just thirty-four years old. In 1891, Barber was granted a pension for his service during the Civil War. He died in his home on East Avenue on 26 June 1925 and is buried in River Bend Cemetery beneath a stone commemorating his service to his country.[34]

James Albert Barber
(Photo: Westerly Historical Society)

Although he is the only Medal of Honor winner born in Westerly, and the only one commemorated on the newly installed mural, Corp. Barber is not the only recipient of the honor buried in River Bend Cemetery.

Although he was born in Thompsonville, Sullivan, New York on 4 November 1843, David Johnson Naylor spent his post-Civil War life in Potter Hill (just across the town line in Hopkinton) and also was buried in Westerly. David J. Naylor was born to Marcus Naylor, a mill operative who born in Lancashire, England, and his wife, Jeanette. By 1850, the family had removed to Connecticut, settling in the town of Vernon before moving to Enfield in Hartford County.[35]

Grand Army of the Republic Gathering at the Westerly Library, 1908
(Photo: Westerly Historical Society)

On 5 August 1864, Naylor was serving as a Landsman for the Union Navy on-board the *USS Oneida* in Mobile Bay, Alabama. During a battle, Naylor, who was acting as powder boy at a 30-pound Parrott rifle, had his passing box shot out of his hands and knocked overboard. He then jumped overboard to recover the box and returned to his station where he continued his courageous acts, aiding the Union in capturing the Confederate ship

Tennessee and damaging Fort Morgan, Alabama. Naylor was issued his Medal of Honor on 31 December 1864.[36] He continued his service until he was discharged at the end of the war.[37]

After completing his service, David Johnson Naylor settled in southern Rhode Island, being accepted into Grace Church in Westerly on 5 August 1866.[38] On Valentine's Day 1867, Naylor married his wife, Martha Thomas, a Westerly native.[39] That same year, he was initiated as a Mason in Franklin Lodge No. 20 in Westerly, and at the time of his death, he was the oldest surviving member of the Lodge.[40]

In 1870, David, Martha, and their daughter, Sarah A. Naylor, were living in Stonington, where David had found work as a mill-hand.[41] The couple later welcomed two more children, Mark W. Naylor (named after David's father,[42]) born in 1875 and Martha "Mattie" E. Naylor, born in 1878.[43] In 1879, David and his family were residing in Stillmanville where he found work in a local mill. By 1880, David J. Naylor and his family had moved to Potter Hill in Hopkinton, where he would live out the rest of his days, working in mills and as a school custodian.

Naylor actively participated in many veteran's events locally including representing the town of Westerly at a Gettysburg demonstration on the battle's fiftieth anniversary and joining the John A. Logan post of the Grand Army of the Republic society. He was also active in the planning of Westerly's Memorial Day exercises, being named to a committee to plan such events in 1916.[44]

David Johnson Naylor succumbed to Pneumonia in the early hours of 7 February 1926 at his home on Potter Hill. Naylor's funeral was said to have "a large attendance of relatives and friends and many floral tributes." He was interred in River Bend Cemetery among his family members.[45] According to his obituary, Naylor was "an esteemed resident of Potter Hill" who was awarded "a number of medals for bravery while he served in the U.S. Navy."[46]

The courageous actions of both James Albert Barber and David Johnson Naylor during the American Civil War should never be forgotten. Now, due in large part to the mural, their legacy will live on for generations to come, much like the acts of valor performed by the servicemen of

Westerly who came after them and those who will continue to bravely defend America.

Getting There: A Brief History of Steamboat and Trolley Travel

"During its thirteen consecutive seasons of operation, the Belle became well-known among travelers looking for a good time."

The murals discussed below can be found on the side of the Martin House building and can be best viewed from the intersection of High Street and Canal Street in downtown Westerly (the New London Steamboat Company Mural) and when exiting downtown Westerly via Canal Street (the Shore Line Trolley Company Mural). Given that the histories of both modes of transport are deeply interconnected, this entry will discuss the story behind both murals.

Although the mural representing the New London Steamboat Company is dedicated to the season of 1893, the story of pedestrian steamboats in Westerly began long before then. In 1868, the Dixon House Hotel, was built on the site of the former Rhode Island Hotel, on Broad Street in the heart of downtown Westerly. The building stood for sixty years before it was destroyed in a fire on 16 April 1928.[47] The hotel became popular with visitors looking to spend time at Westerly's famed beaches. This newfound popularity led to the construction of the steamship *Belle* to carry both hotel guests and Westerly residents to and from Watch Hill.[48] The *Belle* began making daily trips on Independence Day 1869 and thereafter made two round-trips each day for a forty cent fare.[49]

During its thirteen consecutive seasons of operation, the *Belle* became well-known among travelers looking for a good time. The ship also made a stop at Osbrook [a point at the mouth of the Pawcatuck River on the Connecticut side], where Joseph Crandall, better known as 'Osbrook Joe' operated dance halls, bowling alleys, dining halls and bars.[50] At times, riders on the ship would get out of hand, and assistance was needed. A system was developed to warn police as the ship pulled in to Westerly. Just before the on-board band's finale, the *Belle*'s whistle would blow four times as they approached the dock, a signal to the police that they were needed to detain the rowdy individuals causing trouble.[51] It was also said that the ship carried rum from Norwich in kerosene and molasses containers from Norwich, explaining how some riders could end up in such a rambunctious state.[52]

The Belle
(Photo: Westerly Historical Society)

While the *Belle* was the first major steamboat to carry passengers to and from Watch Hill, there were many more that came in the decades that followed. By 1888, Watch Hill was starting to be seen as a luxury summer village by outsiders from around the East Coast and Midwest. With cottages cropping up, a growing number of carpenters, painters, and builders were required to work on the new homes in the area. To shuttle workers back and forth, the ship *Queen City* was purchased. The name of this shuttle was particularly apt, as many of the Midwesterners who purchased homes in Watch Hill came from Cincinnati, often referred to as the "Queen City." At the time, ships were making seventeen round-trips each day between Westerly and Watch Hill. According to the *Providence Journal*, this feat was "unequalled in history."[53]

During the season of 1893, the year referenced on the mural, there were at least two boats in operation between Westerly and Watch Hill. One was the *Surf City*, which was operated by Captain George Greenman between 1890 and 1893.[54] The other ship, the *Martha*, was commissioned by Orlando R. Smith and was named after his daughter. The *Martha* was built at the

Pendleton Dock at Cross and Main Streets and ran to and from Watch Hill in 1893 and 1894.[55] 1894 proved to be the beginning of the end for steamboat transportation locally. That year the Pawcatuck Valley Street Railway began operation providing sudden competition for the steamship companies.[56]

The Martha
(Photo: Westerly Historical Society)

The opening of the Pawcatuck Valley Street Railway in 1894 was the start of a new era in Westerly, a time when trolley transportation became the preferred mode of transportation in the town for the more than twenty-five years.

Originally chartered in 1903, as the Norwich, Mystic, and Westerly Street Railway Company, the above-mentioned leaser of the PVSRC was chartered in Rhode Island on 13 March 1906 as the Norwich and Westerly Railway Company (NWRC). On 12 December 1906, the railway, which "operated with fast cars, railroad roofs, double truck types, and high backed seats built by the Southern Car Company" opened a line from Norwich through Westerly which crossed the state line at White Rock and continued into downtown Westerly.[62] The fare for a trip from Norwich to Westerly was thirty-five cents, which was divided into seven different zones, with each zone costing a nickel to travel between.[63]

Trolleys in Downtown Westerly
(Photo: Westerly Historical Society)

On 1 August 1907, the NWRC suffered a heavy blow with their most serious accident at Avery's Crossing near North Stonington when a passenger car and express car collided head-on. Three were killed and eight were injured in the collision.[64] Still, expansion continued and in 1908 a Pleasant View extension was opened.[65] The lease of the PVSRC on 1 July 1911 by the NWRC, resulted in the creation of the Norwich and Westerly Traction.[66] In December, the PVSRC property was purchased outright by the NWRC after the Norwich outfit built an extension from "Mastuxet Brook through Atlantic Beach (now Misquamicut) to Weekapaug."[67]

The next significant acquisition for the Norwich and Westerly Railway Company came on 1 July 1913, when they leased the Groton and Stonington Company's holdings, creating a sixty-mile-long system stretching from Norwich to Westerly to Groton with branches including Westerly, Watch Hill, Weekapaug, and Ashaway.[68] The tracks in Westerly first entered across a bridge over the state line into White Rock, and then it crossed Pierce Street on a trestle before rejoining street traffic on the corner of West and

Pleasant Streets. Trains then followed West Street crossing the railroad tracks via a bridge then proceeded down Railroad Avenue to the Westerly Train Station. Beyond the train station, trolleys then followed the PVSR tracks up Canal Street to High Street then moved on to Broad Street ending at Dixon House Square.[69]

While the above-mentioned lines were crucial to the transportation revolution in Westerly, their dominance paved the way for their incorporation into a much larger system, the Shore Line Electric Railway Company, which is featured in the newly created mural.

The SLERC was incorporated in 1905 and began operation in 1910.[70] In 1913, the SLERC began acquiring vast amounts of trolley tracks from companies including the Connecticut Company and the New London and East Lyme Street Railway Company. That same year, they purchased stock control of the Norwich and Westerly Traction Company, and on 30 June 1916, the SLERC merged all its holdings except the Connecticut Company, creating a system operating 200 trolley cars over twenty separate routes, encompassing more than 250 miles of tracks. In addition to transporting passengers from town to town, the SLERC also offered a package service, carrying parcels up to fifteen pounds at the same rate as a passenger fare.[71] Although the company appeared dominant after all of their acquisitions, by 1919, it encountered insurmountable struggles. A combination of financial difficulty, an accident on 21 June 1919, and an employee strike that same year resulted in the folding of the SLERC.[72]

The various leases and mergers created a unique issue for passengers. Namely, the numbering systems used for trolleys which caused confusion among riders. At one time, in Westerly alone, there were no less than three trains using the numbers 20 and 24.[73] Despite this issue, the trolley system in Westerly still represented a welcome change, as both residents and visitors could travel to the beach and back quicker than ever before.

Even though Westerly is a shoreline town, many residents prior to the middle of the nineteenth century found traveling to and from the beach to be a struggle given the distance between downtown and the shore. This concern was greatly alleviated, first, by the use of steamboats between the heart of the town and its seaside retreat, and later by trolleys operating between 1894 and 1919. Steamboats and trolleys played a significant role in the growth and development of Westerly and allowed both residents and visitors to move more freely than ever before.

Prompt, Private, Perfect:
The Westerly Automatic Telephone Exchange

The slogan of the Westerly Automatic Telephone Company, "Prompt, Private, Perfect," encapsulated all the advantages the company claimed their service had over the operator-based telephone system. It was prompt because "the connection between subscribers is direct and automatic." It was private, because there was no operator at a central station who would know who you were calling and overhear conversations. Lastly, it was perfect because the service was "instantaneous, direct, free from delays caused by indifferent or overworked operators" and had "continuous service night and day."

The mural discussed below can be found at 15 Canal Street in downtown Westerly.

In a time when telephones are consistently on the cutting edge of technology and form a central part of most people's lives, it is hard to imagine a time when being able to make a private call was considered a new and exciting luxury, but such a time did exist. In 1902, a man by the name of Dr. John Champlin saw the potential of new telephone technology and used his financial backing and eye for innovation to bring Westerly into a new era of communication.

Born in Westerly on 5 October 1863 to Samuel A. and Mary B. (Ross) Champlin,[74] Dr. John Champlin was a well-respected man in his hometown, where he worked as a physician throughout his entire life. Dr. Champlin lived with his wife, Anna E. (Lyon) Champlin, in a grand brick house at 9 Granite Street and his practice could be found at 38 Main Street, in the former Champlin Building, just a short walk away from his front door.[75] By 1902, Dr. Champlin had built a reputation as a strong leader and was greatly respected and admired by his peers. He used this influence to gather support around town for his latest project, the automatic telephone, which he believed would be the future of communication.

The notion of home telephones was not new by this time, as Westerly was served by the Providence Telephone Company; however, many around town felt the service left much to be desired. The PTC used the standard system originally developed by Alexander Graham Bell. This system required the caller to first turn a crank on their telephone box sending an electrical impulse to attract the attention of the operator, who would then inquire about the number the caller was trying to reach. The operator would then connect them to the desired number, completing the time-consuming procedure.[76]

At the start of the twentieth century, there were only thirty-nine phones in all of Westerly with many of them belonging to businesses. Seeing an opportunity to capitalize, Dr. Champlin traveled to Chicago, where he met with an undertaker who had developed a new concept, the automatic telephone, which had caught Champlin's attention.[77] The doctor then returned to Westerly with his new-found knowledge and set out to bring the automatic telephone to his hometown.

The slogan of the Westerly Automatic Telephone Company, "Prompt, Private, Perfect," encapsulated all the advantages the company claimed their service had over the operator-based telephone system. It was *prompt* because "the connection between subscribers is direct and automatic." It was *private*, because there was no operator at a central station who would know who you were calling and could potentially overhear conversations. Lastly, it was *perfect* because the service was "instantaneous, direct, free from delays caused by indifferent or overworked operators" and had "continuous service night and day."[78] Perhaps best of all for Westerly residents, the company's advertisement boasted that their service would cost "less than one half the present rate for long distance" and residential telephone service would cost only twenty dollars per year or five and a half cents per day (equivalent to about $616 annually in 2021).[79]

On 17 February 1902, *The Westerly Sun* published the proposed act being considered by the State of Rhode Island which would create the corporation known as the Westerly Automatic Telephone Company. According to this act, the capital of the corporation would be $25,000 with stock divided into full shares of twenty-five dollars each.[80] The first attempt at gaining a charter from the State Assembly was unsuccessful, but a second attempt led to the corporation's development.[81]

By April 1902, the Westerly Automatic Telephone Company began operations with Dr. Champlin serving as both President and Treasurer, and A.B. Crafts and George C. Bartram serving as directors.[82] That same month, a list of subscribers and their assigned telephone number(s) was published in the *Westerly Sun*.[83] The inaugural subscribers included a combination of residential and business customers, including several banks and local schools. If a caller wanted to speak directly with Dr. Champlin, they could reach him simply by dialing "14-2" or if they needed to check on the status of their train, they could call the New York, New Haven and Hartford Railroad office just by dialing "3-4."[84] The future was approaching rapidly in Westerly.

While many viewed these technological advances as beneficial to the town, not everyone was in support of the new company. In addition to stark opposition from the PTC, some of the town's older and more powerful residents felt that the Providence Telephone Company's service was sufficient. However, in time, the dispute was settled.[85] By July 1902, the equipment for the new system had been ordered and was expected to be installed by that September. Extensions of service to Watch Hill were planned for the following year.[86] In October 1904, after two years of satisfactory service, the Westerly Automatic Telephone Company absorbed the business of the Providence Telephone Company in Westerly, Hopkinton (excluding Hope Valley), Richmond and Charlestown as well as that of the South New England Telephone Company in the towns of Stonington and North Stonington. This essentially gave the company a monopoly on local telephone service.[87] The firm saw continued growth and by 1905, they had twice as many subscribers as both they and the Providence Telephone Company had combined in 1902.[88]

Dr. Champlin continued to serve as President of the WTE until his retirement in 1937, at which time his son, Dr. John Champlin Jr., stepped in as Vice President. Dr. Champlin Sr. saw the great potential of the automatic telephone for Westerly and made his idea a reality. Because of his forward thinking, for a moment in time, Westerly was "the most famous telephone town in the country."[89]

John Champlin and the Westerly Automatic Telephone Company brought the town into the future, making it easier than ever for residents to communicate with one another quickly and easily. This giant leap forward brought about changes still being felt today, and for this reason, Dr. Champlin and his company are rightfully commemorated with a mural in downtown Westerly.

A Park for the People: Wilcox Park's Enduring Legacy

"To argue for the advantages of a public park is unnecessary."

The mural discussed below, which depicts Harriet Wilcox and Wilcox Park can be found near the intersection of High Street and Canal Street in downtown Westerly.

Since the turn of the twentieth century, Wilcox Park has been a fixture of downtown Westerly and remains among the town's most notable features. While many individuals and groups have played a role in preserving the park's beauty and prominence, none were more instrumental in the park's creation than Stephen and Harriet Wilcox.

The story of the Wilcox family and their benevolence in the improvement of Westerly begins many years before the concept of Wilcox Park was ever considered. Harriet Hoxie was born in Charlestown, Rhode Island on 12 January 1829 to Welcome Arnold and Mary (Hoxie) Hoxie.[90] When Harriet was nine years old, her family moved to Westerly, where she would spend much of the rest of her life.[91] In 1865, Harriet married a man named Stephen Wilcox, who was born in Westerly to Stephen Jr. and Sophia (Vose) Wilcox on 12 February 1830.[92]

Throughout their lives, Stephen and Harriet Wilcox accumulated a great deal of personal wealth due to Stephen's skills as an inventor and engineer. Mr. Wilcox initially developed "many important improvements in steam engines," however, his profile grew significantly once he and George H. Babcock innovated a water-tube boiler, known at the time as the "Babcock and Wilcox Type," which was used around the world.[93] Stephen Wilcox was also well-known for his philanthropic efforts, particularly his contributions to local institutions. The Wilcoxes lived for a time in both Providence and New York City before purchasing land in Westerly in 1881.[94] In the 1890's, Mr. Wilcox offered the town of Westerly half of the $50,000 needed to build a library, which was accepted with gratitude.[95] When Stephen died on 27 November 1893, his loving wife, Harriet, continued her husband's charitable pursuits.

Harriet Wilcox   *Stephen Wilcox*
(Photos: Westerly Historical Society)

The project which has come to define the legacy of Stephen and Harriet Wilcox is the park which bears their name. Interest in the establishment of a public park for Westerly reached its peak in 1898. On July 19th of that year, an editorial appeared in *The Westerly Sun* simply titled "Westerly's Park: Why Does Westerly Need a Park?" Many of the arguments made in this piece reflected sentiments which were promoted by contemporary park advocates across America. Some of the more prominent positions included the benefits of people connecting with nature, as well as parks serving as an outlet to prevent members of the working class from falling into wicked habits. According to the author, who is recorded simply as "a Friend of Westerly," a public park "would go much farther toward arresting the tidal wave of intemperance."[96]

Wilcox Park with the Former Westerly High School in View
(Photo: Westerly Historical Society)

Five days later, on 24 July 1898, the *Sun* would publish a lengthy piece announcing that land was now available which would be ideal for a public park. According to this article, "the need of a park is becoming more noticeable." Many of Westerly's most renowned citizens of the time, including Town Council President Crandall and Councilman Biddles are quoted in support of a public park.[97]

On 23 August 1898 a special meeting of the taxpayers of Westerly was held in Armory Hall where a vote was taken regarding whether or not the town should purchase the Rowse Babcock estate on Grove Avenue. In regards to this meeting, the *Sun* claimed "to argue for the advantages of a public park is unnecessary."[98] The principal argument against purchasing this land was an opposition to the tax which would be levied fund the purchase. However, the writer of one letter to the *Sun* noted "With a grand list of over six millions of dollars, a rapidly increasing population, and a community with intelligence and refined taste, it seems rather of an impotant [sic] argument to say we cannot afford it." While the outcome of the August vote is not clear, it was of no matter, as Harriet Wilcox purchased the property from the heirs of Rowse Babcock in October 1898 and presented it to the Westerly Memorial Library Association. It was said at the time that Mrs. Wilcox had an "untiring devotion to the Memorial building," which included taking her husband's place on the Board of Trustees.[99] Plans were then quickly set into motion for the development of a public park in Westerly.

Wilcox Park was initially designed by Warren H. Manning, the first President (1897-1903) of the American Society of Landscape Architects, while other landscape architects expanded upon Manning's initial design including Frank Hamilton's work in 1905, and that of Arthur A. Shurcliff between 1924 and 1937.[100]

On 4 April 1899, the house at 50 and 52 Broad Street was sold to a man named A.L. Chester for ninety dollars ($2,872.16 in 2021), who was given six weeks to move the house as a condition of the sale.[101] In June 1899, Mrs. Wilcox donated a portion of the land to Westerly School District No. 1 allowing the District to build a new high school on the property. The high school built on this land would stand until Ward Senior High School was opened in the 1937. In a letter to the school district, Harriet wrote "The opportunity has now been placed in my hands to assist the people of this school district in providing better and much needed high school accommodations."[102] Mrs. Wilcox continued to contribute to the well-being of Westerly for the remainder of her life.

Harriet Wilcox died in her home at 41 Elm Street on 31 August 1901.[103] The generosity of both Stephen and Harriet Wilcox was championed at the times of their deaths, with many tributes appearing in *The Westerly Sun* extolling their acts of kindness towards the town.[104] While it was initially believed that the Wilcoxes contributed only the $25,000 needed to fund the library's building, it was revealed that they provided more than $100,000 for its construction and maintenance, while paying many of the library's bills.[105]

The immense wealth and philanthropy of Stephen and Harriet Wilcox is obvious through Harriet's last will and testament, which contains fifty-six separate provisions for dividing her estate, including contributions to several churches in Westerly and other enterprises which depended largely upon her aid. In this will, Harriet also bequeathed $150,000 to the Memorial Library Association, as well as a list nearly two pages long detailing the various works of art which were to be donated to the library for their art annex.[106]

Although she lived long enough to see the creation of Wilcox Park (a name which Harriet insisted upon as a tribute to her husband), many important developments followed in the decade after her death. In July 1902, the Westerly Gas and Electric Light Company installed fifteen electric lights on Broad Street for the park and during the same month, a temporary bandstand was built at the intersection of Granite Street and Grove Avenue so that concerts could be held.[107]

While the initial gift of the Rowse Babcock estate served as the catalyst for the park's creation, it was further purchases which allowed it to expand to its current size. In November 1906, the trustees of the park purchased land "from High Street to Grove Avenue" from the estate of Hannah B.W. Brown. Even after her death, this expansion was made possible by Harriet Wilcox, as the purchase was funded by an increase in the value of the funds donated in Harriet's will.[108] In April 1907, land from the estate of Daniel Douglas was purchased by the Memorial Building Association from Joseph T. Murphy.[109]

Over the course of its more than 120-year history, Wilcox Park has been an integral part of Westerly's history. It continues to be the site of many concerts, plays, and other events which are attended by thousands, making it among the most important locations in town.

Musical Traditions of the Westerly Town Band and the Chorus of Westerly

"The Westerly Singers were composed of men from various walks of life, a fact which was well-promoted in The Westerly Sun when they noted that the group 'has in its ranks a carpenter, office executive, printer, gas station owner, mill worker, … a dental surgeon, a forest ranger' and many more."

The murals discussed below are dedicated to the town's musical history, specifically, two important institutions: The Westerly Town Band and the Chorus of Westerly.

As the mural dedicated to it indicates, the Westerly Band is the oldest continuously active civic band in the United States. While details about the band's formation and its earliest years are scarce, most historians agree that the first iteration of the band was founded in 1852, possibly by a man named Stephen Phalens, although there are also references to a man named W.B. Lowry serving as the band's first instructor. Unfortunately, many of this early band's musicians left Westerly to serve in the Civil War, and the group's journey came to a halt. While there are very few remaining records regarding this band, there is little doubt that it existed, as an 1854 program for a performance at the Union Meeting House has been located.[110]

In 1863, in an effort to keep spirits high during the war, a new band was formed with eight musicians, and was led by A.J. Foster.[111] The year 1863 is cited by the Westerly Band as its formation date, which still supports their claim to be the country's oldest continuously active band. By the following year, the band's size had more than doubled, and their performances were highly sought after for various functions around town. The group's membership ballooned, and by 1875, a separate string ensemble was formed by several of the musicians.[112]

A.J. Foster
(Photo: Westerly Historical Society)

Support for the local band was clear, especially after tragedy struck the organization. In 1891, a fire caused massive damage to the Porter-Loveland Block on High Street, where the band's second floor rehearsal rooms were located. The fire destroyed uniforms, instruments and records (the reason for the absence of information regarding the band's origins). The group needed $1,329.50 to replace the destroyed and damaged items. This money was easily raised with support from Westerly citizens.[113]

Competition among local bands was not unheard of, especially during the nineteenth century. According to a popular story from 1896, the Westerly Band and another local outfit, the Sheffield Band, were offered payment to alternate weeks playing in Watch Hill. These shows were funded by the Norwich-Westerly Electric Railroad in hopes that people in town would take the trolley to Watch Hill to hear the bands play. When a dispute over money developed, the Westerly Band played a free concert in town on the same night that the Sheffield Band was paid to play in Watch Hill.[114]

The Westerly Town Band, 3 June 1911
(Photo: Westerly Historical Society)

Another tale of the band's exploits comes from 1933, during the midst of the Great Depression when a parade was organized in Westerly to give the town an emotional lift. The Westerly Band was featured prominently in this parade, heading and closing several divisions, which they were able to do by bussing musicians from the finish line back to the start several times.[115]

More recently, the band has made efforts to expand its range, with young and old working together. For much of its history, the Westerly Band restricted its membership to men, however, the 1950's saw the addition of the first female musician, Paula Richards, to the group.[116] More recently, school musicians have also been encouraged to join the band as a way to expand and diversify the group's membership and to provide young instrumentalists with more experience.[117] The Westerly Town Band, a source of local pride, continues on, with more than a century and a half of uninterrupted rehearsals and performances.

The Chorus of Westerly mural also serves as a reminder of the town's musical legacy. The modern Chorus of Westerly, which was founded in 1959 by George Kent, is not the first choral group to call Westerly home. That distinction may belong to the Westerly Singers, an all-male group established in 1941. Much like the Westerly Town Band, this group halted operations when eight members left in early 1942 to serve in World War II. The group resumed rehearsals in January 1946 when it consisted of twelve men (and advertised openings for "one or two singers" who qualified).[118] The Westerly Singers were composed of men from various walks of life, a fact which was well-promoted in *The Westerly Sun* when they noted that the group "has in its ranks a carpenter, office executive, printer, gas station owner, mill worker, … a dental surgeon, a forest ranger" and many more.[119]

A month later, in February 1946, another unit, the Westerly Choral Club held its first rehearsal at the Westerly Public Library with more than thirty-five people in attendance. The Choral Club struggled, however, as female singers significantly outnumbered male singers, and they were well short of the sixty needed to achieve their goal.[120] It is not known what became of these groups; however, one can assume that some members joined the Chorus of Westerly at the time of its formation in 1959.

In the beginning, when the Chorus of Westerly formed in 1959, membership consisted of one third children aged between eight and sixteen and two thirds adults of all ages, a practice which continues to this day. Initially, adults rehearsed once a week for two hours, while the children rehearsed twice a week for one hour and attended an eight-day music camp each August. This camp was initially held at the YMCA camp, Wind in the Pines, near Worcester, Massachusetts, until moving to Camp Ogontz in Lisbon, New Hampshire in 1965.[121]

In 1960, the chorus included eighty adults and fifty children, and it was during this season that they staged their first musical in front of an audience of 2,500. For over fifty years, George Kent was the driving force behind the Chorus' success, and it was his training with Sir David Willcocks, the director of the King's College Chapel Choir beginning in 1968, which formulated deep connections to the British Choral scene which exist to this day.[122]

Also in 1968, the Chorus held their first concert at the former Immaculate Conception Church (built in 1886), which later became the

Chorus' permanent home and is today known as the George Kent Performance Center. In 1972, it was announced that the church was to be torn down, but a one year lease of the building delayed its demolition until 1973. During the 1972-1973 season, the Chorus performed its first Celebration of Twelfth Night, which went on to become one of its most popular annual shows. The following year, members of the Chorus organized a group known as Center for the Arts with the goal of purchasing the church. This goal was achieved when the building was purchased for $40,000 and then added to the National Register for Historic Places.[123]

During the 1980-1981 season, the Chorus of Westerly embarked on its first tour of Great Britain, which was also attended by the Rhode Island Philharmonic.[124] Just prior to its departure, the Chorus put on the first Summer Pops concert, which was held in Dixon Square with all traffic stopped. The concert was attended by 5,000 spectators. In 1984, it was clear that the (now annual) Summer Pops concert had outgrown the setup in Dixon Square, and the show was moved to Wilcox Park, where it is still held each Summer. That year, the concert had more than 15,000 in attendance. In 1990, it was estimated that the concert was attended by more than 30,000 people.[125]

The group's expansion continued throughout the 1980s, and during the 1984-1985 season, the Chorus hired a full-time manager and opened a new office in downtown Westerly due in large part to a grant from the Rhode Island Foundation. The summer of 1987 also saw the Chorus embark on a highly successful tour of Italy, during which they visited Venice, the Vatican, and Milan. In the latter they performed before more than 13,000 people. By 1991, the Chorus was able to purchase the Center for the Arts building for $165,000, and it was renamed the Chorus of Westerly Performance Hall.[126]

The 1994-1995 season was another special one for the Chorus, as they toured Britain for a second time. During this tour, their performance at St. Alban's Cathedral was recorded live and later broadcast nationwide in Britain.[127]

During the 2005-2006 season, the Chorus of Westerly Performance Hall was rededicated as the George Kent Performance Hall as a tribute to the Chorus' founder and leader for over forty-five years. That same year, Kent was awarded the National Pell Award for Distinguished Achievement in the

Arts, making him one of only thirty-two New Englanders to have won the award.[128] At the end of the Chorus' fifty-second season in 2011, George Kent announced he would be stepping down as music director from the Chorus at the end of the 2011-2012 season. Kent's tenure with the Chorus was celebrated vigorously throughout the season, acknowledging his importance to the Chorus' formation and growth over the course of fifty-three years. In March 2012, after a nation-wide search, Andrew Howell of the University of Rhode Island was appointed the second music director.[129]

Both the Westerly Town Band and the Chorus of Westerly serve as perfect representations of the town's musical heritage and the two murals in downtown Westerly are a fantastic reminder of the importance of both groups, which deserve to be remembered for their contributions and celebrated for their continued success.

"While the granite industry had far reaching implications for the town which continue to this day, it has also brought the community into the national spotlight."

The mural discussed below, which presents a look at Westerly's legacy in the granite industry, can be found in an alley off of High Street in downtown Westerly.

If there is any one commercial field which is inextricably linked with Westerly's history over the last two centuries, it is the granite industry. While granite has had far reaching implications locally which continue to this day, it has also drawn the community into the national spotlight.

The origins of the granite business as a major force in Westerly's economy can be traced back to 1845, when Orlando Smith identified a significant deposit of granite on a parcel of farmland owned by the Babcock family. The following year, he purchased the land and began extracting its valuable resource.[130] Although the first granite in Westerly was excavated eleven years prior in 1834, it was Smith's discovery that resulted in a boom in business which would continue for decades.[131] From the 1830's until the end of World War I, the industry flourished in Westerly.

While there were a number of reasons for the granite industry's strength and continual growth, there were several important factors which combined to create an ideal environment for growth. The late nineteenth century saw an increase in 'garden-like' cemeteries featuring elaborate monuments requiring skilled granite carvers. Additionally, granite companies filled the demand for monuments and memorials at the end of the Civil War. Lastly, the granite found in Westerly has an extremely fine texture making it ideal for delicate and detailed work which these monuments required.[132]

Loading Granite Blocks at the Sullivan Quarry
(Photo: Westerly Historical Society)

Expansion in the granite business meant increased opportunities for laborers in quarries throughout Westerly. This lucrative job market brought about a massive uptick in the number of migrant workers coming to Westerly. The first group to arrive and find work in the quarries were the Irish in the 1850's, followed by Scots in the 1870's.[133] By 1885, eighteen percent of Westerly residents were Irish-born, while ten percent were born in Scotland.

The influx of Scottish immigrants in Westerly was a product of a crowded job market for granite workers in their native country.[134] One company that was established in Westerly, Joseph Newall and Co., was a branch of the D.H. and J. Newall Company of Dalbeattie, Scotland, which formed in 1820, linking the Scottish industry across the Atlantic Ocean.[135] The the 1890's, Finns also began arriving in droves.[136] The group that arrived in the greatest numbers, however, were those from southern Italy. The Italian immigrants who made Westerly their home have left an enduring legacy, with many of their descendants still calling the town home.[137] [For more on Westerly's Italian community, see 75.]

Workers at the Smith Granite Company
(Photo: Westerly Historical Society)

By 1892, nearly four thousand of the town's seven thousand citizens were "in some way tied to the economic well-being of the granite industry in Westerly."[138] Granite's effect on Westerly and the sheer volume of the industry's output continued to grow throughout the nineteenth century. In an 1897 directory, one would find twenty-five granite companies operating in Westerly. The town with the second highest number of companies was Providence with only six.[139] Despite the great number of granite companies in Westerly at the time, it was clear that some were viewed as major players while others were not built to last. One success story was the New England Granite Works, which began operating a quarry as the Rhode Island Granite Works in 1868.[140] The most well-known company, however, was the one founded by Orlando Smith, the Smith Granite Company, which began in 1846 after his purchase of the Babcock farm. Between 1880 and 1898, the company had sales offices in New York, Chicago, Boston, Cleveland, and Philadelphia while employing a staff of four hundred.[141]

The industry saw prolonged success in the early decades of the twentieth century. Unfortunately, by the time the Great Depression struck the nation in 1929, the granite business had begun to fall into decline.[142]

Many of Westerly's smaller companies sold their quarries to larger firms and up-start enterprises. Another catalyst for the industry's downfall was a series of labor disputes, including an extended strike in 1922 which affected the industry deeply.[143] By the start of World War II, most granite companies had closed their doors although a few still remain in operation to this day, albeit on a much smaller scale than during the industry's peak.

One enduring legacy of Westerly's granite history is the notable monuments and buildings carved in Westerly or created using granite extracted from local quarries. These include the famed Private Soldier Monument standing at the Antietam battlefield. This monument, standing over forty-four feet tall and weighing 250 tons, was also displayed at the Centennial Exhibition in Philadelphia in 1876 before it was formally dedicated on 17 September 1880.[144] Altogether, more than one hundred Civil War monuments were carved in Westerly between 1880 and 1900.[145]

Due in large part to the dedicated work of the researchers at the Babcock Smith House in Westerly (authors of the comprehensive and fascinating work *Built from Stone*), it has been determined that the Smith Granite Company was responsible for at least 3,754 monuments standing in thirty-two of the fifty states across America.[146] Several well-known buildings in Westerly were also built using local granite, including the Watch Hill Lighthouse, Saint Pius X Church, the Town Hall, the Industrial Trust Company Building, and the Christopher Columbus monument in Wilcox Park.[147] The wide-reaching impact of Westerly's granite industry is apparent not only in the number of monuments which can still be seen today, but also through its shaping of the town's history.

From Italy with Love: Italian Roots in Westerly

"The arrival of Italian immigrants was due largely to the opportunities for work available in Westerly's burgeoning granite industry. Many of the laborers who made the journey to Westerly from Italy quickly found work in granite quarries, often laboring alongside men from the same villages in their home country."

The mural discussed below can be found on the side of the building at 100 Main Street, which is dedicated to Westerly's Italian heritage.

This mural, which celebrates the culture and traditions which continue to shape the town as we know it, is centered around four important aspects of life for local Italian-Americans: Famiglia (Family), Vino (Wine), Giardino (Garden), and Sopressata. These four articles have long been among the most important to those who migrated from Italy and their descendants.

While the first wave of Italian immigration to Rhode Island began in the 1880's, there was not a significant number of Italians arriving in Westerly until about 1900. In 1880, only fourteen of Westerly's 6,126 residents claimed to have been born in Italy. By 1900, that number had increased to 318 of 7,640, and in 1910, it more than tripled to 1,049 of 8,696.[148] The number of Westerly residents who claimed to have been born in Italy in the federal census peaked in 1920, when there were 1,292 Italians living in Westerly, representing nearly thirteen percent of the town's total population at the time.[149]

The arrival of Italian immigrants was largely driven by the opportunities for work available in Westerly's burgeoning granite industry. Many of the laborers who made the journey to Westerly from Italy quickly found work in granite quarries, often laboring alongside men from the same villages in their home country.

Although the mural promotes four unique features of life that are important to Italians in Westerly, there are three main elements of the Italian-

American story which warrant further analysis: family, community, and preservation of heritage.

Family has, and always will be, very important to Italian immigrants and their descendants. It was not uncommon for several generations to live in the same household together, passing on customs and traditions. Family lore, recipes for meatballs, and techniques for creating the perfect stick of soupy have all been passed down through the years and still live on in local shops.

Also very important to Italian immigrants was the sense of community that developed among their fellow countrymen. Upon arrival in Westerly, Italians were able to join numerous societies which were organized specifically by and for Italian-Americans. These clubs included the Italo-American Civic Club (founded in 1916), the Daughters of Italy (founded in 1925), and the Italian Welfare Club (founded in 1926).[150] However, one club, The Calabrese Club, remains an important representation of the town's Italian roots. Originally formed in 1918 as Societa Cittadini Calabro Americani Club, it was founded by immigrants from Calabria and has been located at the corner of West and Pleasant Streets since 1934. As president George Salimeno noted in 1986, "They [the founders] formed the club to take care of their own."[151] Even today, officers of the Calabrese Club are required to be from Calabria or descendants of natives.[152]

Because many Italian immigrants were practicing Roman Catholics and due to its proximity to Westerly's North End, where immigrants frequently settled, the Church of the Immaculate Conception was the congregation where they usually became members. Even today, the church often holds mass in Italian and the parish maintains a statue of the Saint Angelo of Acri, who originated in the same Italian town where the ancestors of so many Westerly residents were born.[153]

Italian-Americans also sought ways to ensure that their heritage would be properly represented and preserved in their new homeland. One way of doing so was through the creation of the Dante Fund in 1934 "to promote the study of Italian language and literature in the schools of Westerly."[154]

Westerly residents have also taken great pride in Christopher Columbus, a native of Genoa who holds special importance among Italian-

Americans. Since 1947, Westerly has held an annual Columbus Day Parade, a relatively unique event in New England, celebrating not only Columbus, but the "contributions of Italian-Americans in the United States and southeastern New England."[155]

In 1949, a statue of Columbus (built from granite, adding an extra layer of symbolism) was erected in Wilcox Park with an inscription which reads:[156]

"CRISTOFORO COLOMBO, INTREPID ITALIAN EXPLORER WHO LINKED THE OLD WORLD OF OUR FATHERS TO THE NEW WORLD OF OUR SONS."

Despite concerns about Columbus' actions during his explorations including his exploitation of indigenous peoples, he is still revered by many within the town and remains a controversial figure.

The Pawcatuck River and the Colonial Border Conflict

"Although it was assumed that a decree from the King of England would settle the matter, in 1664 a royal commission was sent to New England to assess the basis for the disagreement. This commission decided in favor of the Rhode Islanders, awarding them right to all land on the eastern shore of the Pawcatuck River."

The mural discussed below, which celebrates the history of the Pawcatuck River, can be found on the side of the Walton Block in Pawcatuck and is visible from Donahue Park.

For centuries, the Pawcatuck River has been pivotal in shaping Westerly's physical landscape, as well as its culture. Dutch explorer Adriaen Block (for whom Block Island was named) is believed to have been the first European to travel up the river when he did so during an expedition, c. 1614.[157] Block initially referred to the river as East River, however, the name would later be changed to Pawcatuck. In 1658, the Massachusetts Bay Colony granted Captain Daniel Gookin land on the eastern side of the Pawcatuck, in what is now Watch Hill. Thus began a conflict involving three colonies and lasting nearly one hundred years.[158]

Every Westerly resident knows that the Pawcatuck River now serves as the border between Rhode Island and Connecticut, however, during the early years of Westerly's settlement, the river and its status as a boundary line was frequently called into question. In 1657 and 1660, several wealthier settlers in Providence and Newport combined their funds to make two important purchases from the Native Americans. The first was the Pettaquamscutt Purchase, which incorporated the towns of Narragansett, South Kingstown, and part of North Kingstown. The second was the Misquamicut Purchase, which included Westerly and parts of Hopkinton, Charlestown, and Richmond. These purchases were in direct conflict with claims made by the Connecticut Colony, asserting that its eastern border extended all the way to Narragansett Bay.[159]

Slowly, settlers began occupying the land between Narragansett Bay and the Pawcatuck River. Soon, not only were claims from Connecticut raising questions about the ownership of this land, but the Massachusetts Bay Colony attempted to declare a right to the same property. Between 1661 and 1662, Tobias Saunders and Robert Burdick, two of the settlers from Westerly who claimed loyalty to Rhode Island, were arrested and brought before the General Court of Massachusetts on charges of trespassing. According to the court, the men were not able to properly justify their actions, and thus were fined £40 and held in prison until the fines were paid.

In the closing of the court's letter to Rhode Island, they issued a warning:

"[U]nless you command of your inhabitants that yet continue their possessing at Southertowne* and Pettascomscott (the land east of the Pawcatuck) [to leave] before the last of June next, you may expect we shall not continue to neglect the reliefe and protection of our people thus molested, and shall account it our duty to secure all such persons and estates of yours as shall be found within our jurisdiction until all just damages be satisfied."[160]

* This was the name used at the time for Stonington, Connecticut.

That same year, the State of Rhode Island responded to these claims by stating that those who have settled on the land "have approbation of ye court so to doe…provided they have made fayre and honest lawfull purchase from the native owners thereof."[161]

The issues between the settlers and the colonial governments of Connecticut and Massachusetts came to a head at a meeting of the Commissioners for the United Colonies of New England on 4 September 1662. During this meeting, Captain Gookins, the man originally granted land east of the Pawcatuck in 1658, and others sent a letter to the government of Massachusetts making several disparaging claims about the Rhode Island settlers. In this letter, which refers to the land as "the right of Massachusetts at Paucatucke," the Rhode Island settlers were accused of:

- Acting in pretend authority,
- Building on the land,
- Threatening Captain Gookin's tenants,
- Carrying said tenant to prison and driving away his cattle,
- Cutting the tenant's grass,
- Prophaning the Sabbath, and

- Selling great quantities of liquor to the Pequots.[162]

The letter also noted that a charter bearing the seal of England was sent to some Connecticut residents granting them land on the east side of the river.

The issue became so volatile that King Charles II of England issued a charter to the State of Rhode Island and Providence Plantations in 1663 which laid out the bounds of the colony. This charter included the following description:

"…bounded on the west, or westerly, to the middle or channel of a river there, commonly called and known by the name of Pawcatuck, alias Pawcawtuck river, and soe along the sayd river, as the greater or middle streame thereof reacheth or lyes vpp into the north countrye, northward, unto the head thereoof, and from thence, by a streight lyne drawn due north, vntill itt meets with the south lyne of the Massachusetts Collonie."[163]

Connecticut's main contention had always been that the wording of original agreements pertaining to both colonies described the boundary as the 'Narragansett River' which was the name initially assigned to the Pawcatuck River. Connecticut settlers and lawmakers argued that this term referred to Narragansett Bay, and as a result, they felt they possessed a right to all land extending to the shore of the Bay. For this reason, the 1663 charter included a statement intended to address this confusion, which read:

"[T]he aforesavd Pawcatuck river haven byn yielded, after much debate, for the fixed and certain boundes betweene these our sayd Colonies, by the agents thereof; w hoe have alsoe agreed, that the sayd Pawcatuck river shall bee alsoe called alias Norrogansett or Narrogansett river; and to prevent future disputes, that otherwise might arise thereby, forever hereafter shall bee construed, deemed and taken to bee the Narragansett river in our late Irrupt to Connecticutt"[164]

Although it was assumed that a decree from the King of England would settle the matter, in 1664, a royal commission was sent to New England to assess the basis for the disagreement. This commission decided in favor of the Rhode Islanders, awarding them the right to all land on the eastern shore of the Pawcatuck River.[165] Still, Connecticut persisted, appealing the decision and filing petitions. Initially, they agreed to terms in 1703, however, Connecticut reneged on the agreement shortly thereafter. A settlement in 1728 ended the border dispute between Westerly and Stonington, setting the Pawcatuck River as the dividing line. It was not until 1746 when the matter was finally put to rest completely, with Connecticut accepting the terms laid out in the Rhode Island Charter of 1663.[166]

A Catastrophe: The Hurricane of 1938

"Shortly before 1 p.m., wind and rain began hitting the town, and by 3:30, what began as powerful, but not extreme, winds became forces of destruction. At this point, wind speeds were recorded between 125 and 150 miles per hour in ten minute stretches, with some gusts reaching as high as 200 miles per hour."

The mural discussed below, which showcases the local impact of the Hurricane of 1938, can be found between 29 and 37 West Broad Street in Pawcatuck.

21 September 1938 began like most Wednesdays in Westerly, with people passing through the streets, running errands, visiting the beach, or shuttling to and from work. By that afternoon, however, it became a day which no one who was old enough to remember would ever forget. Shortly before 1 p.m., wind and rain began hitting the town, and by 3:30, what began as powerful, but not extreme, winds became forces of destruction. At this point, wind speeds were recorded between 125 and 150 miles per hour in ten minute stretches, with some gusts reaching as high as 200 miles per hour.[167] The strong gales persisted for several hours, causing untold amounts of damage across the southern coast of Rhode Island and elsewhere.

The devastation caused by the storm was intensified by the fact that, as *The Westerly Sun* reported, "the storm broke so suddenly Wednesday afternoon that many people were caught unawares [sic] in the business district of Westerly and there was a general scurry for shelter." The storm's sudden increase in force caused many drivers to narrowly escape falling trees on Granite and West Broad Streets. Wilcox Park was also brutally ravaged and was described by the newspaper as "a shamble of trees."[168] Causing further harm was the fact that the storm hit its peak at the same time as students were set to be released from local schools. Many of the children remained at school until the storm subsided, including students from Hope Valley who were not able to return home until a bus could arrive after nine o'clock that night.[169]

A House in the Aftermath of the Hurricane, 1938
(Photo: Westerly Historical Society)

When the storm finally came to an end, only then could the wreckage truly be evaluated. One hundred and thirty lives were lost across southern Rhode Island and Connecticut as a result of the storm, fifty-seven of whom were residents of Westerly. The hurricane's impact on the physical landscape was tremendous as well, as 1,018 houses and cottages between Mystic, Connecticut and Narragansett were demolished.[170] Misquamicut was hit harder than any other part of Westerly in terms of loss of both life and property, with forty-one deaths and 369 destroyed homes reported. Of the 369 homes demolished, 282 were located on Atlantic Avenue. Weekapaug was mostly spared, as its rocky shoreline protected many homes from significant damage. Only one death and twenty-three destroyed homes were reported in the area. The extent of the damage in Westerly necessitated the National Guard being called in to aid local police. More than seven hundred National Guardsmen quickly arrived on the scene, and began the search for missing persons with searchlights that could be seen as far as fourteen miles away.[171]

Devastation Caused by the Hurricane, 1938
(Photo: Westerly Historical Society)

The obliteration of virtually all means of communication as a result of damaged electrical systems and telephone lines also caused major problems for the town. Narragansett Electric reported losses of more than one million dollars and the sheer number of supplies needed to restore service was massive. These materials included:

- 1,250,000 feet of copper wire
- 2,000 poles
- 432,000 yards of friction tape
- 25,000 separate pieces of hardware
- 10,000 flashlight batteries

The Hurricane of 1938 was not the first storm to hit Westerly with great force. A hurricane also struck the town in 1815 and brought destruction upon its residents. The earlier storm, however, did not cause as much damage, due mostly to the fact that Misquamicut and Watch Hill were not as heavily settled in 1815 as they were by 1938.[172]

The Hurricane of 1938 and its impact on the town yielded numerous stories which are fascinating, heartbreaking, and uplifting. Many of these stories, while reported on locally in *The Westerly Sun* and other sources, still deserve to be passed down through the decades and remain in the public memory. Below are some of the more intriguing stories that surfaced in the days and months after the storm.

On the afternoon of the storm, a group of women from the Christ Episcopal Church were attending a picnic party at the Lowry Cottage (on Atlantic Avenue across from the Ocean). Unfortunately, as with nearly everyone in town, they were caught unprepared and unaware of the hurricane's approach. Once the wind and rain began to increase in speed and intensity, the women moved to a cottage owned by William D. Wells on the ocean side of Atlantic Avenue, where they sheltered for safety. In a tragic turn of events, all ten occupants perished when the cottage was swept out to sea.[173]

While the women's church group met an unfortunate fate on that terrible day, a miracle story of survival also appeared in the pages of the *Westerly Sun*. During the storm's duration, two babies, both about one year old, narrowly dodged lethal peril. The infants were carried to safety by their parents, who placed them on floating debris and carried them across Brightman's Pond. While one of the children escaped without any physical harm, the other, the child of Mr. and Mrs. Ralph Bliven, was rushed to the hospital after having swallowed a dangerous amount of water. The child was given little chance of survival, but miraculously, made a full recovery and was said to be in "fine condition," shortly thereafter.[174]

In their continued coverage of the storm and its effects on the town, *The Sun* named a group of local boys "heroes of the storm." These boys: Gerald Mason, George Marshall, John Marshall, and Edward Dolan, operated the short-wave radio station on Granite Street, which "gave Westerly its only contact with the outside world for twenty-four hours after the hurricane." The boys pooled their equipment to make a set which was used after the power went out during the storm. Their calls for help were picked up "as far away as Baltimore, Md., and Washington, D.C."[175] Much of the information that appeared in newspapers around the country was provided by the short-wave radio operators.

The damage Westerly incurred from the hurricane's wrath was enormous, and the lives lost in September 1938 should always be remembered. As with many tragedies, the aftermath the town faced brought citizens together and saw many step up to help one another.

"Every year, the two teams meet on the football field on Thanksgiving morning, a tradition which dates back to the first game between the two on the holiday in 1913."

The mural discussed below can be found behind C.C. O'Brien's Irish Sports Bar and Café at 8 Mechanic Street in Pawcatuck, Connecticut.

While many of the murals in both downtown Westerly and Pawcatuck promote unity between the two neighboring towns, there is one which serves to celebrate their differences. At the rear of C.C. O'Brien's, visitors can see a fantastic memorial to the rivalry between the Westerly High School Bulldogs and the Stonington High School Bears.

Every year, the two teams meet on the football field on Thanksgiving morning, a tradition which dates back to the first game between the two on the holiday in 1913.[176] The rivalry itself dates back to 1911 and is the most played series in the United States.[177] It is quite fitting that in a series between two schools that are less than three miles apart, the Thanksgiving Day series is so tight with the Bulldogs holding (as of April 2021) a slight 48-44-9 edge over the Bears (Stonington leads the all-time series 74-69-17).[178] Over the course of the 101 games played between the two on Thanksgiving (the game wasn't played between 1915 and 1920 or in 2020), there have been some thrillers and some lopsided victories (including a 61-0 victory by Westerly in 2018 and a 46-0 win by Stonington in 1914).[179]

In celebration of more than one hundred Turkey Day games, the following is a ranking of the top ten games of all time. Starting the list is a low-scoring affair from more than eighty years ago.

<u>TEN</u>
25 November 1937
Final Score: Stonington 2, Westerly 0

A record setting crowd of 4,000 fans came out to the Stonington Athletic Field to see the brown and white prevail over the Bulldogs. The two teams went to battle on "a treacherous gridiron, which had ice as the base for a two-inch layer of mud."[180] Both teams played stellar defense, and the only points put on the board came in the form of a safety scored by Stonington in the second quarter. The scoring play occurred when Westerly punter Charlie Dolan, intimidated by the Stonington defensive line who burst through on the play, fumbled the snap which bounced into the end zone. Dolan fell on the loose ball, scoring a safety for the opposition which proved to be the deciding points in an otherwise scoreless affair.[181]

The 1937 Bulldogs
(Photo: Westerly High School Yearbook, Westerly Public Library)

NINE
24 November 1960
Final Score: Westerly 6, Stonington 6

Coming into this game, Stonington had won six of the previous seven Turkey Day games, including a 45-0 demolition in 1955, so there was little reason to think the Bulldogs would play the Bears so closely. It didn't help Westerly's case that they came into the game with a record of 3-7-1 on the season while Stonington, led by coach Woody Douville, boasted a record of 7-1-1. Westerly's lone score came on a 16-yard run from Ed Bruno, while Stonington responded with a score of their own on a run from Bill Previty from just one foot out. The score stood at 6-6 going into the second half, and both teams held the opposition at bay. While Stonington threatened late in the fourth quarter, an interception by Charlie Dufour snuffed out their rally. The game concluded with the score at six apiece.[182] Westerly may not have come away with a victory, but given how overmatched many felt they were, it was certainly a moral victory for the Bulldogs.

Charlie Dufour, 1960
(Photo: Westerly High School Yearbook, Westerly Public Library)

EIGHT
24 November 1927
Final Score: Westerly 0, Stonington 0

Much like the game which came a decade later, this scoreless tie was a product of stout defensive efforts from both teams. What made this game even greater than the 1937 edition is that the Stonington Bears, who were poised to claim the championship of the Southeastern Connecticut and Southwestern Rhode Island League that season, came into the game as the heavy favorites while Westerly came into the game with a record of 2-3-3 (including a 12-0 loss to Stonington earlier that season). According to *The Westerly Sun* the final score was "a complete upset of pre-game dope" as the Bears were "favorites by at least a couple of touchdowns."[183] Despite the Bears' powerful running attack from their "three C's" Cragan (left halfback), Croning (right halfback), and Cowan (fullback), Stonington failed to take advantage, and the game ended in a deadlocked 0-0 tie before 2,500 fans. In his recap published in *The Senior*, sports editor Edwin Sawyer [for more on Edwin Sawyer, see page 191.] proclaimed: "The much-touted Stonington eleven was played completely off its feet and, with a few minutes more to play, the game, without a doubt, would have been Westerly's."[184]

Although the game ended without a score, it was enough for Stonington to take the league championship as well as the league trophy which was donated by a Mr. Ellington, owner of a sporting goods store in New London.[185-]

SEVEN
22 November 1962
Final Score: Westerly 15, Stonington 12

Perhaps more so than any previous game between the two, this edition of the annual Turkey Day classic was personal. In 1961, Stonington upset the Bulldogs 16-6, handing Westerly its first loss of the season. Much had changed since the 1961 season, as Westerly entered Thanksgiving with a disappointing 2-6 record. One of their two victories, however, showed the tenacity that the blue and white could exhibit. Just one week before Thanksgiving, the Bulldogs handed South Kingstown High School a stunning loss. The Rebels, a Rhode Island football powerhouse came into the game with a 6-1 record against the Bulldogs' 1-6. *The Westerly Sun* proclaimed that the Rebels should have won by "five or six touchdowns." Westerly would not be denied and they carried their momentum into their Thanksgiving Day matchup against their rivals. [186]

The two teams met for a 10 a.m. kickoff at the rain-soaked Ward Avenue Field in Westerly in front of 2,500 dedicated fans. Westerly took an early lead on a safety when Charlie Brooks tackled Stonington's Bruce Greene in the end zone, however, the Bears responded with two touchdown runs from John Rezendes in the second quarter. Stonington led 12-9 going into halftime, but the Bulldogs scored on a 47-yard catch by Nap Liborio, giving them the 15-12 lead, which they held on to for a stellar victory.[187] With their loss from the previous year avenged, the Bulldogs brought the Jeff Moore Memorial trophy back to Westerly.

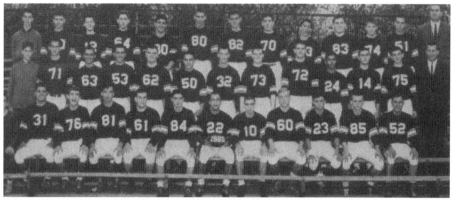

The 1962 Bulldogs
(Photo: Westerly High School Yearbook, Westerly Public Library)

SIX
25 November 1982
Final Score: Stonington 7, Westerly 0

With this loss, a decade of dominance by the Bulldogs came to an end. From 1971 through 1981, Westerly won eleven straight games against Stonington. While some games were close (such as 1978, when Westerly escaped with a 2-0 win), others were runaways (the Bulldogs crushed their rivals, 53-8, in 1973). To say that Stonington needed a win over Westerly would be an understatement, and on a cold November day, the Bears delivered. The 115th meeting between the two teams came down to the wire. Both teams held up on defense, preventing either side from gaining an edge on the scoreboard. Heading into the fourth quarter, the rivals were at a standstill, tied 0-0. With only 2:28 remaining in the game, Bears quarterback Steve Dolan hit his target, throwing a 39-yard pass to Gregg Bell for the game's lone score. The Bears dominated Westerly's passing game throughout, holding them to four first downs and only twenty-one passing yards. For the Bears, Dolan, who passed for 154 yards was awarded the trophy for 'outstanding player.' As *The Westerly Sun* proclaimed, "Stonington will now wipe the dust off the Jeff Moore Trophy that has been in the Westerly High showcase for 11 years."[188] For Westerly, the loss capped off a disappointing season which saw them finish with a record of 2-7-1.

FIVE
28 November 1940
Final Score: Westerly 7, Stonington 0

On eight different occasions, including the aforementioned 1982 game, the Westerly-Stonington Turkey Day game has ended with a final score of 7-0, six of which were won by the Bears.[189] What made the 1940 edition so thrilling is the way in which the Bulldogs scored the only touchdown of the game.

3,500 fans gathered at Westerly's Craig Field for the annual tradition despite the wet and windy conditions.[190] The muddy field and the intense wind prevented both teams from executing their offensive game-plans, leading to a defensive struggle for much of the game. Further hampering the Bears' efforts was the loss of "their play-calling and blocking back," Johnny Guekel, who left the game when he suffered a serious wrist sprain just three minutes in.[191] Towards the end of the first half, Westerly's left halfback, "The Bradford Blitzkreiger" Joe Capalbo, received a punt from the Bears' punter, Johnny Dion, and thanks in large part to stellar blocking by his teammates, Capalbo was able to run the ball back seventy-two yards for a touchdown. Capalbo then put a dot on that exclamation point by kicking the extra point through the uprights to give his team a 7-0 edge. Stonington attempted to rally in the game's final minutes, employing several forward passes (a strategy which was used far less frequently then than it is today). This last push for a score was extinguished when Westerly's Benny Servideo made a spectacular one-handed interception.[192] Given Stonington's recent dominance of their rivals, this win came as a shock to many.

The 1940 Bulldogs
(Photo: Westerly High School Yearbook, Westerly Public Library)

FOUR
24 November 1988
Final Score: Westerly 21, Stonington 21

This game may have ended in a 21-21 tie, but for much of the game, it appeared to be a one-sided affair. Before an estimated 7,500 fans, the Bulldogs (7-3) took on the Bears (2-7) with Westerly coming in as heavy favorites, however, expectations did not equate to reality.[193] Despite averaging 198.5 yards per game on the ground, Westerly was held to eighty-four yards on twenty-nine attempts by Stonington's defense.[194] At the end of the first half, Westerly held a slight edge, 13-7. The Bulldogs led 21-7 with only six minutes to go in the game, and to many, it seemed as though a Westerly victory was imminent. This was not to be, however, as the Bulldogs fumbled twice and the Bears took advantage of the opportunities with which they were presented, converting both turnovers into touchdowns to tie the score at 21.

The Brown and White's quarterback Heston Sutman was named the most valuable player for his fantastic performance which saw the junior rush for 122 yards, throw for ninety-three, and score all three touchdowns (two on the ground and one through the air). Sutman also ran for a two-point conversion that tied the score late in the game. The game, which *The Westerly Sun* called "one of the most—if not the most—exciting games (minute for minute) in the 76-year history of Stonington-Westerly football, ended with the two feelings of both joy and despair." While Westerly coach Jim Murano said "All I've got is this empty feeling," the MVP Sutman called it "the game of his life—'til next year."[195]

Westerly's Quarterback, Chad Gwaltney, Prepares to Hand the Ball Off in the 1988 Matchup.
(Photo: Westerly High School Yearbook, Westerly Public Library)

THREE
23 November 2000
Final Score: Westerly 24, Stonington 17 OT

The first Turkey Day game of the new millennium also gave rise to another first in the long-standing rivalry: an overtime game. In 1998, Rhode Island developed a protocol for tied games which would allow for overtime play. Connecticut did not have any such rules at the time, which is why the 1999 edition of the annual game ended in a 14-14 tie.[196] The thriller was played before 3,500 fans in Westerly, and saw the game's Most Valuable Player, Brian Lynch, score in overtime on a ten yard run to seal the victory for the Bulldogs.

Westerly (who would go on to finish the season 11-3 after winning the Superbowl game) opened the scoring with a record-setting ninety-one yard run by J.R. Lamotte, and went up 14-0 when quarterback Chris Reale scored on a run from four yards out. At the end of the first half, the Bulldogs held a 14-7 lead. The Bears came back and tied up the game on a twenty-eight yard pass by Mike Mellow which made the score 17-17 with 9:28 left in the game. Neither side could put the game away in regulation and for the first time, a game between Westerly and Stonington went to overtime. Lamotte's scoring run in OT brought the game to an end and gave Westerly its thirty-eighth victory over Stonington on Thanksgiving Day.[197]

Frank Chiaradio, Captain of the 2000 Bulldogs
(Photo: Westerly High School Yearbook, Westerly Public Library)

TWO
27 November 1969
Final Score: Stonington 29, Westerly 26

A record setting crowd, estimated to be between 7,000 and 8,000 was on hand to watch this game, the best Thanksgiving Day game between the Westerly and Stonington up to that point. Stonington was led by quarterback Bob Goodman who completed twelve of his seventeen passes for 194 yards and accounted for twenty-eight of the team's twenty-nine points. The Bears' offense was also powered by running back Dave Weber, who ran for 100 yards, averaging 7.8 yards per carry. Westerly was coached by Jim Gulluscio, who had a record of 1-9 in his first season leading the Bulldogs while Stonington's coach, Bob Anderson, evened his record against Westerly at 4-4 with this victory.

Al Savage, One of Three Captains of the 1969 Bulldogs
(Photo: Westerly High School Yearbook, Westerly Public Library)

Although Stonington got off to a 14-0 lead, the Bulldogs came back with a vengeance, trailing Stonington 21-20 at halftime. The Blue and White finally took the lead on a 49-yard touchdown drive, bringing the score to 26-21 in their favor. In the fourth quarter, Goodman struck once again, running the ball in from the one-yard line and hitting Mike McCue for the two-point conversion, giving the Bears a 29-26 lead. With little time remaining, Westerly had a chance to come from behind one final time. The Stonington defense, however, stymied the Bulldogs' efforts and held on to the lead keeping the Jeff Moore Memorial Trophy in Connecticut for another season.[198]

ONE
26 November 1981
Final Score: Westerly 13, Stonington 12

After losing to Westerly (5-3 entering this game) in the previous ten Thanksgiving Day games, Stonington looked poised to finally overtake their rivals, however, it was not to be on this day, thanks in large part to the efforts of Westerly's Quarterback, Rob Sciro. The bright sunny day brought fans out in full force, with an estimated crowd of 7,200 in attendance to witness the greatest Turkey Day game in the sixty-eight-year-old series.

In addition to playing Quarterback and amassing 120 rushing yards, Sciro was also Westerly's best defensive weapon throughout the game. While playing defensive back, Sciro intercepted three Stonington passes and recovered a fumble. Going into the game, Bulldogs coach Jim Murano's plan was to shut down the Bears' rushing attack, a plan which was executed to perfection as Stonington was limited to seventy-eight yards on thirty-four attempts. Despite Westerly's defensive dominance, Stonington entered the fourth quarter with a 12-7 lead. A seventy-five-yard scoring march engineered by Sciro was capped off by a nine-yard run for a touchdown by Ziggy Suminski.[199] The Bulldogs held on to their one-point lead, walking away with a 13-12 victory and extending their winning streak to eleven Turkey Day games over the Bears. Sciro's efforts and the fourth quarter comeback performed by the Bulldogs truly make this the greatest Turkey Day game Westerly and Stonington have ever played.

Coach Murano and the 1982 Bulldogs
(Photo: Westerly High School Yearbook, Westerly Public Library)

Westerly's Lost Village of Stillmanville

"The textile industry in Westerly, however, did not flourish until the middle of the nineteenth century. At that time, one man had such an influence on the area that the entire neighborhood surrounding where the mill buildings still stand today became known as Stillmanville, in honor of the proprietor, Oresmus M. Stillman."

The mural analyzed below, which depicts the historic mills of Pawcatuck, can be found on the side of C.C. O'Brien's Irish Sports Bar and Restaurant in Pawcatuck. While the mural does not refer to specific mills in Westerly, this article discusses one of the most important mill communities in town.

It often has been said that Rhode Island was at the forefront of the American Industrial Revolution which began shortly after 1800. While this is true, Rhode Island's role in the rise of the textile industry can be traced back to 1790. It was in this year that British industrialist Samuel Slater came to Pawtucket and installed the first successful Arkwright cotton-spinning machine, the most up-to-date technology, in America.[20] The textile industry in Westerly, however, did not flourish until the middle of the nineteenth century. At that time, one man had such an influence on the area that the entire neighborhood surrounding where the mill buildings still stand today became known as Stillmanville, in honor of the proprietor, Oresmus M. Stillman.

While the parameters of the Stillmanville neighborhood have never been officially defined, the epicenter was undoubtedly the lower portion of Canal Street which runs along the Pawcatuck River, where the Pleasant Street Hill comes to an end. Today, as was the case throughout the nineteenth century, the mill properties are separated into two distinct areas divided by the river. On the Westerly side of the river stands a complex of buildings currently owned and operated by the Darlington Fabrics Company. On the opposite side of the river, in Pawcatuck, a large multi-story building that had been abandoned for decades, stood until recently, where it served as a relic of the neighborhood's industrial history.

Oresmus M. Stillman
(Photo: Westerly Historical Society)

The area once known as Stillmanville is now more commonly known as the "North End" of Westerly. Today, it is among the most densely populated areas of the town. However, at the turn of the nineteenth century, the district's population was a mere fifteen residents. Before 1750, some settlers in Westerly had used water power from the Pawcatuck River, however, it was around 1798, when a man named Samuel Brand built a woolen mill roughly half a mile north of downtown Westerly, along the Pawcatuck River where Canal Street runs today, that the textile industry truly took off locally. The mill was sold to Sanford Taylor before passing through various hands over the next two decades. At some point prior to 1820, Brand's mill was replaced by a mill owned by William Stillman Jr. and Stephen Smith. [201] In addition to owning and operating the mill, Stillman was also an innovator, having been granted a patent for a cloth-shearing machine on 8 April 1815. [202]

Stillmanville
(Photo: Westerly Historical Society)

On the Pawcatuck side of the river, John Schofield purchased a former sawmill and linseed oil mill in 1806 that was constructed by John Congdon. Schofield then developed it into a carding and fulling wool mill.[203] Then, in August 1827, the White Rock Manufacturing Company began construction on a canal from the Pawcatuck River to Stillmanville which was completed in May 1828 at a cost of about $10,000. This canal, which has long since been filled in and built over, is where Canal Street's name was derived.[204]

The year 1831 was a crucial one for the development of Westerly's growing textile industry. It was in this year that Orsemus M. Stillman purchased Schofield's woolen mill in Pawcatuck. Stillman then constructed a bridge over the river, connecting Schofield's former mill with the Stillman and Smith mill in Westerly. Shortly thereafter, the two mills were combined to create a single manufacturing company. In 1848, the original mill buildings were replaced by two red-brick buildings standing three stories tall, which survive today. O.M. Stillman then proceeded to purchase several large tracts of land in the area surrounding his mills, eventually expanding them into a large mill village which would come to bear his name.[205]

Beginning in the middle of the nineteenth century, Irish, English, and Scottish immigrants, many of whom had prior experience in factories and mills during the United Kingdom's own Industrial Revolution, began emigrating to Westerly en masse to secure jobs in the booming textile industry. During this period, buildings began to crop up in Stillmanville. In an 1855 atlas of Westerly, very few buildings can be seen in the area, however, by 1870, there were more than one hundred buildings in the neighborhood.[206] Many of the houses which were constructed during this period were typical of those found in mill villages throughout New England: very near to the industrial center, built close together, and designed with "very little ornamentation."[207] Despite the lack of "ornamentation" in these homes, it has been noted that "Stillmanville was not a typical corporate-owned and corporate-built mill village characterized by nearly identical workers' houses."[208] These houses were later also popular among the Italian immigrants who came to Westerly in large numbers between 1900 and 1955. [For more information on Italian immigration to Westerly, see page 63.] The popularity of the Stillmanville/North End among Italian immigrants was due largely to its proximity to both the mills and the granite quarries, the two largest employers of immigrants in the area.[209]

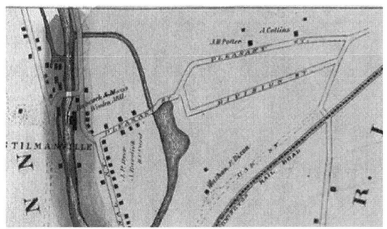

Stillmanville in 1855

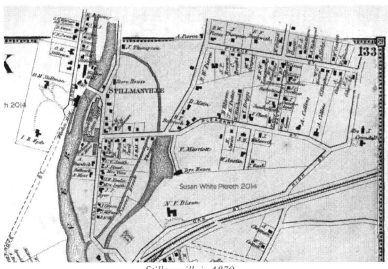

Stillmanville in 1870

While the influx of immigrant labor was a significant factor in the textile industry's prolonged success in Westerly, another factor worthy of mention is the 1837 arrival of the Stonington and Providence Railroad, which stopped in Westerly just a short distance from the Stillmanville Mill. [For more information on railroads in Westerly, see page 29.] The location of the railroad's terminal allowed the companies operating local mills to load and unload freight to and from other areas with relative ease. According to a report produced for the National Register of Historic Places for Westerly's North End: "Becoming part of an interstate rail network not only facilitated travel for people doing business, visiting, or living in Westerly Village and environs, but also gave local manufacturers the distinct advantage of ready access to suppliers of raw materials and to regional and national markets for finished products."[210]

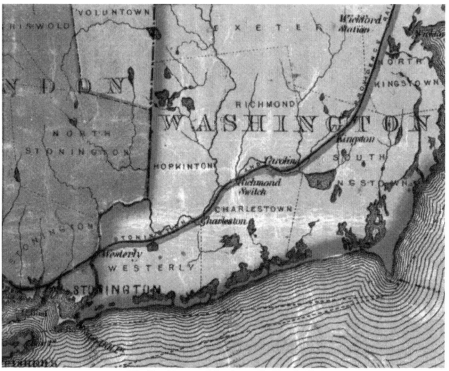

The Providence and Stonington Railroad, 1860
(Photo: Library of Congress, Geography and Map Division)

Stillmanville as Depicted on a Map Dated 1911
(Photo: Library of Congress Map Collection)

O.M. Stillman continued to operate his enterprise until 1870, when Jesse L. Moss and Rowse Babcock III acquired an ownership interest in the Stillmanville Mill.[211] The company was renamed the Westerly Woolen Company and continued under the ownership of the same company until the 1880s, despite Babcock's death in 1872.[212],[213] The mill was then sold to Louis W. and Warren O. Arnold, who retained the Westerly Woolen Company name until the early twentieth century. In 1918, Frederick F. Fowler, President of the Westerly Textile Company, acquired the property, with the intention to use it to produce automobile tire fabric.[214] The exact arrangement of this sale is not known, as Fowler purchased the properties on both sides of the river for ten dollars and "other valuable considerations."[215] Regardless, Fowler did not hold the property for long, as he sold it to the Ninigret Mills Company in March 1919.[216] Eventually, the mill properties were sold to the George C. Moore Company. Today, the plant is still operated by Moore Company in conjunction with Darlington Fabrics.[217]

Chapter III
Momentous Days in Westerly's History

Over the last three and a half centuries, there have been several extraordinary days, weeks, and months in Westerly's history.

The stories contained within this chapter fall into three distinct categories: events that were only impactful locally and were virtually unheard of outside of Westerly, those that were nationwide in scale and were distinctly American, and those that were experienced worldwide. The latter two categories are just as important as the former one because they showcase how events of great importance on a large scale were embraced in Westerly.

Not all of these events were pleasant for the people of Westerly, and some of these more harrowing events may have been experienced by those who are reading this book. This is especially true of the Blizzard of 1978, a week-long event that has taken on folklore status throughout New England. Despite occurring more than forty years ago, many still remember the storm's impact on the region.

Another troubling period in local history lasted from late 1918 to early 1920, a time when the entire nation and many parts of the world were in the grips of a deadly influenza pandemic. In the wake of the COVID-19 pandemic, much can be learned from the past. This is especially true given Westerly's response to the 1918 influenza epidemic which allowed the community to fare much better than many other towns across America.

In regards to events that were, and still are, celebrated across the entire world, two which are highlighted in this chapter are Christmas, particularly how those in Westerly celebrated the season in years past, and the coming of both a new century and a new millennium in 1900 and 2000. The examination of how the town embraced the arrival of two new years separated by a century is particularly fascinating in that the levels of celebration were at entirely opposite ends of the spectrum.

A nationwide event that was embraced in Westerly was the Centennial of the signing of the Declaration of Independence on 4 July 1876. Much like the Bicentennial one hundred years later, Westerly showed pride in its country in numerous ways throughout the day.

One last event that is covered in this chapter is one that was both local and out of this world entirely at the same time. In January 1925, a total solar eclipse was visible throughout much of the northeastern United States. Prior to the eclipse, which lasted just over two-and-a-half minutes, it had been determined that Westerly was among the best vantage points in the whole world for witnessing the event and for that reason, the town was inundated with curious visitors for several days.

The events discussed in detail throughout the chapter were of varying lengths with some taking place over the span of multiple years while others were over in a matter of mere minutes. Still, the impact these events had on the town was monumental and elicited emotions that were, in many ways, uniquely Westerly.

July 4, 1876: A Centennial Celebration

""At 4 o'clock in the morning, all the bells of the village commenced ringing, which was kept up for half an hour. Then a company of boys drove through the principal streets of the village, ringing bells and blowing horns."

As America draws nearer to the 250th anniversary of the signing of the Declaration of Independence, how Westerly celebrated the American Centennial on 4 July 1876 is certainly worthy of being studied more closely.

Leading up to the big day, it was apparent to all that there should be a momentous celebration. In the weeks prior to July Fourth, the Westerly Town Council voted and approved several measures, including granting permission to Everett Barnes and others to "ring hand bells on the streets of this village on the morning of 4 July 1876 from 4 o'clock to 5 o'clock or longer."[1] Additionally, the Council granted permission to all persons who wished to light fireworks on the property of the heirs of Rowse Babcock, east of Grove Avenue (today in Wilcox Park), and the land of Edward F. Vose on High Street to do so. In the event that the festivities got out of hand, the Town Council also appointed a special police unit to "preserve order at the Westerly Driving Park." This police unit was to serve without pay.[2]

The Centennial celebration began early in Westerly, as one review noted: "At 4 o'clock in the morning, all the bells of the village commenced ringing, which was kept up for half an hour. Then a company of boys drove through the principal streets of the village, ringing bells and blowing horns."[3] Later, at 8 o'clock, a parade of "Antiques and Horribles," a form of parade which originated in New England in the 1850's satirizing politicians and public figures, began.[4] The Westerly parade, however, had a particularly comical and self-deprecating tone. The procession was led by a man imitating President Ulysses S. Grant. This was followed by a replica of the famous Antietam statue with a moveable head and lower jaw which was drawn by eight oxen, as well as a display called "Going to the Centennial" which depicted a husband and wife from the country in a shabby carriage. The

Parade began at Armory Hall (on the land where McQuade's Marketplace now stands), proceeded through Westerly and Pawcatuck, and concluded at Dixon House Square on Broad Street.[5] A map of the approximate route can be seen on the following page.

At the parade's conclusion, the Declaration of Independence was read followed by an oration delivered by Gideon X. Squills LL.D. The entertainment for the afternoon was then held at the Westerly Driving Park. At noon, a baseball game was played between "a picked nine" and "Our Boys" the latter of which won the contest 12-7.[6] Following the game, there were horse races attended by more than eight hundred spectators which were "characterized by accidents" including two disabled carriages and one runaway horse. The horse owned by W.H. Chapman apparently became frightened at one point and ran into the crowd. Thankfully, there were no injuries from the incident.[7]

Although a sack race was planned for the afternoon, this was changed to a foot race, with a five dollar prize. Closing out the afternoon's revelries was a tightrope walk by a professor Dernier, who walked over Deep Hollow. The Westerly Brass Band furnished the music throughout the events. As the day turned into night, fireworks provided by the Antiques and Horribles Committee were launched from Grove Avenue, thus concluding the day-long observance.[8]

One intentional absence from the Fourth of July celebration in Westerly was alcohol. An article which appeared in the *Wood River Advertiser* several weeks after the Fourth noted, "There was an almost total absence of any appearance of intoxication during the day, the beer shops were voluntarily closed by their keepers. Only one arrest was made during the day for disorderly conduct."[9]

There was also a significant, albeit quieter, celebration of the Centennial held in White Rock. The day began with an invocation by Reverend J.G. Noble, Pastor of the Broad Street Christian Church and was followed by a reading of the Declaration of Independence by Reverend John Evans of First Baptist Church. This then led up to an oration by Reverend C.T. Douglass and a prayer read by J.W. Willetts of Pawtucket. After these readings, there was a dinner, a sack race, gymnastics, and a tub race on Pawcatuck Lake, as well as music by the White Rock Band throughout the day.[10]While the Centennial celebrations in Westerly were certainly exciting for their time, and properly commemorated an important date in our nation's history, the Fourth of July celebrations just twenty-four years later in 1900 showcase just how much progress was made in the late nineteenth century. On 4 July 1900 the steamer *Martha* was run between Westerly and Watch Hill five times throughout the day, and it was said that the electric cars in Watch Hill were constantly full and were run double their usual schedule.[11] Local merchants were also flooded with customers all day. According to one account "Tribly, the popcorn man, was in his element. All day long his melodious voice told of the food." The soda fountains in town were said to have done big business as a result of the intense heat. The heat also led to large crowds at the bathing beaches. Other events of the day included a picnic held by St. Michael's Church, a celebration for the opening of a new house at the Misquamicut Golf Club, and two baseball games played by the White Rock team at Riverside Park against teams from Wakefield and Jewett City.[12]

While the way the Fourth of July is celebrated may have changed since 1876, the sentiments remain the same. Nearly a century and a half later, many in Westerly still spend the day celebrating the history of our great nation and our town which we hold so dear.

"In 1885, the Westerly Roller Rink, which later became Bliven's Opera House, was the site of an afternoon party on Christmas afternoon. All who attended were given an umbrella and a photo album, and attendees were treated to live music and skating as well as the opportunity to meet Santa Claus in person."

When thinking of Christmas and the holiday season, it's hard not to envision beautifully decorated stores, familiar songs of the season, (and despite the rise of online shopping), people drifting between stores trying to find the perfect gift. These images perfectly describe the scenes visible in Westerly over the last century and a half which persist to this day.

At its very core, Christmas is a religious celebration, and for this reason, celebrations in Westerly often took place at local churches and with various religious groups. Through the early twentieth century, Christmas activities at local churches often were held throughout the week leading up to, and sometimes after, the holiday.

In 1873, at least seven local parishes held Christmas events. Three of these churches, the Calvary Baptist Church, the Seventh Day Baptist Church, and Christ Episcopal Church, held their festivities at Armory Hall on Main Street.[13] Only two churches had detailed descriptions of the events to be held published in local newspapers.

The Methodist Church held a festival on Christmas Day which was to include "a tree, a supper, and perhaps some literary exercises."[14] The Congregational Church was set to hold a festival with entertainment at the church.[15]

In the 1890's, it was fairly common for churches to bring in a preacher from out of town to conduct Christmas masses. In 1893, preachers from as close by as Woodville and as far away as Rochester, New York, made their way to Westerly for the holiday.[16] According to an account by Sallie Coy, in the first decade of the twentieth century, schools in Westerly held reenactments of the biblical story of Christmas, a practice which continued for many years. Religious aspects of Christmas have continued to be popular in Westerly, such as when, in 1949, *The Westerly Sun* highlighted the manger scene produced by the Church of the Immaculate Conception. [17],[18]

Christmas has always brought people together, and as a result, throughout history, parties and entertainment have been central to local holiday celebrations. In 1885, the Westerly Roller Rink, which later became Bliven's Opera House, was the site of an afternoon party on Christmas afternoon. All who attended were given an umbrella and a photo album, and attendees were treated to live music and skating as well as the opportunity to meet Santa Claus in person.[19]

While it may seem odd that such an event would be held on Christmas Day, at the turn of the century, observance of Christmas did not usually begin until Christmas Eve and often lasted through New Year's Day.[20] Children's Christmas parties were also quite common at the time, as Sallie Coy also recalled attending a party at a home on Elm Street, where children wore their finest outfits and were treated to "ice cream, animals [cookies], Santa Clauses, trees and stars."[21]

Christmas carols and concerts of holiday music could always be found on calendars throughout December in Westerly. In 1927, there was a Christmas Song Festival held at the United Theater which was put on by the YWCA. The event was held for the benefit of the community, as donations for the People's Mission, a local charity group, were collected.[22] [For more on the People's Mission, see page 318.] In addition to these concerts, in later years entertainment could be found at Christmas dances held at Westerly High School as well as shows by the Chorus of Westerly who performed Mozart's Mass and the annual Christmas Pops Concerts.[23]

Christmas is also a holiday centered around gift giving, making shopping and advertising a significant part of holiday preparations. While local stores composed the bulk of advertising in Westerly's newspapers before 1900, retailers as far as Providence also promoted their products, likely in anticipation of Westerly residents traveling to the city by train for a day of shopping.[24] In the 1890s, items as varied as domestic and imported fruits, canned turkey, chicken, tongue, ice skates and sleds could be seen advertised in *The Westerly Sun*.[25]

In the era before electric lighting was commonplace, many people would walk the streets with only the lights in window displays to guide them, as gas lamps often did not provide nearly enough visibility.[26] Despite this, or perhaps because of the well-lit shops, people would find themselves walking downtown past beautifully decorated stores with magnificent displays.[27]

By the early 1900s, a shift in gift-giving trends can be seen based upon the items advertised most prominently in local newspapers. Gift ideas for children were hardly in short supply, as there were promotions for Dunning's "Toy Wonderland" at 42 Main Street (between the Washington Trust building and the former *Westerly Sun* offices today) and numerous stores showcasing their confections and candy for both children and adults. For adult loved ones, Silverstein Brothers on West Broad Street advertised their selection of "Christmas furs."[28] For those looking to unwind after a busy holiday, they could easily go downtown to see a specially priced Christmas matinee moving picture at Ancient Order of Hibernians Hall on Union Street.[29]

One look at *The Westerly Sun* in December 1927 and the economic prosperity of the period before the Great Depression would be clear. Over the course of the month, the newspaper published a Christmas shopping guide several times, providing readers with the ultimate roadmap for local shopping. The wide range of items featured included handmade needle crafts, singing canaries, cigars, and even suggested giving a child the gift of a savings account at one of Westerly's many local banks.[30]

By this ti-me, Christmas shopping had become more of an event than ever before, a fact all the more apparent by Santa Claus' appearance at the P.H. Opie Company. The store invited children to come meet Santa and "shake hands with him."[31]

In the post-World War II era, automobiles were accessible to the masses, resulting in Christmas events held all across town. In 1949, *The Westerly Sun* published a column dedicated to the noteworthy decorated doorways which all could go see. That same year, the Christmas spirit was on display, as the Westerly Parent Teacher Association conducted a program in which they gave donated gifts to 115 children in foster homes. They were aided in their efforts by students from Westerly High School who held a tag day and raised eighty dollars which they used to purchase toys to donate.[32]

Although much has changed over the last 150 years, much of what has made Christmas such a special time of year has remained the same. Each year, people across Westerly are brought together by their love for one another and the joy that the holiday inspires.

The Start of a New Day, a New Century, and a New Millennium: New Year's Day in 1900 and 2000

"While Westerly seems to have honored the approach of 1900 in a fairly reserved manner, the coming of the new millennium at the end of 1999 was an entirely different matter."

All across the world, the dawn of a new year is celebrated with great anticipation and excitement. The joyous feelings are amplified significantly when it comes to the start of a new century and, even more so, a new millennium. While it is quite possible that there were festivities of some sort in Westerly at the start of the seventeenth and eighteen centuries, little is known of these events, and therefore, the focus of this article will be on how the town celebrated the arrival of the start of the twentieth century in 1900 and the new millennium in 2000.

1900: The Dawn of the Twentieth Century

Despite the excitement surrounding the coming of a new century, the evening of 31 December 1899 was a relatively quiet one in Westerly. The indifference of people throughout the town was noted in the *Westerly Sun* on New Year's Day when they claimed "The Holiday [was] Practically Ignored in Westerly."[33] The same newspaper also published a list of 'Happenings of the Year' which noted that "the past year has been an uneventful one in the history of Westerly."[34] Despite the perception of a mild response, events of note did take place throughout the evening.

As the year 1900 approached, several stores in downtown Westerly held special New Year's sales, as most were attempting to relieve themselves of leftover Christmas stock.[35] Aside from the retail establishments of Westerly, perhaps the busiest venues in town were the churches. In several religions, watchnight services are held on New Year's Eve and extend into early New Year's Day. A watchnight service is a mass which begins late in the evening and allows Christians to review the year, make confession, and prepare themselves for another year of faith.[36] Several local churches held services for this purpose. At the Church of Our Father, Westerly's Unitarian church, several musical selections with violin and vocal solos were performed, and a sermon was delivered.[37] At the Church of the Immaculate Conception, there was a solemn high mass sung "promptly at midnight."[38] It was later said that the church was filled nearly beyond capacity for this service. The Advent Church on Pleasant Street also held services which were well-attended. Despite being advertised on New Year's Eve, there were no watchnight services held at Grace Church.[39] Lastly, there was a watchnight service held at the People's Mission, a local charitable society, which was met with "much enthusiasm."[40]

(Photo: Westerly Sun)

Outside of the church services and retail establishments, Westerly residents did not engage in any noteworthy festivities for the coming of the twentieth century. In fact, much of Westerly carried on in much the same manner on New Year's Day as they had on any other day. The only exceptions were the library, which was closed for the day, the Westerly Cash Market which was closed between 11 a.m. and 4 p.m., and the Rhode Island Granite Works, which suspended work for the day.[41] The latter was said to have been closed owing to the many Scottish employees who celebrated New Year's Day as a "cherished holiday."[42]

2000: Y2K and the New Millennium

While Westerly seems to have honored the approach of 1900 in a fairly reserved manner, the arrival of the new millennium at the end of 1999 was an entirely different matter. As many will recall, the biggest news story leading up to the end of 1999 was the concern regarding the Year 2000 problem. 'Y2K,' as it was known, was a possible computer bug which had the potential to cause major data loss and the shutdown of important technological networks worldwide. Many will also recall that, despite the panic, few, if any, serious problems materialized. Leading up to New Year's Eve 1999, Y2K concerns were addressed publicly in Westerly. On December

28th, Town Manager Pamela Nolan informed *The Westerly Sun* that she was confident that the town was prepared for any issues which could arise.[43] In the unlikely event of any immediate problems, police chief Bruno Giulini stated that the police and fire departments were staffed at the same level as a peak summer weekend.[44]

Establishments across Westerly embraced the coming of a new millennium by hosting events and offering specials. Restaurants such as Three Fish (now the site of Bridge Restaurant) and the Weekapaug Golf Club offered special deals, while venues including the Andrea Hotel (which held a 'Millennium Party') and the Watch Hill Inn (which promised dancing and live entertainment) also exhibited the holiday spirit.[45] Although these events were intended for adults, there were also many activities provided with younger crowds in mind. Beginning at 4 p.m. on New Year's Eve, children were treated to face painting, magic shows, and a kids' carnival. The First Night program also hosted a special fireworks show at 6 p.m. "for those who have trouble keeping their eyes open until midnight."[46]

Millennium Events Year 2000 - 2001

December 31, 1999 Westerly Town Hall

3 P.M. rain or shine

Chairpersons: Charles McGrath & Dan LaPointe

Millennium Ceremony Schedule

Prayer for the Universe : Councilor Anne Schwer

Town of Westerly Mission Statement: Town Council

Veterans Honor Guard

Bristol Ready Volunteers

National Flag raised by Veterans / Legislators in Washington D.C.

State Flag raised by Legislators: Senator/ Representatives

Town of Westerly Millennium Flag raised by Mrs.Susan Latz

Councilor Richard Comolli and other Councilors present with Year 2000 Events Committee

Presentations:

Oldest Citizen: Finita Abbruzzese born August 7, 1896

Youngest Citizen: as of Midnight January 1, 2000

Piggy: Neil Winchenbach Creator / Gina Pellicano recipient

"Grand Olde Flag" etc. sung by Mrs. Jane Gencarelli

- Sign the Millennium Book until midnight -

- See the Millennium Dove by Anastasia Troyan -

- Toast the New Year with Sparkling Cider -

The Goal For The New Millennium 21st Century

LOVE. PEACE. UNITY

(Photo: Westerly Sun)

The countdown to the new millennium in Westerly officially began at 3 p.m. on December 31st with a ceremony held on the steps of the Town Hall. The event opened with a "Prayer for the Universe" read by Councilor Anne Schwer which was then followed by the Town of Westerly Mission Statement read by the Town Council.[47] This was followed by the raising of several flags including the Town of Westerly Millennium flag and the presentation of awards to the oldest (Finita Abbruzzese, born 7 August 1896) and youngest (born by midnight on December 31st) citizens.[48] The ceremonies concluded with attendees signing the 'Millennium Book.'[49]

As the day progressed, various events were held throughout downtown Westerly. The train station was transformed into a 1920's speakeasy and was the setting for an interactive murder mystery.[50] In the library gallery, visitors were invited to "meet" Roger Williams and at 9 p.m., a 'Count Down to Midnight' dance party was hosted by the YMCA.[51] The night turned out to be a cold but clear one, with the temperature hovering in the mid-20's all evening and no sign of snow.[52] As 1999 turned to 2000, all remained normal at the start of the new year. *The Westerly Sun* reported: "Despite some extraordinary predictions, Saturday, 1 January 2000, found local citizens doing ordinary things."[53]

Although they were celebrated in two very different ways, the events honoring the arrival of each new century were very much a product of their times. The year 1900 was welcomed in a very subdued and reserved manner, with Westerly residents embracing a Victorian approach with a quiet celebration. The year 2000, on the other hand, was anticipated with open arms in a more excited way. In the end, the events were similar in that they served as a time for all to reflect on the past year and to bring families and friends together.

A Royal Host: The Solar Eclipse of 1925

"Leading up to the day of the eclipse, New Haven Railroad officials reported that 4,500 round trip tickets had been sold for the train dubbed the "Eclipse Special." In addition to those who came from Connecticut, New York, and other points south, there were many who arrived on one of the six special trains from Boston, Providence, and Attleboro which ran to and from Westerly in the days prior to the event."

For several days in January 1925, Westerly was the host for more than five thousand visitors who arrived in droves to witness a rare and momentous event, a total solar eclipse. Several days were spent preparing for the thousands who descended upon the town to view the eclipse. Despite the time and effort required to brace for the influx of people, the event lasted a mere two minutes and thirty-two seconds.[54] Although brief, Westerly's hospitality and charm left a positive impression on those who chose the town as their viewing destination.

Leading up to the day of the eclipse, New Haven Railroad officials reported that 4,500 round trip tickets had been sold for the train dubbed the "Eclipse Special." In addition to those who came from Connecticut, New York, and other points south, there were many who arrived on one of the six special trains from Boston, Providence, and Attleboro which ran to and from Westerly in the days prior to the event.[55] In order to coordinate locations, transportation, and other logistics, an eclipse committee was formed by the Westerly Board of Trade (one of the groups which would later form the Ocean Community Chamber of Commerce). The committee was chaired by Frank W. Coy and included other prominent local businessmen including Arthur I. Perry, James M. Pendleton, Arthur M. Nash, and Daniel F. Larkin.[56]

Several landowners in Westerly offered up their properties for viewing, and the committee eventually settled on Foster Farm (now approximately 85 Beach Street) as the principal location for visitors arriving by train. Due to inclement weather in the days prior to the eclipse, the highway department was tasked with clearing snow from a large space on the property. As a means of limiting congestion, cars were not allowed on the farm. Passengers arriving on later trains were taken to a space across from Vose Park (on the Granite Street hill).[57] Meanwhile, many Westerly residents planned to view the eclipse from Hinckley Hill in Pawcatuck. William A. Wilcox, who owned nine acres of land on the hill, opened up his property to those who wanted to see the eclipse. Additionally, the firm of Thorpe and Trainer granted access to a lot of land they owned at Misquamicut Hills, a series of bluffs off of Shore Road, as a potential viewing location.[58]

The committee issued a plea to the people of Westerly to supply vehicles to transport those arriving by train and to guests at the hotels downtown.[59] According to *The Westerly Sun*, rides were provided by "scores of automobiles including buses, jitneys, trucks fitted up especially to carry a number of passengers and private cars loaned by their owners."[60]

When the day of the eclipse finally arrived, all of the preparations by the town and the committee paid off, and the event went as smoothly as possible, garnering praise from many who visited. The first special train bringing passengers to Westerly arrived at 8:10 a.m. and contained mostly college students and professors.[61] In an effort to allow their employees to witness the momentous event, most local businesses did not open until after 10 a.m., including banks that stated they would open at 10 a.m. and close at 12:30 p.m. (the early closing time was due to the eclipse falling on a Saturday).[62] The town was well-protected, as members of local Battery E served as military police, providing assistance to the Westerly Police Department. Local Boy Scout troops were tasked with guiding pedestrians throughout the town and directing traffic. Some viewers began arriving at Vose Park and other areas on the Granite Street hill as early as 7:20 a.m. when they were seated on an old grandstand available for the occasion.[63]

Amenities were provided throughout the morning to accommodate watchers. Due to the cold weather, the town hall, the library, and the Colonial Club were all made available as places where people could warm up. As for food, Harry A. Littlefield informed the eclipse committee that he would be opening his Shore Dinner House in Watch Hill for those who were in the area. Hot dog and coffee stands were also present at all popular viewing locations.[64]

SIGNS AND WONDERS
1925

Photograph and Copyright by Frederick W. Goetz,
Highland Falls, N.Y.
DIAMOND RING
OF THE
SOLAR ECLIPSE - JAN. 24, 1925.

The 1925 Solar Eclipse
(Photo: Library of Congress Prints and Photographs Division)

Several notable individuals made their way to Westerly to see the phenomenon, including Percival P. Baxtor, former Governor of Maine and Alfred C. Lane, Professor of Geology at Tufts University, who brought his students down for the event. The most notable name mentioned in the days leading up the event, however, was Thomas Edison. Unfortunately, Edison was unable to come to Westerly due to illness. Edison's son and daughter made the trip, however, and they were said to have stayed at the Rhode Island Hotel.[65]

At 9:54 a.m. on 24 January 1925, those looking towards the sky witnessed a solar eclipse which lasted, at its peak, for just over two and a half minutes.[66] Witnesses at Foster Farm were treated to messages broadcast by the dirigible *Los Angeles*, which was carrying a group of government officials and scientists. The messages were conveyed by a radio tractor which was set up at the farm.[67] The response to Westerly's hospitality was overwhelmingly positive in the days following the eclipse. Dr. Leonard T. Troland, former President of the American Optical Society, was quoted as saying that the event put Westerly on the map. An article in the *Boston Advertiser* referred to Westerly as "a royal host."[68] Much of the praise was given to those who worked to ensure the event ran without issue, and the success was attributed to careful planning and hard work.

(Photo: Westerly Sun)

For several days in early 1925, Westerly was considered a must-visit destination. The events leading up to and after the solar eclipse of January 24 left an impression on many visitors and provided them with memories that would last a lifetime.

The Week Westerly Stood Still: The Blizzard of 1978

"The snow continued to fall throughout the evening, and Governor J. Joseph Garrahy declared a snow emergency for the State of Rhode Island. Members of Westerly's 169th Military Police Company spent the night checking Interstate 95 for stranded motorists. Those who were located were transported to the armory on Dixon Street. Overnight, twelve deaths due to the storm were reported in Rhode Island, although none were in Westerly."

If you were to ask anyone in New England over the age of 50 about the Blizzard of 1978, chances are, they could tell you numerous stories from the week that Rhode Island stood still. Westerly was deeply affected by the storm, as was the entire northeastern United States. Preparations began on Sunday February 5th and it was not until Monday of the following week, February 13th, when life fully returned to normal. Below is a day by day look at the Blizzard of 1978 in Westerly.

Sunday, February 5th

At 5 a.m. on Sunday morning, WPRO, the Providence-based radio station, issued its first Winter Storm Watch, which served as an early indication of what was to come. At 5 p.m. that evening the station issued a Heavy Snow Watch, predicting more than six inches of snow, while cautioning listeners to the potential of heavy gales.[69] Late in the day, low temperatures caused the fish ladder at the Potter Hill Dam to freeze over, and a picture of this scene appeared in *The Westerly Sun* the following evening.[70]

Monday, February 6th

The evening edition of the *Sun* referred to National Weather Service reports which suggested that up to sixteen inches of snow could fall in Westerly between Monday and Tuesday, a figure that turned out to be an underestimate. The *Sun* made it clear that this storm would be more impactful than the one which had struck the state two weeks earlier.[71]

At 10 a.m., snow began to fall heavily in Westerly, making travel from difficult to impossible.[72] By noon, Coastal Flood Warnings were issued for Narragansett Bay, indicating that tides could rise as high as two to four feet above normal.[73]

A School Bus in the Snow at the Intersection of East Avenue and Wells Street
(Photo: Westerly Sun)

The Superintendent of Westerly Public Schools, Felix J. Torromeo, announced that afternoon kindergarten would be cancelled and all Westerly schools were to be dismissed at 1 p.m. Despite the early dismissal, the school system still encountered multiple issues. At the height of the storm, elementary school students were stuck on immobilized school busses in several areas including Chestnut Street, Woody Hill Road, Beach Street, and Upper High Street.[74] In some cases, students did not arrive home until as late as 5 or 6 p.m. Westerly Police Chief James R. Gulluscio noted that he fielded about thirty calls from concerned parents when their children did not arrive home when expected. Additionally, approximately two hundred students were left in the gymnasium of State Street School with only one teacher's aide around 2 p.m.[75]

At 7 p.m. that evening, the negotiating committee for Council 94 of the American Federation of State, County, and Municipal Employees, led by Director Giovanni Folcarelli, met to discuss whether or not union workers would go on strike over a contract dispute. Disaster was narrowly averted, as the 12,000 union members did not begin their strike during or directly after the storm.[76] The snow continued to fall throughout the evening, and Governor J. Joseph Garrahy declared a snow emergency for the State of Rhode Island. Members of Westerly's 169th Military Police Company spent the night checking Interstate 95 for stranded motorists. Those who were located were transported to the armory on Dixon Street. Overnight, twelve deaths due to the storm were reported in Rhode Island, although none were in Westerly.[77]

A Man Walks through an Abandoned Downtown Westerly
(Photo: Westerly Sun)

Tuesday, February 7th

The snow finally let up at noon on Tuesday, at which time measurements were taken, and it was determined that Westerly received between twenty and twenty-four inches of snow.[78] An application to Washington D.C. signed by Governor Garrahy was accepted and on Tuesday morning, President Jimmy Carter officially declared the state a disaster area.[79] At 4:30 that afternoon, the President further declared Rhode Island a Federal Emergency Area.[80]

Throughout the day, winds remained strong, with gusts over fifty miles per hour, creating dangerous snow drifts and piling on to already massive peaks. Temperatures also remained dangerously low, with an overnight windchill of just ten degrees.[81]

Newspaper and television reports of the storm brought updates to Rhode Islanders who steadily began to realize the havoc the blizzard wreaked on the entire state. According to authorities, as many as one thousand cars were stranded along several roadways.[82] Captain Frederic Ward of the Military Police reported that there were still fifteen stranded motorists who remained at the armory that evening. At the storm's peak, 2,100 Narragansett Electric customers had lost power, but by 9:30 a.m. on Tuesday morning, service had been restored to all but 275 of those customers. All schools and town hall buildings were closed for the day.[83]

At 6 p.m. a fire was reported at Pal's General Store in Misquamicut. Misquamicut Fire Chief Martin Bralich stated that "horrendous roads complicated matters." Despite the poor conditions, two Misquamicut Fire trucks with tire chains and one truck from the Westerly Fire Department managed to reach the site of the fire. Some of the firefighters were said to have arrived on foot and one even made use of a snowmobile to access the scene. It took forty men forty-five minutes to fight the blaze, which was blamed on a "faulty electrical cable."[84]

The Fire at Pal's General Store
(Photo: Westerly Sun)

<u>*Wednesday, February 8th*</u>

Federal troops arrived in Rhode Island from Fort Benning, Georgia throughout the day on Wednesday. The troops were assigned to Rhode Island after President Carter's confirmation that the state was a Federal Emergency Area. Because of its status as an emergency area, Rhode Island was required to fund only twenty-five percent of the cost of the equipment required to clear the streets.[85]

Schools remained closed, as many roads were still considered impassable. Highway crews continued their dedicated work ensuring that most main roads in Westerly were cleared by the start of the day, although secondary roads were still covered in snow.[86]

Locally, banks and some stores reopened, but restaurants throughout town were still shuttered on Wednesday. By this time, some establishments had not had the opportunity to shovel their sidewalks, forcing pedestrians, at times, to walk in the streets of downtown Westerly.[87]

Thursday, February 9th

After another day of cleanup efforts, Westerly began its return to relative normality. By Thursday, most local stores had reopened. According to *The Westerly Sun*, the supplies of "milk and basic foodstuffs" were "adequate" as were gas and heating supplies, which were essential to keeping homes warm during the extremely cold temperatures.[88]

Pedestrians were seen flocking to stores and restaurants in the downtown area throughout the day on Thursday, another sign that the town had begun to come out of its snow-induced hibernation. Residents were urged to clear their sidewalks, as mail service was set to resume for the first time all week. After an hour-long conference with Chief Gulluscio, Public Works Director James H. Crowley, Town Manager John F. Donnoe, and Superintendent Torromeo determined it would be best to keep Westerly schools closed until Monday.[89]

It was also reported that normal police activities were being conducted using both volunteer and Army National Guard four-wheel drive vehicles and police cruisers. Most of these actions involved transporting doctors and nurses to and from Westerly Hospital. For the first time since the snow began to fall, some employees of the Westerly town garage on Beach Street were given a reprieve after many had worked forty hours straight without much opportunity for sleep.[90]

Friday, February 10th

While Westerly Public Schools remained closed, other local school districts, including Stonington and North Stonington, resumed classes for the final school day of the week.[91] Travel throughout the state was severely hindered due to roadblocks set up by Rhode Island State Police. On Interstate 95 in North Stonington, cars heading northbound beyond East Greenwich were halted and not allowed to proceed.[92] Areas in northern Rhode Island had received significantly more snow, including Burrillville, which reported a total of thirty-three inches.[93]

The ban on travel beyond East Greenwich caused many truckers to be stuck in place when police prevented them from continuing on to their intended destinations. Those who were interviewed claimed that a three-day layover was something they had never seen before, and the cargo carried by these drivers risked spoiling. They also realized that even if they made it through Rhode Island, they would face issues in Massachusetts, which had also issued a non-emergency driving ban.[94]

Over the weekend, day-to-day life in Westerly returned to normal, due in large part to the tireless efforts of Westerly town employees. On Monday, students were finally allowed to return to school.

The Week That Was

While Westerly survived the storm without significant loss of life or property, other communities were not as lucky. According to the United States Department of Commerce, the American Red Cross reported ninety-nine deaths and 4,587 injuries caused by the storm, while 39,000 people required shelter.

Although Massachusetts reported the greatest storm-related damage, Rhode Island was the state that felt the second largest impact. The Red Cross recorded the following statistics for Rhode Island:[95]

- 26 deaths
- 232 injuries or illnesses
- 50 hospitalizations
- 15 single-family homes reporting major damage
- 15 single-family homes reporting minor damage
- 66 shelters operating
- 9,150 persons sheltered
- 52,317 victims and workers given mass care

Long-term effects of the storm were also notable, as snow drifts damaged seawalls and protective dunes, leaving beaches open to further harm by future storms.[96]

The Blizzard of 1978 left Westerly buried under nearly twenty-four inches of snow, the tireless efforts of town workers, citizens, and emergency personnel allowed the community to survive relatively unscathed. While many will remember where they were when the storm hit our town, the strong response which averted tragedy should be celebrated. The Blizzard of 1978 should be remembered locally for way the community came together and survived one of the greatest storms the town had ever seen.

"All of Westerly Seems to be Awakened to the Situation": The Influenza Epidemic of 1918-1920

"For several weeks, it seemed that Westerly had weathered the storm that swept across the nation in 1918; sadly, however, this was only the beginning. Just before Christmas, a second wave swept over the town, and on December 23rd, it was reported that there were one hundred new cases and the Red Cross was once again asked to supply masks."

More than one hundred years ago, the town of Westerly, and all of America, faced a pandemic the likes of which had rarely been seen in American history. Now more than ever, the story of the so-called "Spanish Influenza" epidemic is relevant to the struggles faced by many as we, as a society, attempt to navigate life in the time of COVID-19. The story of a community that did all it could to survive and showed strength in the face of great danger serves as an important lesson that must be remembered.

Despite the name given to the illness, Spanish Influenza, or more commonly, Spanish Flu, the illness was first identified in the United States in March 1918 when an Army cook at Camp Funston in Haskell County, Kansas, became the first confirmed victim. Within just two days, there were 522 men at the camp who were reported as sick.[97] Due largely to the United States' involvement in World War I, the virus spread rapidly to other army camps before eventually ravaging Europe.

The name "Spanish Flu" was likely derived from the fact that newspapers frequently reported the effect of the pandemic in Spain, a country that remained neutral in World War I. These news stories as well as reports of the severe illness suffered by King Alfonso XIII of Spain at the hands of the virus led to the proliferation of the nickname that has persisted.[98] Although more than a century has passed, the exact origins of the illness have not been definitively located, there is little to no evidence to suggest Spain was the point of origin.[99]

The 1918 Influenza Pandemic, like many epidemics, struck in waves. The first wave, which lasted throughout the first half of 1918, was relatively mild and had no notable impact on the town of Westerly. The second wave, which began in September 1918 and lasted until the end of that year, was a very different story. *The Norwich Bulletin* first reported on September 20th that "there are cases of influenza in Westerly, but no quarantine has been ordered by the Superintendent of Health."[100]

The first death recorded during Westerly in 1918 that was attributed to influenza was three days later on September 23rd.[101] The first death specifically identified as being caused by "Spanish" Influenza was recorded on October 4th. Over the next two weeks, thirty-eight deaths were attributed to influenza in some way.[102] It was reported on October 1st that physicians were receiving as many as one hundred calls per day.[103]

One week after it had been reported that no quarantine measures had been taken, there were indications that this was likely to change. Dr. Samuel C. Webster, the Superintendent of Health for the Town of Westerly (and soon to be a prominent figure in the community), ordered the closing of all schools, churches, theatres, and the "juvenile department" of the Westerly Public Library. The closing of schools must have seemed to be a foregone conclusion, as it was stated that there were 382 absences attributed to illness at local schools the day before the order was put in place.[104]

The interruptions to the local workforce were felt almost immediately. It was reported that "boys under 15 are reading metres [sic] for the Westerly Light and Power Company" and girls were doing the same in New London. It was also noted that trolley cars were not running on schedule, much to the chagrin of passengers. There was no official record of the number of cases in Westerly at the end of September, as Influenza was not considered a reportable disease at that time, and therefore, no tally of cases was taken.[105]

At the start of October, further measures were taken to mitigate the spread of the virus, including many which are similar to those taken by Westerly residents a century later. Saloon keepers were notified to not allow men to congregate in groups and failure to comply with these orders would result in immediate closure until the epidemic passed.[106] While saloons were allowed to remain open with limited patronage, soda fountains, including those inside pharmacies, were ordered to close their doors at once. This caused some to question the rationale of allowing bars to keep their doors open while others were prevented from conducting business.

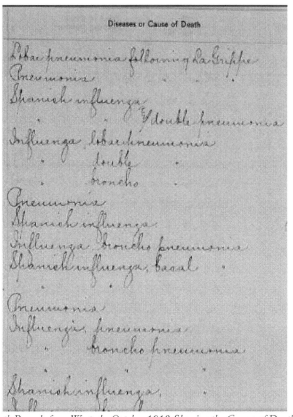

Death Records from Westerly, October 1918 Showing the Causes of Death

To better enforce the measures being implemented, the Westerly Town Council swore members of the Sanitary Corps (later known as the Westerly Ambulance Corps) in as police constables providing them with the authority to enforce regulations which were meant to prevent the spread of influenza.[107]

This was a much-needed action, as several members of the police force had been unable to work due to illness.[108] One recommendation that may sound very familiar to many readers came when local health professionals implored citizens to wear face masks when caring for those who were ill. Masks were being made by the Westerly chapter of the Red Cross and according to an account in *The Norwich Bulletin*, the masks were "not to be soaked in any chemical but are designed to protect the wearer from bacteria floating in the air."[109]

Within just five days, it was apparent that further actions were needed to continue to protect the community. Both the (then vacant) Beach Street School as well as the Pleasant Street School were converted into makeshift hospitals to handle the growing number of Influenza cases. This led one news source to proclaim: "The need for a fully equipped hospital has been made plain."[110] Additionally, members of the Sanitary Corps, most of whom held full-time jobs, gave up their employment to dedicate themselves to caring for the sick.

Their resolve in the face of an epidemic did not go unnoticed, as it was said: "The Sanitary Corps…has shown the result of thorough training and concerted action." In addition to the temporary constables enforcing compliance with local orders, the Rhode Island State Guard was contracted to patrol "the most infected section of the town" to prevent unnecessary home visits, especially in places where sickness was rampant.[111]

By the second week of October, it was apparent that the situation was rapidly becoming "all-hands-on-deck" in Westerly, and citizens began to step up and do their part for the community. A group known as the Women's Motor Corps was formed to take doctors to and from the sick, carry supplies to emergency hospitals, transfer nurses, and do work of an emergency nature while remaining on-call both night and day. Several retired doctors and nurses returned to work to offer assistance wherever they were needed, and in noting the seriousness of the issue, it was said "all of Westerly seems to be awakened to the situation."[112]

Despite the grim outlook, especially as the death rate in Westerly was reported as being "very high," Dr. Webster reported on October 8th that the number of new cases was decreasing, suggesting that the preventative measures were successful in curbing the rise of new cases.[113] One week later, on October 15th, the outlook had hardly improved. One local resident perhaps put his reaction best when he recorded in his diary that day: "Influenza very alarming in Westerly. Many deaths."[114] It was reported the same day that barrooms (which had since been closed), soda fountains, schools, theatres, and the library all remained closed. In spite of all these concerns, Dr. Webster still reported "a material decrease in the number of cases."[115]

The number of cases continued to fall and three days later, only two influenza deaths were reported, a decrease from days prior.[116] The closing of many businesses and places of gathering impacted several local institutions, including the Westerly Historical Society which canceled their October meeting due to the epidemic (an act they would repeat in January 1919 for the same reason).[117]

As the number of cases fell each day, the beginning of November allowed many to step back and truly assess the impact of the illness on the community. Dr. Webster made a report to the Westerly Town Council early that month, and in doing so, he painted a rather jarring image for those in attendance. It must be noted that there was not any type of testing for influenza in 1918 and therefore, a diagnosis could only be derived from an examination of symptoms and the opinion of a physician. Bearing this in mind, the fact that Dr. Webster reported an estimated 1,000 cases and roughly one hundred deaths due to influenza was reason for great concern. In 1910, the population of Westerly was 8,696 and it had risen to 9,955 in 1920, and therefore, it can be surmised that there were approximately 9,703 residents in 1918 (assuming consistent growth over the decade).[118] Therefore, about 10.3 percent of the town was stricken with influenza and 1.3 percent perished as a result of the virus. Dr. Webster reported there were still sporadic cases and some deaths in the week prior, but there were "very few new cases."[119]

In 1918, there were 231 deaths recorded in Westerly, more than one hundred over the ten year average of 130 between 1907 to 1917.[120] The official death records for the town of Westerly for 1918 show fifty-eight deaths that were attributed to influenza, however, there were likely several in which influenza was an underlying cause but it was not listed as the official cause of death.[121] In terms of who was most affected by the illness, it was reported: "The majority of cases were in the thickly populated Italian section and so it was said, due to the unsanitary conditions."[122] Of the 58 deaths recorded in 1918 that were attributed to influenza, the average age at death was just 26.8 years.[123]

For several weeks, it seemed that Westerly had weathered the storm that swept across the nation in 1918; sadly, this was only the beginning. Just before Christmas, a second wave swept over the town, and on December 23rd, it was reported that there were one hundred new cases and the Red Cross was once again asked to supply masks.[124]

In a retrospective account by Dr. Albert Spicer who was a young boy at the time of the pandemic, "Many local people were stricken right after Christmas," and he recalled his father, also a doctor, hiring around-the-clock nurses to care for his patients.[125] The virus struck at home for Spicer as well, as his mother was taken ill and was bedridden for more than three weeks with double pneumonia. In his most telling memory, Dr. Spicer claimed: "I remember my dad telling of picking up *The Westerly Sun* every night to check the obituary column and finding eight to ten names of people that had died, oftentimes close friends of the family."[126]

1919: The Second Wave

By the start of 1919, it was apparent that Westerly was facing a major epidemic that was to be treated as a significant threat. On January 1, it was reported that the Washington Trust Company was particularly hard hit as twelve employees were absent with illness and former employees had to be called in for assistance. Interestingly, in this second wave, many of the homes that were hit in the first wave were now immune while other neighborhoods were impacted to a greater degree.[127]

When it became clear that a community-wide effort would be required to combat the sickness, many of the groups that provided invaluable assistance during the first wave, namely the Red Cross, the Rhode Island State Guard, and the Women's Motor Corps, were ready to begin work again when needed. Despite a spike in cases appearing just prior to Christmas, Westerly schools resumed classes after Christmas, although schools across the river in Pawcatuck were ordered to close.[128]

One area which was deeply impacted was Block Island, where there were fifty-one reported cases and it was said that many in Westerly had relatives on the island. Most startling, however, was the report of 700 cases in Westerly at the start of 1919.[129]

By the second week of January, church services on Saturdays and Sundays were being canceled due to the growing threat of the spread of influenza.[130] Very little was reported on the epidemic for the remainder of January. On February 4, it was written that influenza was now considered a reportable disease, and therefore, official statistics could be kept. At that same time, Dr. Webster reported only eleven cases in January.[131] Based on how the epidemic was reported after January 1919, it appears that the town was hit hardest just during the Christmas season in 1918, before the disease rapidly vanished from the public eye.

The diary of thirteen-year-old Helen May Clarke of nearby Mystic, Connecticut provides a unique perspective on how the illness was treated. In an entry from July 1919, Helen recalls her experience as she was stricken with the illness. According to her account, her grandmother "slapped mustard plasters on [her] chest, salt pork around [her] throat, and [used] a horrible ointment that smelled like skunk oil." She also recounts being given herbal teas with sulfur and molasses as well as "sirup [sic] of onions."[132]

As 1919 wore on, fewer and fewer cases were reported, and by November, only one case was reported with no fatalities at that time.[133] Overall, the number of Influenza-related deaths in 1919 was significantly less than in 1918 as there were only sixteen deaths attributed to the illness that year.[134]

1920: The Epidemic Comes to an End

As is often the case with influenza, there was a seasonal pattern that developed, and as a result, there was yet another wave. The 1920 wave, however, would have a much smaller impact on the town than the 1918 and 1919 versions. In early February, it was stated that there were no reported cases, however, it was speculated that there may have been several milder cases that were simply not reported.[135]

Just a few weeks later, it was said that there were thirty cases in Westerly.[136] The smaller numbers were explained by Dr. Webster when he spoke before the Town Council in April. At that time, he proclaimed that he firmly believed the current strain of influenza differed from that which struck the town in 1918.

According to the Superintendent, only five of the sixteen physicians in Westerly reported cases to him, and because of his belief that it was a different illness, he did not report these as part of his monthly health report in order to avoid causing unnecessary panic. Interestingly, of the fifty-three cases that had been officially reported by the start of April, thirteen were in Bradford.[137]

Overall, there are many parallels that can be drawn between the local response to the 1918-1920 influenza epidemic and how the COVID-19 epidemic of 2019-2021 has been handled in Westerly. As always, lessons of the past must be applied whenever possible so that we may learn from the situation and continue to improve as a society.

Chapter IV
The People Who Made History in Westerly

At its very heart, history is driven by the people that make it. The articles in this chapter tell the stories of the people that made Westerly's history.

The most prominent figures in Westerly's history have been written about at great length, and therefore, the articles in this chapter aim to tell the stories of those who made monumental contributions but were previously excluded from the narrative.

This chapter begins with the story of Anna Thornton Williams, a woman born into slavery in Kentucky who became a successful businesswoman and eventually made her home in Westerly. In 1920, she was the first woman to cast her ballot in the presidential election in Westerly after the passing of the Nineteenth Amendment.

Following an account of the life of an individual born into bondage is the story of Charles Perry, a man who fought to abolish such an injustice in the United States.

Throughout this chapter, there are stories of individuals who made Westerly a better place for the people who lived there. One such story is that of Dr. John Gordon Anderson, the founder of the Margaret Edward Anderson Hospital, where many Westerly residents were treated over a span of four decades. Another noteworthy individual who selflessly saved lives in Westerly was Henry M. Morris, a man who rescued several people who were stranded during the Hurricane of 1938. Additionally, there is Marshall Drew, a man who survived incredible hardship at a young age, enduring the sinking of the *Titanic* and later finding a place for himself in Westerly's art community.

Ultimately, it is Westerly's people that create its history and the lives captured on the pages that follow are just some of the many who shaped the town that we know today.

She Hath Done What She Could: Anna Thornton Williams and Her Historic Vote

"According to The Westerly Sun, *which was on the scene for the momentous occasion: "Williams did not say for whom she voted, but as she came from the voting place and was congratulated by a* Sun *reporter for being the first to vote, she remarked: "Washington left principles for everybody,"*

"FORMER SLAVE FIRST TO VOTE" read the headline in *The Westerly Sun* on 2 November 1920. The individual the headline referred to was Mrs. Anna Thornton Williams, the first woman to cast a ballot in Westerly after the Nineteenth Amendment was ratified in August 1920.[1]

Today, there stands a grave marker in River Bend Cemetery for Mrs. Williams which reads "ANNA THORNTON WILLIAMS, BORN A SLAVE IN KY, 1856, SHE HATH DONE WHAT SHE COULD."[2] Anna Williams, born into bondage, lived a full and fascinating life both before and after her historic vote.

On 27 February 1856, Shumake (or possibly Benjamin) Williams and Amanda (King) Williams, a slave on the plantation of Andrew and Rachel McClure in Nicholasville, Kentucky, welcomed to the world a daughter, Anna.[3] According to records from later in Anna's life, it is believed that her father was born in England, however, very little is known about her early life and the lives of her parents.[4] What is known is that she was the granddaughter of Hiram King, a Civil War veteran and a slave of a man named Isaac Shelby.[5]

Although an official record has not been located, Anna claimed that in either 1872, when she was just 16 years old, or 1873, she married a man by the name of Walker Thornton.[6] Within the next five years, Anna and Walker moved eighty-five miles north to Cincinnati, Ohio, where Walker worked as a barber while Anna found work in a confectionery for some time before settling into a lifelong career in beauty and hair care.[7]

Although they were frequently recorded in Cincinnati, Anna and Walker actually settled just outside the city in the town of Miami in Clermont County, Ohio.[8] On 5 June 1885, Anna gave birth to her only child, a son named Charles Walker Thornton. Interestingly, this son's name was given as Charles Jr. on his birth record, although his father was listed as Walker Thornton.[9]

The marriage between Anna and Walker appears to have been a difficult one, as they were separated by 1890. Three years later, in March 1893, Walker applied for a license to marry his second wife, however, Anna requested an indictment against Walker and presented a certificate showing that she married him in 1873 and that they were not legally divorced.[10]

MRS. A. THORNTON,

Mrs. Anna Thornton, 1900
(Photo: The Colored American)

Between 1894 and 1907, Anna lived in Cincinnati and was variously described as a hairdresser, dermatologist, manicurist, and a scalp specialist, reflecting a wide range of specialized knowledge.[11] During this time, she was consistently living on Fifth Avenue in Cincinnati while operating her business out of her home. An account published in the *Colored American* on 17 November 1900 speaks glowingly of Anna's business acumen. The article states:

"The city of Cincinnati is blessed in having as one of its citizens, Mrs. A. Thornton, who, from a poor Kentucky girl, has risen to a commanding position in her profession."[12]

According to that same account, Anna's business was the largest dermatology parlor in Cincinnati and she was acknowledged as the leading scalp specialist in the city. Perhaps most notably, the article proclaims "She stands out as a shining example of the possibilities [for] women of the race."[13]

Anna found herself in Watch Hill in the summer of 1895, having traveled there with a woman named Ada Humphrey. Although the reason for her trip is unclear, it may have been during this 1895 visit that she initially became attracted to the community.[14]

Anna's second husband, George Lewis Williams was a barber at Harvard University who spent the summers in Watch Hill where he found seasonal employment cutting hair. Given that Anna was both a hairdresser and manicurist, it is a virtual certainty that this line of work and their time spent in Watch Hill is what brought them together.[15] Anna Thornton married George L. Williams in Westerly on 7 September 1904 at the Broad Street Christian Church.[16]

Despite being married, it is possible that the couple lived apart for the next three years, as Anna remained in Cincinnati until at least 1907.[17] On 25 May 1908, George and Anna purchased a house at 21 Newton Avenue, and it was in this home that Anna would live for nearly the rest of her life.[18]

By 1910, George and Anna were fully settled in Westerly, living in their new home on Newton Avenue where Anna was a self-employed scalp specialist, operating out of her home. According to the census from that year, Anna described herself as 'mulatto' and indicated that her father was born in England, giving credence to the possibility that her father was a white Englishman.[19] A decade later in 1920, Anna reiterated that her father was born in England.[20] On 18 November 1919, Anna was granted a divorce from George L. Williams on the grounds of "neglect to provide."[21]

It is not clear how profitable Anna's business was, however, she made enough to offer contributions to causes which mattered to her. In 1909, she made a donation to the Abraham Lincoln birthplace farm in her native Kentucky,[22] and in 1915, a donation was made to the Tuskegee

Normal and Industrial Institute in the name of Charles W. Thornton through Mrs. Anna Thornton Williams.[23]

In 1920, Anna was described as a dermatologist and was working on her own account while continuing to live at 21 Newton Avenue. Interestingly, in the 1920 census, Anna was enumerated as white, however, given that all other respondents on the same page were listed as white, it is possible that this was an error.[24] That November, Anna Thornton Williams cast her historic ballot, becoming the first woman to vote in the town of Westerly.[25]

According to *The Westerly Sun*, which was on the scene for the momentous occasion: "Williams did not say for whom she voted, but as she came from the voting place and was congratulated by a *Sun* reporter for being the first to vote, she remarked: "Washington left principles for everybody," which would indicate in itself that she stood for the grand old party."[26]

Whether or not she definitively voted for the Republican candidate and eventual winner, Warren G. Harding, is unknown, but given that according to later published tallies, Harding won the town of Westerly 2,070-490 (approximately 80.8% of voters), this supposition was a fairly safe bet.[27]

After that significant moment in 1920, Anna Thornton Williams continued to live in Westerly for several more years. In 1925, she was once again recorded living alone at 21 Newton Avenue.[28] On 27 May 1929, Anna was admitted to the Howard State Hospital for Mental Diseases in Cranston, Rhode Island.[29] She was listed at the hospital in both 1930 (when her occupation was given as 'mending') and 1935.[30]

Anna Thornton Williams passed away at the State Hospital on 6 September 1936. She was later interred at River Bend Cemetery in Westerly.[31] Anna lived a historic life and in spite of the likely troubles and hardships she almost certainly faced, she was able to live a long, and hopefully fulfilling life. In other words, as her gravestone reminds us: She hath done what she could.

Charles Perry, Ardent Abolitionist

"In addition to supporting prominent opponents of the slave trade in America, Charles Perry also actively aided the escape of runaway slaves as part of the Underground Railroad. Perry was known to have harbored escaped slaves at his home before moving them to his brother Harvey's home in North Stonington. On his land, Perry constructed a number of stone cottages with sod roofs where the fugitive slaves could hide until their next stop."

Although slavery is a significant part of the history of the United States, it was less prominent in New England than in most other parts of the nation. As a result, slavery was uncommon in Westerly throughout much of the town's history. In 1790, there were ten slaves recorded in the town across four households. In every census record available after 1790, not a single slave was enumerated in Westerly.[32] While slavery was far from prevalent locally, there were still citizens in Westerly who opposed the practice being used throughout the country. Perhaps the town's most notable and ardent supporter of abolition was a man by the name of Charles Perry (1809-1890), a friend of Frederick Douglass, and a renowned opponent of the slave trade.

Charles Perry was born in Westerly on 27 September 1809 to Thomas and Elizabeth (Foster) Perry.[33] Charles was from a long line of Perrys descended from Edward Perry who was born in Devonshire, England c. 1630 and settled in the Massachusetts Bay colony where he became one of the nation's first Quakers.[34] In 1825, at the age of fifteen, Charles Perry published what is widely considered to be the first newspaper published in Washington County, Rhode Island, the *Bung Town Patriot*. The newspaper was a laborious effort, with Perry carving the type and advertisements from wood blocks on his own. The paper contained poetry, advertisements, news, shipping announcements and other features.[35] The following year, when he was only sixteen years old, Charles Perry succeeded his recently deceased father as the cashier at the Washington Bank (later known as Washington Trust), a position he held for the next fifty-five years. [For more on the Perry Family at Washington Trust, see page 293.] Perry was selected by a meeting of the directors on 29 March 1826 and was officially appointed at the annual meeting on July 4th of that year. In 1836, Charles Perry was named the Director of the Washington Bank, and upon his retirement as cashier in 1881, he was selected as President.[36]

Charles Perry was raised by Quaker parents and continued the family tradition by becoming an ardent Quaker himself. In 1844, he served as assistant clerk at the Rhode Island Quarterly Meeting of Friends, and throughout his life, he held other positions of importance at local Quaker meetings.[37] Although Charles Perry was once described as "progressive in his political views as well as in business," he never sought public office. Perry was also very active in various causes and was once described as "a strong advocate of temperance, an uncompromising abolitionist, and was active in many movements of civic and moral reform."[38] He was said to have had a deep love of education which led him to be a vehement supporter of improved schools in Westerly.[39]

While Perry supported a great many causes throughout his life, perhaps his strongest conviction was that slavery should be outlawed in the United States. At his home on Margin Street in Westerly, Perry hosted well-known abolitionists such as Benjamin Lundy, and most notably, Frederick Douglass.[40] On 7 December 1868, Douglass delivered a lecture hosted by the Young Men's Christian Association at the Westerly Armory titled "William, the Silent."[41] According to a copy of the lecture maintained by the Library of Congress, Douglass spoke that night about William I, Prince of Orange.[42] One story conveys that Perry actually shielded Douglass when a man who opposed the abolition of slaves hurled eggs and water at Douglass during his speech to the Westerly Anti-Slavery Society.[43]

In addition to championing leading challengers to the slave trade in America, Charles Perry also actively aided the escape of runaway slaves as part of the Underground Railroad. Perry was known to have harbored escaped slaves at his home before moving them to his brother Harvey's home in North Stonington. On his land, Perry constructed a number of stone cottages with sod roofs where the runaway slaves could hide until their next stop.[44] According to one tale, a runaway slave once showed up at the Perry residence and, wanting to help the man, Charles rolled him up in a rug in the back of a farm wagon and took him to the next stop in Ashaway.[45] Often times, Perry's Quaker beliefs intersected with his opposition to slavery.

In a letter dated 24 September 1845 to his friend and fellow Quaker, Thomas B. Gould of Newport, Perry refers to anti-slavery lecturer Abby Kelly being carried out of a meeting in Ohio. Perry, a 'Wilburite'[46] wrote that he hopes it was Guerneyites (a branch of the Quaker faith that held views opposite of his own) who performed the act.[47] In 1863, Perry and his cousin, Ethan Foster, went to Washington to speak with President Lincoln in support of four fellow Quakers who were jailed for refusing the Union draft "as a matter of conscience."[48]

In 1848, Charles Perry married Temperance Foster, the daughter of Thomas and Phoebe (Wilbur) Foster, and a granddaughter of eminent Quaker preacher John Wilbur, the leader of the Wilburites.[49] The couple were the parents to five children, four of whom, Mrs. Elizabeth (Perry) Foster, Mrs. Phebe (Perry) Buffum, Charles Perry Jr., and Arthur Perry, were living at the time of Charles' death in 1890.[50] Temperance (Foster) Perry died on 27 November 1861, leaving Charles as a widower for the final twenty-nine years of his life.[51]

The Perry family was relatively well-off in the middle of the nineteenth century. In 1850, Charles owned $2,000 (approximately $68,000 in 2021) worth of real estate in Westerly.[52] By 1870, the value of Charles' real estate had increased significantly to $30,000 (approximately $607,000 in 2021) while he claimed to hold $20,000 in his personal estate as well.[53]

By all accounts, Charles Perry was a well-respected man in Westerly, and was well-known for championing various causes about which he was passionate. Even those who contested these same causes could see the virtue in their opponent. Charles Perry died in Westerly on 29 May 1890 and he is buried in River Bend Cemetery next to his wife, Temperance.[54]

Excellence in Medicine: The Margaret Edward Anderson Hospital

"During his medical career, Dr. Anderson became well known for his diagnostic abilities and he was recognized throughout New England for his medical knowledge and surgical skills. He would also publish articles including some of which appeared in The American Journal of Surgery.*"*

Today, if you are injured or need urgent medical care, the state-of-the-art Westerly Hospital is the only emergency room in town, however, this was not always the case. For nearly four decades, a second hospital operated in Westerly before closing its doors in August 1963.[55] This facility, the Margaret Edward Anderson Hospital, was located on Westerly-Watch Hill Road and was managed by a well-known and highly-respected physician by the name of Doctor John Gordon Anderson.

Margaret Edward Anderson Hospital, c. 1927
(Photo: Westerly Sun, Westerly Public Library)

While the story of the Margaret Edward Anderson Hospital is a fascinating one, the man who was the driving force behind it is just as important. In 1873, Dr. Anderson's father, John C. Anderson, the son of Alexander and Elsie (Forest) Anderson, left his home in Aberdeen, Scotland to make a new life for himself in the United States. Eventually, John settled in Westerly where he worked as a stonecutter.[56] Around 1888, he married an immigrant from Kincaidshire, Scotland named Margaret Edward.[57]

John and Margaret Anderson would become the parents to three boys, the second of whom was born in Westerly on 29 December 1892, and given the name John Gordon Anderson. The family remained in Westerly where the boys were all born and raised. In 1913, John G. Anderson graduated from Westerly High School.[58] After his graduation, John went on to attend the University of Rhode Island (then known as Rhode Island State College) where he studied Applied Science.[59] Anderson's interest in medicine was apparent during his studies in Kingston, as the 1917 yearbook gives his nickname as "Doctor" and notes that he delivered a prize speaking essay on immunization.[60]

The career path of John G. Anderson took a turn after his studies at Rhode Island State College when he enlisted in the military and served in the Army Medical Corps. After completing his military service, Anderson was accepted to Harvard Medical School, where he graduated at the top of his class.[61] John's superb performance at Harvard helped him to receive offers for several high profile opportunities.

In 1922, he served as an intern at both Boston City Hospital and Rhode Island Hospital.[62] That same year, Dr. Anderson was chosen for a three-year appointment at the Mayo Clinic and he also later served on the staff of the New York City Hospital.[63] Eventually, Dr. Anderson would be named the first Chief of Staff at the Westerly Hospital when it opened in 1925.[64] Despite all of his accomplishments, it was Dr. Anderson's work at another local hospital that would form the greatest part of his legacy.

In 1925, at the conclusion of his stint at the Mayo Clinic, Dr. Anderson returned to his hometown where he established a hospital in his home at 23 Cross Street. This hospital would be Anderson's primary focus until Christmas Day 1927 when a more ambitious project came to fruition. It was then that he opened the Margaret Edward Anderson Hospital, named in honor of his mother, at the former Tristam Babcock Homestead on the bank of the Pawcatuck River on Watch Hill Road. [65],[66]

Dr. John Gordon Anderson, 1917
(Photo: University of Rhode Island Yearbook)

At the time of its opening, the hospital had five private rooms and one room with three beds, additional rooms brought the total capacity to twenty beds. The hospital was staffed by five nurses, including the superintendent of nurses, Mary I. Patton, who would become Dr. Anderson's wife.[67]

The hospital's third floor was devoted to obstetrical cases with a dedicated delivery room.[68] During his medical career, Dr. Anderson became well known for his diagnostic abilities and he was recognized throughout New England for his medical knowledge and surgical skills.[69] He would also publish articles some of which were published in medical journals including *The American Journal of Surgery*.[70]

Of the 132 deaths recorded in Westerly during 1928, the hospital's first full year of operation, fifteen were recorded at the Margaret Edward Anderson Hospital.[71] These numbers would decrease over the history of the hospital, with only eleven recorded in 1932 and five in 1946.[72] These figures may have been the product of several factors including the advancement of medical technology, decreased patient totals, or a decrease in the number of life-threatening cases taken on by the hospital.

Dr. Anderson was not the only highly decorated doctor employed by the hospital. Dr. John D. Camp, a radiologist at the hospital, was awarded the gold medal from the Radiological Society of North America for his contributions to the field in 1949.[73]

DR. ANDERSON

Dr. Anderson c. 1982
(Photo: Westerly Sun)

The Margaret Edward Anderson Hospital closed in August 1963 for unknown reasons.[74] It is notable, however, that the hospital closed just as the Westerly Hospital opened a new wing, and it is quite possible that the Anderson Hospital was no longer necessary. On 9 March 1968, the hospital building and the land it was built upon were sold to Dr. Anderson's son, Marshall.[75] The legacy of Dr. Anderson's Hospital has lasted for more than half a century since the facility's closing however.

Dr. John Gordon Anderson died in Westerly on 13 February 1982, but his memory lives on in a unique way.[76] While the exact number of births at the hospital is not known, it is a near certainty that many of those born at the Margaret Edward Anderson Hospital are still living today.

The Artist Who Survived the *Titanic*

Years later, Marshall would tell friends that he was having donuts and cocoa when the list of survivors was being compiled and as a result, his fate was unknown to his family back in New York. In fact, the Brooklyn Daily Times reported on April 17th: "All Greenport is fearful that James V. Drew and Marshall, the 5-year-old son of William J. Drew, brother and partner of James Drew, are among the Titanic's dead."

While Westerly has seen its share of fascinating individuals over its more than three-hundred-and-fifty-year history, perhaps no one had a more interesting story to tell than Marshall Drew, a survivor of the sinking of the *R.M.S. Titanic*. Although not born in Westerly, Marshall's family had connections to the town's granite industry, and he spent the last several decades of his life in his Dunn's Corners home.

Marshall Brines Drew was born on 30 March 1904 in the town of Greenport on Long Island, New York to William John Drew, a granite worker, and his second wife, Annie Eliza Brines. William was born in 1864 in Constantine, Cornwall, England.[77] Upon the death of his first wife in 1894, William moved from Greenport to Westerly, where he found work at the Smith Granite Company. It was in Westerly where he met his second wife, Annie, a Westerly native and daughter of Irish immigrants.[78] The couple returned to Greenport, where Marshall was born the following year. Annie passed away just weeks after Marshall's birth, leaving William as a single parent. Believing he was not able to properly care for his son alone, William asked his childless brother, James Vivian Drew, and his wife, Lulu, to raise Marshall in Southold, New York. Together, William and James operated a successful marble monument business on Long Island.[79]

In the fall of 1911, James, Lulu, and Marshall travelled on the *Olympic* to England, where they would spend several months celebrating the holidays with relatives in Cornwall. Then, on 10 April 1912, the family, looking to return to New York, purchased tickets for the maiden voyage of the *Titanic*, a decision made more out of convenience than a desire to travel aboard the massive ocean liner. Marshall, along with his aunt and uncle, boarded the ship at Southampton as second-class passengers, where they were assigned ticket number 28220. The trip cost £32, 10s for the three passengers (worth approximately £3,750 or approximately $5,300 in 2021).[80]

On the evening of 15 April 1912, the *Titanic* struck an iceberg, sinking the ship resulting in the death of 1,513 passengers.[81] When the impact occurred, James Drew was on the deck having a cigarette while Marshall and Lulu slept in their cabin on the lower decks. Once he realized what was happening, James returned to the family's room and escorted his wife and nephew to lifeboat number ten (some accounts claim it was number eleven) and said his goodbyes. Despite his assurances to the contrary, Lulu knew that she was unlikely to ever see her husband again, a premonition which sadly proved true, as James Vivian Drew perished when the ship sank into the north Atlantic.[82]

Memorial Gravestone for James Drew
(Photo: Westerly Historical Society)

In the lifeboat, Marshall fell asleep, and when he awoke he witnessed the approach of the *Carpathia*, the nearest ship which proceeded to pick up the stranded passengers and give them passage back to New York.[83] Years later, Marshall would tell friends that he was having donuts and cocoa when the list of survivors was being compiled. At the moment, his fate was still unknown to his family back in New York.[84] In fact, the Brooklyn Daily Times reported on April 17th: "All Greenport is fearful that James V. Drew and Marshall, the 5-year-old son of William J. Drew, brother and partner of James Drew, are among the Titanic's dead."[85] Upon hearing this, William went to Manhattan and stayed near the White Star Line offices, awaiting word of his son's fate.[86] William's eventual joy in learning of the safety of his son was short lived, as the death of his brother, James, was confirmed. The following year, the widowed Lulu Drew visited Westerly where she met and married Richard Opie, a local shipbuilder. The couple would live the rest of their days in Dunn's Corners, where she would die in 1971.[87]

Five years after Marshall's safe return to New York, his father succumbed to tuberculosis, leaving his son without a living biological parent at the age of thirteen.[88] During the 1920's, Marshall exhibited a talent for art, and in 1928, he graduated from the Pratt Institute in New York City then attended Columbia University for a time.[89] During the 1930's, Marshall married a woman from Connecticut named Mary and on 27 March 1937, their only child, a daughter, Elizabeth 'Bette' Drew was born.[90] Marshall Drew went on to become a teacher, specializing in art, and teaching at Grover Cleveland High School in Brooklyn for thirty-six years.

After retiring from teaching, Marshall continued to give art lessons and host events and exhibitions. He would spend much of his time practicing painting and origami.[91] In October 1946, he purchased land on Boston Post Road in Westerly from Richard and Lulu Opie, although he would continue to be identified as being from New York until 1962, when he appears to have settled in Westerly permanently.[92] Still, he spent many summers in Southold, New York with his great uncle, Henry Christian, a Civil War veteran.[93]

While living in Westerly, Marshall Drew gave art lessons in his home studio and enjoyed photographing local scenes immensely. Upon his death, he left more than ten thousand photo slides to the Westerly Camera Club. He was also fond of singing songs while strumming away on his ukulele sitting outside his home in Dunn's Corners. On Friday mornings, he could often be found at local coffee shops, conversing with his friends from the art community.[94]

Marshall Brines Drew died on 6 June 1986 in Greenport, New York while visiting friends. At the time of his death, he was one of an estimated twenty remaining survivors of the sinking of the *Titanic*.[95] In 2003, a hat band purchased by James Drew for his nephew while on board the *Titanic*, sold at auction for $53,000, allowing his story to live on in the public memory.[96] Marshall is buried in River Bend Cemetery in Westerly where his gravestone reads: "Teacher • Artist • Friend, Survivor R.M.S. Titanic 4-15-1912," serving as a loving reminder of the man for all who knew him.[97]

Henry M. Morris, Hero of the Hurricane of 1938

"While down near Shore Road, the men noticed the faint light of a candle in the distance, the only sign of survivors which emanated from the Weekapaug Inn. Morris' actions upon observing this far off beacon of hope earned him wide-ranging recognition for his bravery."

Early in the morning on 22 September 1938, just hours after the most powerful hurricane in memory had devastated the Westerly coastline, a local carpenter and senior Red Cross lifeguard named Henry M. Morris was out with Westerly Police Lieutenant George Madison and patrolman Arthur B. Kingsley searching for survivors.

While down near Shore Road, the men noticed the faint light of a candle in the distance, the only sign of survivors which emanated from the Weekapaug Inn. Morris' actions upon observing this far off beacon of hope earned him wide-ranging recognition for his bravery.

Henry M. Morris was born in Westerly on 15 September 1911 to Henry Bradford and Carrie (Lovett) Morris.[98] Throughout his childhood, Henry lived with his family on Shore Road and attended schools in Westerly. Although census records suggest Morris completed four years of High School, no record could be found of his graduation from Westerly High School.[99]

By 1930, at the age of 18, Henry was working as a carpenter and living with his divorced mother in their home on Shore Road.[100] By 1935, Henry married his wife, Calista Kenyon, and they started a family together. At that time, he had found work as an operator at a dye mill in Bradford (likely the Bradford Dyeing Association), but shortly thereafter, he returned to his career as a carpenter.[101]

In late September 1938, tragedy struck the town of Westerly, as it was bombarded by an immensely powerful hurricane that destroyed much of the coast. Around 1 a.m. on 22 September 1938, while Henry M. Morris was out with Westerly Police officers looking for survivors,[102] Theodore Billings (38),

Leon Bliven (64), William Wheeler (49), Ella Rewick, and Lawrence Miller (51) were taking refuge at the Weekapaug Inn.[103]

Morris, having seen the candle the refugees placed in a window, immediately made his way to the hotel. Upon arriving there, he found that what had once been tennis courts now formed a wide breachway, separating the hotel from his position.[104]

Undeterred, despite the twenty-five mph winds, Morris, Kingsley, and Madison formulated a plan. First, the men tossed a mattress into the water to test the current, and when they saw it "float away like a match in the raging current," they judged it impossible to use a boat for the mission.[105] Their next course of action was to tie a rope around Morris' waist so that he could safely swim back and forth across the breachway.

When Morris arrived at the other side of the breachway, he wrapped the rope around himself and one of the survivors and swam back across. He completed this feat four more times, rescuing all five survivors.[106] Upon arriving back on shore with the last evacuee, Morris collapsed from exhaustion and was taken to Westerly Hospital, where they found he had bruises from debris in the rough waters.[107] Morris returned home the following day and was roundly lauded as a hero in the community.

After his daring rescue, Morris resumed his work as a carpenter, eventually moving with his wife and two children to Weekapaug Road in Westerly.[108] Fifteen months after his successful rescue mission, Henry M. Morris' heroism and bravery were recognized, as he was awarded the Carnegie medal for valor presented by the Carnegie Hero Fund Commission.[109]

The Carnegie Hero Fund, established in 1904 by industrialist Andrew Carnegie, was created with the intention of rewarding those who performed heroic deeds. Initially, the recipients were chosen by a twenty-one-member commission in Pittsburgh which utilized Carnegie's depiction of a hero as the basis for their decisions.[110]

As of 2018, the Commission has awarded more than 10,000 medals out of more than 90,000 candidates. Based on the tales of Morris' exploits, it is quite clear that he met the Commission's requirement that the candidate for an award "must be a civilian who voluntarily risks his or her life to an extraordinary degree while saving or attempting to save the life of another person."[111]

On 3 January 1940, in a ceremony held in the Ward Senior High School Auditorium, Henry M. Morris was presented with a bronze medal and $500 for "a worthy purpose as needed" by the Carnegie Hero Fund Commission.[112] Morris, a boy scout as a child, received the award from Harold R. Williams, Chief Executive of the Narragansett Council of Boy Scouts.[113] Upon being informed in October 1939 that he was to receive the medal, he claimed: "It had to be done and I did it, with the aid of the other fellows."[114]

The week after he received his Carnegie medal, Henry M. Morris was treated to an event that *The Westerly Sun* described as the "real party."[115] Morris and one hundred thirty other locals gathered for a dinner at the Elm Tree Inn in Pawcatuck hosted by the Westerly Chamber of Commerce.

At the dinner, when presented with a barometer, Morris stated "You may rest assured that I will value this gift more even than the Carnegie medal, for it is given to me by the folks of my own home town."[116] Celebrations of Morris' heroism continued throughout the evening, as he humbly acknowledged the efforts of patrolman Kingsley (who was seated at Morris' table) and Lieutenant Madison.[117]

Morris' bravery was never forgotten by the people of Westerly, and he remained a well-known presence in town for the rest of his life. On 2 May 1944, Morris enlisted in the United States Navy, and he remained on active duty until his discharge on 5 November 1945, following the end of World War II.[118]

He also served in the United States Engineering Corps and was at one time a top-ranking Civil Engineer Corps Officer candidate for the Society of American Military Engineers.[119] Morris and his wife, Calista, were also the owners of several local businesses, including the Pine Lodge Motor Court on Post Road, and the building contractor firm of Morris and Turano.[120]

Later in his life, Morris entered the arena of local politics. In 1958, he campaigned unsuccessfully for a term on the highway commission and in 1960, he ran as a Republican candidate for the position of Sixth Councilman in Westerly. [121] Eventually, Morris served as president of the Westerly Town Council. [122]

In February 1950, Morris and Turano was awarded the contract to build the first Fire Station for the Dunn's Corners Fire Department. Morris' association with the Fire Department would continue for the rest of his life, after he was added as a member in 1952. [123] Between 1970 and 1976, he served as the Department's Chief Engineer. [124] Henry M. Morris died on 6 August 1976 at the age of 64. [125]

After more than eighty years, the legacy of Morris' brave act lives on. He is still remembered as one of the heroes of the Hurricane of 1938 as well as a prominent and respected member of the community.

Horace Vose, Turkey King

"1896 turned out to be quite the year for Horace Vose. In addition to his shipments to President Cleveland, he also provided turkeys for President-elect William McKinley. On top of that shipment, Vose was also asked to ship a turkey from North Stonington to Queen Victoria. The article covering this request mentioned that although Vose had hoped to receive a note from the Queen of England, no such note ever arrived. After many years of shipping turkeys domestically, Vose expanded his scope and was known to ship turkeys to Europe and South Africa from time to time."

In mid-November in the year 1873, a package departed the Westerly Railroad Station bound for Washington, D.C. The destination of this package was not just any building in Washington; it was to be sent directly to the White House, where its contents could be enjoyed by President Ulysses S. Grant. Inside the large wooden crate was a turkey to be served on Thanksgiving courtesy of Westerly's own Horace Vose.

Thus began a tradition that would last for nine presidential administrations spanning four decades.[126] Each year thereafter until his death in 1913, Horace Vose sent the President of the United States (as well as the Vice President) local turkeys for both Thanksgiving and Christmas, and therefore, the turkeys that were enjoyed at the White House each year were shipped directly from Westerly.

Horace Vose was born in Westerly on 12 May 1840 to Charles Babcock and Mary Jane (Thompson) Vose.[127] From an early age, Horace was surrounded by farms and the animals that lived on them. In 1860 and 1865, he identified himself as a farm laborer and farmer and by 1870, his profession was given as "stable keeper."[128] In 1872, Horace married Susan Amanda Cheseboro and they would spend the rest of their lives as residents of Westerly.[129]

In 1873, Rhode Island Senator Henry B. Anthony, being acutely aware of the positive reputation of turkeys from southern Rhode Island, contacted Horace Vose, by then a highly regarded dealer of livestock, about sending a turkey to President Grant.[130] Even after beginning his tradition of providing the presidential turkey, Vose was more well-known locally as a horse dealer than a turkey farmer.[131] In fact, Vose did not raise turkeys himself but simply bought and sold them throughout the area.[132]

The very first turkey sent to the White House was purchased from the farm of Horace Brightman and weighed a hefty thirty-six pounds.[133] Vose was assisted with his deliveries by Senator Anthony who had a close relationship with President Grant, having twice been elected as President Pro Tempore, the Senate's highest post.[134] Upon Anthony's death in 1885, Vose was assisted by his neighbor, Senator Nathan F. Dixon III.[135]

It was said that the turkeys procured by Vose "won a sound reputation, not only for themselves but for Horace Vose, who soon acquired the title of the "Turkey King.""[136] After dining on the turkey, President Grant sent Vose a note expressing his gratitude.[137] Every year thereafter, Vose was said to have received a similar note signed either by the President himself or his secretary.[138]

For many years, Horace Vose served as a jack-of-all-trades in Westerly, working as an auctioneer, ice dealer, horse dealer, and livery owner.[139] Vose often traveled far and wide to obtain the livestock which he would deal in Westerly, as there are accounts of his presence as far west as Iowa.[140] Horace Vose was also fairly prolific locally as a horse trader and seller and one advertisement for a joint sale of 'trotting stock' described his property as "Mr. H. Vose's large and commodious stables nearly opposite [the] railroad station."[141] Notably, although the turkeys that Vose supplied were shipped from Rhode Island, they often were brought in from Virginia, Kentucky, Iowa, and other states.[142]

For forty years running after the initial delivery in 1873, Horace Vose continued to send turkeys to the White House twice each year. Apparently, by 1893 the tradition had grown in scope and efficiency as one newspaper article mentions that Senator Dixon was to serve as Chairman of the "Turkey Committee."[143] Still, Vose's act remained relatively unknown for several years, as there are virtually no accounts of the presidential turkey shipment between 1873 and 1893.

Horace Vose made good on his desire to provide the finest turkeys to the White House no matter who was serving as the chief executive at the time. As one account claimed: "In the matter of turkeys, Vose was a hidebound non-partisan."[144] Another story noted, in 1896 Vose shipped a turkey to President Grover Cleveland, a Democrat, along with a note reading: "I voted the Republican ticket this fall. Did not have quite as good business as I hoped, the last year, but I want to be sure you have a good Rhode Island turkey, so I send you a half blood, wild one, which please accept."[145]

It was said that when Cleveland had passed through Westerly several years prior, Vose introduced himself and the president "gave his [Vose's] big, sun-browned hand an extra pressure and expressed pleasure at meeting him." Vose never failed to receive a note of thanks from President Cleveland and they served as a point of pride for the Turkey King, who framed the notes which were "the pride of the entire community."[146]

The Year 1896 turned out to be quite the year for Horace Vose. In addition to his shipments to President Cleveland, he also provided turkeys for President-elect William McKinley.[147] On top of that shipment, Vose was also asked to ship a turkey from North Stonington to Queen Victoria.[148] The article covering this request mentioned that although Vose had hoped to receive a note from the Queen of England, no such note ever arrived.[149] After many years of shipping turkeys domestically, Vose expanded his scope and was known to ship turkeys to Europe and South Africa from time to time.[150]

Throughout his lifetime, Horace Vose gained a reputation as a highly-regarded livestock supplier with a keen eye for quality. It was said that a presidential turkey delivered by Vose never weighed less than twenty-five pounds. A particular method was strictly adhered to, namely: "When killed and dressed for shipment to the White House, the turkeys were left with head, wings, tail-feathers, and feet all on for this was the method of preparing the very finest birds for market."[151]

One result of Vose's growing reputation and notoriety he received from providing the presidential turkeys is that he "became very wary of strangers, seldom allowing any about his grounds."[152] On 20 December 1913, Horace Vose died in Westerly after suffering from a heart ailment. He was buried in River Bend Cemetery alongside his wife and children.[153]

SHIPPING A THANKSGIVING TURKEY TO THE PRESIDENT

Horace Vose Shipping a Turkey, 1901
(Photo: Ladies' Home Journal)

It was said that after Horace Vose's death, Rhode Island turkeys fell below presidential standards and turkeys were shipped to the White House from elsewhere in America.[154] Although it is unfortunate that the tradition died with Vose, in the annals of local lore it will be forever remembered that for forty years the leader of the United States of America dined on Westerly turkeys every Thanksgiving and Christmas.

Continuing Faith: The History of Westerly's Jewish Community

"From the late nineteenth century through the first decade of the twentieth century, there was another wave of Jewish immigration to Westerly, which led to discussions regarding the formation of a congregation. The result was the founding of the Congregation Sharah Zedek on 14 October 1908."

Although they have always composed a relatively small portion of the town's overall population, the Jewish citizens of Westerly have played a substantial role in shaping the community into what it is today. In this piece, there is a closer look at the history of Westerly's Jewish community and their many contributions over the last 150 years.

The man largely believed to have been Westerly's first Jewish resident was Abraham Englehard, a successful dry goods store owner. His store opened in the 1860's and remained in operation locally until at least 1893.[155] The belief that he was Jewish originates from advertisements in the *Narragansett Weekly* for Englehard's store which note that he was closed on Saturdays and in 1863, he was also closed for Rosh Hashana. [156]

Englehard's store being closed on Saturdays was not unusual, however. In fact, closing on Saturdays was a fairly common practice locally, which contributed significantly to an influx of Jewish immigrants in the latter half of the nineteenth century. Westerly and Hopkinton were home to many Seventh Day Baptists, who celebrated their sabbath on Saturdays, much like the practitioners of Judaism. Because of this, Rhode Island blue laws requiring businesses to be closed on Sundays contained an exemption for the two towns, allowing business owners to close on Saturdays and reopen on Sundays. This unique practice enticed many early Jewish immigrants to settle in Westerly and open businesses. [157]

After Englehard, there was a slow but steady stream of Jewish migrants to Westerly which led to the formation of a sizeable community. One of these immigrants was Jacob Stern, who initially found work at Englehard's store in the 1860s, before opening his own store, the famed Bee

Hive on the corner of Broad and High Streets, in 1879. Over the next several decades, Stern became a prominent local figure. [158]

The weddings of Stern's three daughters, who were themselves quite popular in town, were held at Bliven's Opera House. [159] Another noted migrant was a man named Louis Tuch, who arrived in Westerly in the 1870's and operated a successful clothing store with his brothers-in-law, Theodore, Herman, and Max Samuel, until 1926. [160]

Beginning in 1881, there was a significant migration of Jews from Eastern Europe including many who settled in Westerly. Some were peddlers who sold their wares while riding through town on horse-drawn carriages.[161] By 1890, the majority of the Jewish immigrants to Westerly had become part of the upper middle class, allowing them to open several successful businesses. At the beginning of the twentieth century, Westerly was visited by Rabbi Bernard Drachman, who chronicled his stay in his autobiography "The Unfailing Light." In his account, Drachman describes his time in Westerly as "three delightful days," and gives a detailed account of the local Jewish population. [162]

From the late nineteenth century through the first decade of the twentieth century, there was another wave of Jewish immigration to Westerly, which led to discussions regarding the formation of a congregation. The result was the founding of the Congregation Sharah Zedek on 14 October 1908. The original members who signed the charter were Lewis Solomon, David Ribner, Sender Soloveitzik, Solomon Soloveitzik, Morris Soloveitzik, and Harry Soloveitzik.[163] Prior to this development, there were various holy day celebrations held in locations throughout downtown Westerly, but there had never been a formal group which oversaw these observances.

After forming a congregation, the group then faced their next issue: finding a permanent home for worship. This problem was solved on 5 December 1917, when the congregation purchased their current synagogue on Union Street. This building, constructed in 1872, had previously served as an Episcopal Church before being sold to the Ancient Order of Hibernians, from whom Sharah Zedek purchased the site for ten dollars.[164] Before establishing their permanent home, Jewish residents worshipped in synagogues on Canal Street, where most of the town's Jewish settlers resided. By early 1918, there were thirty-five Jewish families in Westerly, a number which increased to forty by 1954.[165]

Union Street
(Photo: Westerly Historical Society)

Throughout the 1930s and 1940s, the congregation initiated efforts to raise funds for various causes including the Jewish Hospital in Denver (still operating today as the leading respiratory hospital in America) and aid for Jewish refugees in Europe who were facing persecution by the Nazis.[166] In May 1946, a sisterhood organization was formed, and in the ensuing decades, the group has performed a great deal of charitable work to benefit the community.[167] During this period, another notable congregant was Abraham Soloveitzik, an editor for *The Westerly Sun*. Soloveitzik was a noted supporter of Westerly's Boston Marathon winner, Ellison M. "Tarzan" Brown.[168]

Union Street
(Photo: Westerly Historical Society)

In Sharah Zedek's early years, the synagogue was considered an Orthodox Shul, a status which it retained until the 1940's. Throughout the 1940's and 1950's, there was a split within the congregation between those who practice Orthodox Judaism and those who chose to observe Conservative Judaism. [169] The divide led to the creation of two distinct groups within the same building, with the Orthodox practitioners on the lower level, while the Conservative worshippers congregated upstairs in the sanctuary. This divide did not last long. By the end of the 1950's, the synagogue practiced conservative Judaism exclusively.[170]

For many years, the temple also maintained a school, which by September 1953, had twenty-one students enrolled. At that time, the advanced classes (for older children) met on weekday afternoons, while the kindergarten group met on Sunday mornings.[171]

In the ensuing decades, the number of worshippers waned, with only twenty members in total being registered in 1968.[172] Declining membership resulted in fewer services. At one point, Sharah Zedek only held services for High Holidays.[173] Since the 1980s, however, a resurgence in the number of congregants has caused the temple to now hold services at least once per month. In 2008, the congregation celebrated its 100th anniversary.

Although the Jewish population of Westerly has decreased over the last century, the devotion and strength of the community has remained. The contributions of Westerly's Jewish citizens are worthy of celebration and the continuing faith of these individuals and families has added to Westerly's diversity and contributed to the sharing of ideas and beliefs.

Chapter V
A Sporting Legacy

Tracing back to the baseball teams of the 1860's more than one hundred and fifty years ago, there have been accounts of sporting events held in the town of Westerly. Since that time, there have been numerous legendary games, seasons, and careers and Westerly has been the home to many athletes of note.

Considering that New England is the cradle of many sporting innovations in America, it should come as little surprise that there have been many noteworthy competitors who once called Westerly home. Some of the most notable accomplishments of Westerly natives include:

- Managing a Major League Baseball team in a World Series
- Participating in a Little League World Series
- Being the Starting Pitcher for a Major League Baseball All-Star Team
- Winning two Boston Marathons
- Competing in the Olympics
- Throwing a touchdown pass in the National Football League

In the following chapter are the anecdotes behind these momentous accomplishments. The chapter opens with a detailed history of the football program at Westerly High School, beginning with their earliest known games in 1893 and chronicling their history up to the present day. Although he did not play for his hometown Bulldogs, Don Panciera is, as of this writing, the only Westerly native to play in a game in the National Football League. His career and the path he took to the NFL are also presented in this chapter.

No sport has had a longer history in Westerly than baseball, and there are several local players and teams of note that made an impact on the national stage. Eddie Sawyer, a Westerly High School graduate, managed the "Whiz Kid" Philadelphia Phillies to a National League Pennant in 1950 and was lauded in his hometown for his accomplishments. The same year that Sawyer captained the Phillies to the World Series, a team of young men from

Westerly participated in the fourth Little League World Series. Although neither Sawyer nor the Westerly boys came away victorious, their exploits remain a celebrated part of local history. Twelve years later, another Westerly High School graduate, Dave Stenhouse, found himself as a Starting Pitcher for the Washington Senators. Stenhouse's strong 1962 season resulted in his selection to the 1962 American League All-Star team where he faced off against future hall of famers Orlando Cepeda, Bill Mazerowski, Roberto Clemente, and Willie Mays.

Closing out this chapter is the story of Tarzan Brown, a two-time winner of the Boston Marathon. Brown also qualified and competed at the 1936 Olympics in Berlin and qualified for the 1940 Olympics before they were cancelled at the outbreak of World War II.

The sporting legends of Westerly, while not as well-known as some of the more famous heroes in the annals of sports history, help to shape the identity of the town they called home and in the process, also created a powerful legacy.

125 Years of Football at Westerly High School, 1893-2018

"On 20 October 1893, a group of young men from Westerly High School took to a makeshift field on the Moss Street Grounds (home to the William Clark Thread Mill) in Pawcatuck where they would defeat a visiting team from Mystic by a score of 18-0. This accounts for the first game played by a team from a Westerly high school in which the score is known."

In the fall of 1886, a squad of boys from Westerly High School took the field to play a game of football against a local team. Beyond this fact, very little is known about the first football team to represent Westerly High School.[1] What is known is that the team must have disbanded at some point before 1893, because that fall, *The Westerly Sun*, in describing a newly created Westerly High School team, claimed that it was the unit's first season.[2] As a result, the following article, a transcribed version of a presentation delivered before the Westerly Historical Society on 29 September 2019, chronicles the history of football at Westerly High School from 1893 through 2018.

Over the course of their 125 year history, the Westerly High School football team, originally known simply as the "Blue and White," has seen a significant amount of success on the gridiron. The team has won ten or more games on eight occasions, the same number of undefeated seasons they have accumulated.[3] Additionally, Westerly has won sixteen State Championships.[4] In order to showcase the wide span of the Bulldogs' success, below is a discussion of some of the most notable periods in the history of Westerly's football team.

1893-1900: The Beginning of a Legacy

On 20 October 1893, a group of young men from Westerly High School took to a makeshift field on the Moss Street Grounds (home to the William Clark Thread Mill) in Pawcatuck where they would defeat a visiting team from Mystic by a score of 18-0.[5] This accounts for the first game played by a team from a Westerly high school in which the score is known. The second game of this season was played in Kingston against the Rhode Island School of Agriculture Aggies (later known as the University of Rhode Island Rams). Westerly would avenge the 6-4 loss handed to them by the Aggies later in the season when they defeated the college squad by a score of 16-8. This result was not without controversy, however, as the Aggies protested a referee's call in the fourth quarter and refused to finish the game out of protest. The score stood, however.[6]

The 1899 Westerly High School Team
(Photo: Westerly Public Library)

Between 1893 and 1908, the Westerly High School team played against several local college teams in addition to URI, including Bryant and Stratton College (later known as Bryant University), Brown University, and the Westerly Business College. On Thanksgiving morning in 1893, Westerly battled Providence High School to a 10-10 tie in a game played on the Beach Street Grounds. The game was apparently quite popular, as an advertisement published prior to the game notes that "large teams leave Dixon House Square for the grounds at 9:45."[7] In 1895, the Westerly boys found a permanent home at Riverside Park, an aptly-named field located on Canal Street along the banks of the Pawcatuck River. Today, the field is home to National Grid. Westerly played their home games at Riverside Park from 1895 to 1905 and again from 1910 to 1922.[8] From 1905 to 1908, the team returned to the Beach Street Grounds for unknown reasons and the school did not field a team in 1909.

In 1899 and 1900, Westerly won back to back Rhode Island State Championships compiling a record of 10-0-3 over the two seasons.[9] More impressively, the Westerly boys surrendered only twelve points in total over the thirteen games, while holding their opponents scoreless in eleven of those games. These seasons, capping off a successful stretch throughout the nineteenth century, represent one of the more successful eras in Westerly football history.

1917: A Season of Dominance

In 1917, the Westerly High School football team had perhaps their most all-around dominant season. From 1917 to 1933, the team was coached by Dwight Harold Rogers who ended his career as a coach with a winning percentage of 62.2%, making him one of the most successful coaches in Westerly's history. The 1917 season began with a low-scoring affair, when the high schoolers defeated a team of Westerly alumni, 6-0. They then strung together three shutout wins of 25-0, 22-0, and 20-0 against East Greenwich Academy, Bulkeley High School (New London) and Windham High School (Willimantic) respectively. The only team to truly test the Bulldogs after those victories was the New London Vocational School which dropped a game to Westerly, 7-6. After winning a rematch against the vocational school, 20-0, Westerly went on to put up two of the most lopsided scores the school had ever seen before or since.[10]

On 9 November 1917, the Bulldogs traveled to Providence to play a game against LaSalle Academy. The outcome of this contest was never in question. Westerly's fullback, Wilcox, scored four touchdowns on the way to an 80-0 demolition of the Providence boys. As if that victory were not enough of a statement, the Bulldogs followed it up with an even more powerful game against Stonington at Riverside Park on November 16th. Calling this contest a beatdown would be an understatement. Westerly's quarterback, Geoffrey Moore, scored seven touchdowns, while Wilcox put up four more. At the time of the final whistle, the scoreboard read 122-0 in favor of Westerly.[11] It must be noted, however, that the Bears were severely undermanned, as most of their first string players had left for military service in World War I leading Stonington to stumble through a challenging season. Westerly then played a much closer game against an alumni team on Thanksgiving, walking away with a comparatively closer 14-0 win.[12]

By the end of the 1917 season, Westerly had racked up a number of seemingly unbreakable records. They finished the season with nine wins and no ties or losses and outscored their opponents by a total of 316-0. This was good for an average of 35.1 points per game, a strikingly high number by today's standards, and simply unheard of in 1917.

The 1918 Bulldogs
(Photo: Westerly Historical Society)

1944-1946: The Goose Runs Loose

After more than two decades of mixed results for the Bulldogs, the team found its footing and played fantastic football between 1944 and 1946. During this stretch, Westerly bulldozed their way to a record of 24-4-3 over three seasons.[13] The team's success was at least partially due to the play of one of the greatest talents in Westerly's illustrious history. In 1944, fullback John "Goose" Gentile, the leading scorer in the Southern Division of the Rhode Island Interscholastic Football League, was named a Rhode Island First Team All-State selection. Prior to the start of the 1945 season, Gentile, along with several members of the Bulldogs football squad, were called to military service at the tail end of World War II. The Goose maintained a year of eligibility, however, and in 1946, he played even better than his stellar 1944 season. After scoring eighteen touchdowns in 1946, including four in a single game against North Providence, Gentile was named once again to the First All-State team.[14] The 1946 season came to a close with Westerly collecting its second consecutive State Championship.

The 1964 Bulldogs Run onto the Field
(Photo: Westerly High School Yearbook, Westerly Public Library)

1964-1965: Augeri Leads the Bulldogs to the Promised Land

The 1964 season marked the beginning of perhaps the greatest coaching career in the history of Westerly High School. After a disappointing 1963 season in which the Bulldogs finished with an unimpressive 3-7 record, the school brought in a coach by the name of Sal Augeri. Augeri's career was so successful that he became the namesake of the field where Westerly plays their home games today.

In his first three seasons at the helm for Westerly, Augeri led the team to an astounding 24-2-2 record, including two consecutive seasons without a loss in 1965 and 1966 and three straight State Championships from 1964 to 1966.[15] During the course of Augeri's tenure (1964-1968, 1971-1976), the Bulldogs went a stellar 78-27-3. While the teams of the mid-1960's were incredibly impressive and brought the Bulldogs a well-deserved reputation for success, they were not the most dominant teams that Augeri put on the field.

Bulldogs Fans Celebrate the Perfect Season in 1973
(Photo: Westerly High School Yearbook, Westerly Public Library)

1973-1974: The Glory Years

As hard as many found it to believe, the success of the Bulldogs in the mid-1960's was only the beginning. Between 1973 and 1974, Westerly did not lose a single game, earning a record of 23-0 over the two seasons. Not only was Westerly winning their games, they were winning them handily. Over the course of both seasons, they outscored their opponents 855-120, scoring more than seven times the amount of points they surrendered.[16] For perspective, if Westerly gave up only one touchdown in every game they played, they would have won each game by a score of 49-7. In 1973, Westerly's season was capped off with a thrilling 28-20 victory over the defending champions, Middletown, in the Division II Championship Game.[17]

In 1974, the Bulldogs scored an average of thirty-six points per game while allowing their opponents to score only six per game.[18] Nine of Westerly's twelve victories during that season were by at least three touchdowns and not a single official game was won by less than eight points (the Injury Fund game ended with a score of 13-6). Unlike the 1973 Championship Game, in which Westerly scored a close victory, the outcome of the 1974 title game was never in doubt, as the Bulldogs rolled over Warren by a score of 39-14.[19] During this period, support for the team was very high, with games being broadcast live on the radio on 103.7 WERI, allowing fans across town to hear every game.[20]

1984-1985: Defense Wins Championships

Interestingly, by the 1980's, a pattern emerged in which the Bulldogs found their greatest success in the middle of each decade. Westerly won State Championships in 1935, 1945, 1946, 1964, 1965, 1966, 1973, and 1974. This trend would continue into the 1980's. In 1984, the Bulldogs began the season with seven straight victories before dropping their final two games to East Greenwich and Stonington. Westerly would earn a chance at redemption, however, meeting East Greenwich in the Class B Championship Game. Vindication would have to wait however, as Westerly was handed a heart-breaking 13-6 loss.[21]

Westerly got their revenge the following season, defeating East Greenwich 7-6. That game was one of twelve victories in 1985, a season in which the team would go undefeated. Unlike the teams of the 1970's which were driven by a high-scoring offense, it was the Westerly defense which often led the team to victory. Over a span of twelve games, the team allowed only twenty-seven points against them, good for an average of 2.25 points allowed per game.[22] In eight of their twelve wins, the Bulldogs did not allow a single point to their opponents. After a tight 7-0 victory over Stonington on Thanksgiving Day, Westerly finished off their perfect season with a thrilling 9-7 win over Coventry to claim another Class B State Championship.[23]

1984 Team MVP Scott Morgan Goes Up for a Catch
(Photo: Westerly High School Yearbook, Westerly Public Library)

2000-2005: Piling up the Wins

Although Westerly fielded excellent teams during the 1990's, including championship squads in 1991 and 1996 that took down undefeated opponents to claim their division championships, the teams from 2000 to 2005 warrant further analysis. The first six seasons of the twenty-first century comprised the most successful half-decade in Westerly football history. During this stretch, the team went 58-16, an average of just under ten wins per season. From 2000 to 2002, the Bulldogs would face off against another dynasty, West Warwick, in the Division II Superbowl. Westerly would go on to capture the championship in the first two meetings in 2000 and 2001 while narrowly missing out on a third consecutive title after they dropped a tough loss to the Wizards, 9-7.[24] Despite finishing the seasons with 8-3 and 9-3 records in 2004 and 2005, the Bulldogs missed the playoffs both seasons. Westerly would not earn another postseason berth until 2011 but they lost in the Division II semi-final game to Central High School.[25]

Today: Bulldogs on the Rise

The last several seasons have been marked by renewed success for Westerly, including a 9-2 campaign in 2018. Westerly's success can be at least partly attributed to their play at running back in 2017 and 2018. During those seasons, Tristan Turano had perhaps the greatest statistical seasons in Westerly High School history, when he racked up 4,038 rushing yards and scored sixty-two touchdowns. He also had nine games in which he rushed for at least 200 yards.[26] With their recent success on the gridiron, there is every reason for fans to be optimistic about the future of Westerly High School football.

Don Panciera: Westerly's Own NFL Star

"After three seasons of college football, Don Panciera made the decision to take his game to the professional level. In the spring of 1949, the Westerly native was drafted into both the National Football League and their upstart rivals, the All America Football Conference. In the NFL draft, Panciera was selected in the fourth round, forty-first overall by the Philadelphia Eagles. In the AAFC draft, he was selected in the sixth round by the New York Yankees."

While Westerly has quite a long history of success on the football field, there is only one man born there who is known to have played in the National Football League. Although he did not play his career at Westerly High School, Don Panciera was always associated with Westerly, the town where he was born and raised. After a stellar college career at Boston College and the University of San Francisco, Panciera went on to play in parts of three seasons in the National Football League, making him Westerly's only known professional football player to date.

Donald M. Panciera was born in Westerly on 23 June 1927 to James L. and Westerlina (Campo) Panciera, both immigrants from Italy.[27] From 1932 to 1943, he attended Immaculate Conception School, an experience which would profoundly impact his worldview throughout his life.[28] As his wife, Patti, noted: "Don was very Catholic. He always had a rosary in his pocket and felt he wasn't dressed without it. He was very religious and felt comfortable in a Catholic school."[29] After the ninth grade, Panciera, already a standout football player, was recruited to attend and play for La Salle Academy in Providence, starting his sophomore year in 1943. Panciera continued to live in Westerly, taking the train to Providence on school days. Every night, he would not arrive home until seven or eight o'clock and on game days, it was much later.[30]

Despite the challenges he faced playing for a school across the state, Panciera succeeded beyond all expectations at La Salle. With the Westerly native under center, the Rams won a share of the Rhode Island State Championship all three years he attended.[31] In 1944 and 1945, Panciera received first-team All-State honors. While Panciera's entire tenure was a success, the 1945 team stands out as one of the greatest in state history. That season, La Salle had seven shutout victories and outscored opponents 203-9.[32] The amazing season was capped off with a trip to New Orleans, where the Rams squared off against Holy Cross Prep, the Louisiana State Champions. The game was generally considered to be for the mythical "Catholic High School Championship," an unofficial designation for the best Catholic school in the country.[33] The game, played on a muddy field, ended in a 6-6 tie- a somewhat disappointing conclusion to a magnificent season.[34]

Don Panciera as a Coach at Boston College, 1959
(Photo: The Heights Newspaper)

As a result of his success on the gridiron, in 1999 Panciera was among those named by *Providence Journal* sportswriter John Gilooly as one of the one hundred most significant people in Rhode Island high school sports history of the twentieth century.[35]

After graduating from La Salle in the spring of 1946, Don Panciera was recruited to play both quarterback and defensive back for the Boston College Eagles.[36] On October 5th, the Eagles secured their first of five consecutive victories with Panciera under center when they defeated Michigan State, 34-20. In the following contest, they defeated the Merchant Marines team by a lopsided score of 56-7. After a close 14-12 victory over Villanova, the Eagles traveled to New York City to face off against New York University. That game was decidedly less competitive, as Boston College crushed the Violets, 72-6 before a crowd of 8,000 at the Polo Grounds.[37] In addition to his passing duties, Panciera also kicked four extra points for the winners.[38] One week later, the Eagles escaped with a 20-13 triumph over Georgetown when their Westerly-born quarterback tossed two touchdown passes in the fourth quarter.[39]

After a loss against a strong Tennessee team, the Boston boys clashed with Alabama, winners of the 1945 Rose Bowl. In that game, Panciera intercepted a pass on the one yard line with less than two minutes to play, sealing the 13-7 win for the Eagles.[40] Boston College then suffered defeat in their final game against Holy Cross by a score of 13-6.

Largely because of their quarterback's strong play, the Eagles finished the season with a record of 6-3 and were ranked sixth nationally in passing offense and for one week, they were ranked seventeenth in the nation.[41]

Following the 1946 season, Panciera and other BC teammates caused a minor controversy when they followed assistant coach Ed McKeever to the University of San Francisco. The departure of several players caused Eagles coach Denny Myers to accuse teams of "stealing" his players. Myers asserted that an unnamed player, presumed to be Panciera, was offered $300 a month and transportation for four vacations in exchange for coming to USF.[42] The claims were never substantiated and Panciera remained in San Francisco for two seasons. At the time of his transfer, USF was a program on the rise. On the west coast, Panciera was given the opportunity to start at quarterback and defensive back immediately. During his career at USF, the Westerly thrower played with two future football hall of famers, Gino Marchetti and Bob St. Clair.[43]

Panciera Stares Down the Defense with Boston College
(Photo: Boston College Yearbook)

Prior to Panciera's arrival, USF went a meager 3-6 in 1946, but with him under center, they improved to 7-3 in 1947 and were even ranked twentieth in the nation for one week. In 1947, the team was ranked seventh nationally in passing offense.[44] The following season was still highly productive for Panciera, as the Dons were ranked fourth in the nation in passing offense and once again achieved a record of 7-3.[45]

After three seasons of college football, Don Panciera made the decision to take his game to the professional level. In the spring of 1949, the Westerly native was drafted into both the National Football League and their upstart rivals, the All America Football Conference.[46] In the NFL draft, Panciera was selected in the fourth round, forty-first overall by the Philadelphia Eagles.[47] In the AAFC draft, he was selected in the sixth round by the New York Yankees.[48]

Ultimately, Panciera chose to sign with New York, where he started all twelve games at quarterback for the Yankees. With the Rhode Islander under center, the Yankees went 8-4 in the regular season, securing a spot in the playoffs, where they lost their only game, 17-7.[49]

Despite the constant moving necessitated by a professional football career, Don Panciera retained his deep connections to his birthplace. On 2 January 1950, he married Miss Gloria Bruno at Immaculate Conception Church in Westerly.[50] At the end of the 1949-50 season, the AAFC was absorbed by the NFL. However, the New York Yankees were not taken in by the league and most players were divided between the New York Giants and New York Bulldogs. Those whose rights were not purchased, including Panciera, were entered into a dispersal draft involving the thirteen NFL franchises.[51] It is clear that the Philadelphia Eagles still saw talent in Panciera, as they drafted him for a second time, this time in the seventh round. Unfortunately, by the time he signed with the Eagles on 26 June 1950, the team already had three other quarterbacks on their roster. Although there was speculation that he would make the team as a defensive back, Panciera was cut by the Eagles before the season got underway.[52]

After being cut by the Eagles, Don Panciera found himself at the University of Connecticut pursuing a degree in physical education. His time on campus was short, however, as on 6 November 1950, Panciera announced that he had signed with the Detroit Lions. The Lions called him for assistance after losing five of their first eight games on the season. The Lions determined that Panciera would be ideal to fill their need at defensive back, especially considering they had future Hall of Famer Bobby Layne as their starting quarterback. In total, Panciera played four games for the Lions, where he secured a single interception.[53]

Initially, Panciera was signed once again by the Lions prior to the 1951 season, however, on August 11th, he was cut loose from the team.[54] After his release, Don sat out the remainder of the 1951 season. In July 1952, his career was reinvigorated once more after he signed a contract to play quarterback for the Chicago Cardinals.[55] Panciera found his way into eight games with the Cardinals in 1952. Unfortunately, he was less than successful with the Cardinals, completing only 36.5% of his passes and throwing nine interceptions to his five touchdowns while leading the Cardinals to a record of two wins and six losses.[56] Panciera's best week with the Cardinals came in a 34-28 loss to the Pittsburgh Steelers when he completed seven of his sixteen passes for 191 yards and three touchdowns. In spite of his sub-par performance, the Cardinals signed Panciera to a contract in July 1953. However, he was no longer with the team by August 17th, when he made his way north to sign with the Toronto Argonauts of the Canadian Football League.[57]

Don Panciera's stint in Toronto was brief, playing only one game for the Argonauts at quarterback and defensive back. On September 22nd, the team released him from his contract.[58] In his last attempt at a career in professional football, Panciera signed with the Ottawa Rough Riders of the CFL and after playing in one pre-season game, he was released for the final time.[59]

Don Panciera hung up his cleats after playing parts of five seasons in professional football. For the 1955 season, he served as player-coach for a team from Fort Devens in central Massachusetts.[60] This experience would begin the former quarterback's foray into coaching. From 1956 to 1958, he served as an assistant coach at the University of Dayton and in 1959, he returned to Chestnut Hills to serve in the same capacity for Boston College.[61] In 1960, Panciera returned to his home state, serving as assistant coach at the University of Rhode Island for one season.[62]

In 1960, Don Panciera found a new passion in automobiles. For seven years he served as a district manager for General Motors. In 1967, he was granted a franchise, Panciera Chevrolet in Wakefield, which he owned and operated for thirty-one years before retiring in 1998.[63] According to his wife, Patti, Panciera attributed his success in business to his football background. She recalled: "He used to say he owed his success in business to what he learned from sports. He had a strong work ethic, was a workaholic and was fiercely competitive." In 2008, Panciera was inducted into the Rhode Island Interscholastic League Hall of Fame.[64]

On 9 February 2012, Don Panciera passed away in Westerly at the age of eighty-four.[65] Many who knew the man personally look back on his life fondly and while he will be remembered as the only known man born in Westerly to ever play in the NFL, he will also hold a legacy as a native son who lived his life doing what he loved.

Eddie Sawyer: Captain of the Whiz Kids

"Pride for the hometown hero was high in Westerly. On 3 October 1950, the Westerly Town Council issued a resolution of congratulations for winning the pennant and wished him luck in the World Series. After the end of the 1950 baseball season, Eddie Sawyer returned to Westerly where he was given a hero's welcome. The so-called 'Eddie Sawyer Day,' was held on 8 January 1951 and included a wide range of celebrations and ceremonies."

The Philadelphia Phillies are among the oldest franchises in Major League Baseball beginning play in 1883.[66] The first six decades of the franchise's history were marked by ups and downs (mostly downs). Although they won the National League pennant in 1915, they were mired in futility thereafter, winning only 41.2% of their games over the next thirty-three seasons. That all changed when Westerly's own Eddie Sawyer was brought on as the team's manager.

Edwin Milby Sawyer was born in Westerly on 10 September 1910, the middle child of Scottish immigrants, Robert G. Sawyer, a stonecutter, and his wife, Isabel Milby.[67] Edwin, or Eddie, as he came to be known, developed an aptitude for sports at a young age. When he was ten years old, as one story goes, he worked as a batboy for a visiting semi-pro team playing exhibition games against Westerly teams. It wasn't until later in life he learned that the team was actually the Boston Red Sox (who did not play on Sundays), playing under assumed names to avoid being discovered.[68]

Eddie attended Westerly High School beginning in 1924, graduating as part of the Class of 1928. While in high school, he was a four sports athlete, running track and playing baseball, football, and basketball. Eddie proved to be quite well-liked, as he was voted most popular, served as Class President, and was named Captain of the baseball team. In his senior yearbook, it was said that he was a "Shining example of the perfect athlete combined with personality plus."[69] Westerly won the Rhode Island State baseball championship in 1927, due in large part to Sawyer's skilled pitching.

Despite the fact that he was successful both academically and athletically, Eddie did not have the financial resources to attend college.[70] After graduation, he was given a tryout with a baseball team in Winston-Salem, North Carolina, but he did not make the team's roster and returned home to Westerly, where he found work as an assistant caddy master at a local golf course while playing semi-pro baseball for the Westerly Independents.[71]

Three years after graduation, Eddie learned that Ithaca College in New York would extend tuition credit to incoming students allowing them to work their way through college. Upon discovering this, he applied and was accepted to the school. In order to pay for his tuition, Eddie tended furnaces, swept gyms, and worked as a short-order cook for a fraternity house. In addition to all of his hard work, he was able to succeed academically, obtaining a bachelor's degree and membership in the Oracle Society (Ithaca's version of Phi Beta Kappa, the nation's oldest academic honor society) in 1935. While at Ithaca, he pitched and played outfield for the school's baseball team, was the star halfback of the football team, and even was a part of the school's hockey team.[72]

During his summer off from college in 1934, he played summer college league baseball in Malone, New York and was eventually signed to play for the Norfolk Tars, the Class B team for the New York Yankees (comparable to modern day AA level).[73] Upon signing, Eddie was given a $1,000 signing bonus, which he promptly justified by leading the Tars to the Piedmont League pennant batting .361 in 102 games.[74]

After graduating from Ithaca, Sawyer went on to attend Cornell University, where he earned a Master's Degree in biology, while playing for the Class A Binghamton Triplets of the New York-Penn League. On 8 July 1935, he married his wife, Pauline "Polly" Bassett, a New York girl who was a classmate in the Physical Education department at Ithaca. Their wedding day was not without its troubles, however. The wedding was intentionally scheduled for an open date on the Triplets' schedule, but just forty-eight hours before he was to be married, Eddie learned that the League had ordered Binghamton to play a makeup game in Scranton on his wedding day. Showing dedication to his craft, Eddie rushed from his own wedding to Scranton where he played in the game that same night (while his wife was not pleased with this decision, they remained married for sixty-two years, suggesting he was forgiven).[75] Despite his efforts to make it to the game, the contest was shortened by rain and completed at a later date.

Eddie Sawyer continued to find success with the Triplets through the 1936 season when he hit .313 over 142 games, and because of this, he was called up to the Oakland Oaks, the Yankees' Pacific Coast League team. In Oakland, Eddie's shortcomings as a player, specifically his slow speed coupled with a separated shoulder, diminished his chances of making the major leagues. After the 1937 season, he decided to give up baseball. He then started teaching physiology and biology at Ithaca College while working towards his PhD.[76]

His love for the game would not let him stay away for long, however. In 1938, he resolved to give baseball one more chance, returning to Binghamton for another season. Before the season began, Eddie told his wife that if he did not hit over .300, he would quit baseball. At the end of the year, his batting average settled at .299, however, he did not give up. (For the record, one additional base hit would have given him an average of .301) Before the 1939 season, the Yankees asked Sawyer to be a player-manager for the Class C Amsterdam (NY) Rugmakers. He had another stellar season, leading the league with a .369 average while driving in 103 runs. Although the Rugmakers finished in first place, they lost the League Championship 3-2 to the Rome Colonels. The following season, Eddie Sawyer returned to play for and manage the Rugmakers, hitting .329 and leading the team to the league title. In 1941, he was named the player-manager of the Norfolk Tars hitting .277 in 128 games before returning to play and manage the Triplets. In 1942, he remained in Binghamton until the end of the 1943 season, when he officially retired as a player.[77]

In addition to playing and managing for several different baseball teams, Eddie also coached football at Binghamton North High School and served as the assistant football, baseball and basketball coach at Ithaca College while also serving as the college's Assistant Athletic Director.[78]

Sawyer's managerial style was often described as 'laid-back' and 'hands-off.' He rarely held meetings with players, and tried not to complicate the game with intricate signs.[79] He was also known for not showing his frustration on the field, only being ejected from major league games 'four or five times' early on in his career.[80] Despite letting his team approach the game in their own way, one of his players once claimed he "gets 20 percent more out of a team than any man I ever saw."[81]

In 1944, Eddie left the Yankees organization because he did not feel he could move up the managerial chain. He knew a man by the name of Herb Pennock who was about to bring him in to the Red Sox organization when Pennock suddenly left Boston to manage the Phillies organization. Sawyer was brought in for the 1944 season to manage the Phillies' Class A team in Utica. When he took over, the team did not have a nickname, so Sawyer opted to call them the Blue Sox.[82] Eddie remained with Utica through the 1947 season, winning the regular season pennant in 1945 before dropping to seventh place in 1946. In 1947, the Blue Sox smashed through the league, winning the pennant by ten games and eventually finishing as league champions.[83] Sawyer's success was rewarded and he was named the manager of the newly acquired Class AAA Toronto Maple Leafs. An even bigger opportunity was fast approaching.

In July 1948, the Philadelphia Phillies were floundering, sitting firmly in seventh place. The team fired manager Ben Chapman and promoted Sawyer to the major league position. In many ways, Sawyer was the antithesis of Ben Chapman, a man known for his aggressive nature and persistent racism. In doing so, Eddie Sawyer became the league's second youngest manager at thirty-seven years old.[84] He would also simultaneously serve as the team's third base coach, a rarity in the game.[85] Success was not immediate. In 1948 the Phillies went 23-40 under Sawyer and finished in sixth place, 25 ½ games out of first place.[86]

The 1949 season saw the Phillies make significant strides, finishing with a record of 81-73. While the team still finished in third place, it was their first winning season since 1932, and their highest finish since 1917, before six of the team's eight position players had been born.[87] At the end of the season, after seeing his team's performance, Eddie Sawyer vowed that the Phillies would win it all in 1950.[88]

Sawyer's prophecy nearly proved to be true. In 1950, Sawyer's Phillies, sporting his newly designed red pin-striped jerseys, finished 91-63-3 and took the National League pennant. The first-place finish did not come without drama. Although the Phillies did not relinquish their hold on first-place after July 25th, their lead in the National League was down to one game over the Dodgers, who they played in the final game of the season. If the

Phillies lost, they would be forced to play a playoff series against the Dodgers. This situation did not come to pass, as the Phillies took the final game 4-1 in ten innings. After winning the pennant, thirty thousand fans met the team at the 30th Street railway platform.[89]

Edwin Sawyer at Home with His Mother
(Photo: Westerly Sun)

The Phillies had ended their season in a hitting slump and that slump extended through the playoffs, ultimately leading to their World Series loss to the New York Yankees, Sawyer's former employer. The series was a low-scoring affair, as no World Series up to that point had seen fewer runs scored than in 1950. After the end of the series' final game, it was said that Sawyer was the first man out of the dugout to congratulate the Yankees.[90] Despite the season's disappointing end, Eddie Sawyer was named the 1950 Manager of the Year.[91] He was also named the Coach of the Year by the Rhode Island Association of Sportswriters and Sportscasters.[92]

Pride for the hometown hero was high in Westerly. On 3 October 1950, the Westerly Town Council issued a resolution of congratulations for winning the pennant and wished him luck in the World Series.[93] After the end of the 1950 baseball season, Eddie Sawyer returned to Westerly where he was given a hero's welcome. "Eddie Sawyer Day" was held on 8 January 1951 and included a wide range of celebrations and ceremonies. During one such ceremony, Sawyer was given the key to the town, which was carved out of light pink Westerly granite and inscribed "Westerly, R.I., 1951."[94] Throughout the course of the day, Eddie "made a marathon whirl of all the public and parochial school houses in Westerly and Pawcatuck" speaking before more than 3,200 children. Also included were lunch and dinner receptions, as well as a program held in the High School auditorium which was attended by more than four hundred citizens and was broadcast on local radio stations. Sawyer did not come to the events alone, as two of his coaches and the Vice President of the Philadelphia Phillies were also in attendance, as were Eddie's parents.[95]

A few months later, the Phillies opened up their 1951 season. Unfortunately, this season was not nearly as successful, and the team finished in fifth place with a record of 73-81. After the less than stellar campaign, Sawyer clamped down during Spring Training in 1952, proclaiming there would be "no wives, no automobiles, no golf, no gambling, no swimming, and a strict curfew."[96] Despite the coach's new hardline stance, the Phillies wilted to a record of 28-35 by June 27th. On that day, Sawyer resigned as manager of the Philadelphia Phillies (some sources suggest he was fired, but regardless, the split appears to have been mutual.) Sawyer remained on the team's payroll for the remainder of the year and he served as an advisor, evaluating the franchise's farm system.[97]

After the 1952 season came to an end, there were rumors that he was to be considered to manage the Pittsburgh Pirates, but Sawyer denied these claims, saying he was done with baseball for good. This was a promise he seemed to keep, at least for the next several years. From 1953 to 1958, he worked as a salesman for a golf ball manufacturer, eventually being named the Vice President of Sales. In a shocking turn of events, Eddie Sawyer was once again named the manager of the Philadelphia Phillies in July 1958. Sawyer's influence could not help the struggling team and they finished in last place with a record of 69-85.[98] The Phillies were 40-46 when Sawyer took over, and therefore, they went 29-39 under his management. The 1959 season followed a similar course, with the Phillies finishing in the basement once again at 64-90. Despite the team's struggles, Sawyer was signed to a new contract on 25 September 1959 and seemed poised to continue on as the team's manager for the foreseeable future.

The 1960 season opened with a Phillies loss to the Cincinnati Reds. After the game, Sawyer stepped down as manager, famously quipping "I am 49 years old and want to live to be 50."[99] This would be the end of Sawyer's final stint as a manager at any level. Eddie Sawyer finished his Major League managerial career with a record of 390-423 (.480), placing him seventh all-time among Phillies managers (as of 2021).[100] Much like years past, Eddie Sawyer found it difficult to stay away from baseball for too long. In December 1962, he rejoined the Phillies as a scout, holding this position until 1966. In 1968, he was announced as a full-time scout for the newly created Kansas City Royals, who began play in 1969. Sawyer's expertise paid off, and Kansas City was the most successful of the four teams that began play that year and the only one to not finish last in their division.[101] On 1 January 1974, Eddie Sawyer officially retired from baseball after four years as a scout for the Royals.

On 14 October 1980, Eddie Sawyer threw out the ceremonial first pitch at Veteran's Stadium in Philadelphia, kicking off the 1980 World Series which would be the first ever won by the Phillies when they defeated (ironically) the Kansas City Royals. He then spent much of the 1990's caring for his wife, Polly, who was often ill, and he routinely turned down speaking engagements across the country, preferring to remain out of the spotlight.[102] On 22 September 1997, Eddie Sawyer died in Phoenixville, Pennsylvania at the age of eighty-seven. He was survived by his wife, two daughters, five grandchildren, and three great-grandchildren.[103] Sawyer's legacy can be easily summarized by one of his well-known quotes: "Baseball gets in your blood. There's more to working than just making money. What good is all the money in the world if you don't enjoy yourself?"[104]

Westerly's Boys of Summer in the 1950 Little League World Series

"Between the two games against Wellsville, Garafolo struck out nineteen batters in eleven innings. With that victory, the team punched their ticket to Williamsport, leading The Westerly Sun *to refer to the team as the "Cinderella Club" of the Little League World Series."*

Since the 1860's, baseball has been played on fields across the country, making it one of the most popular sports in our nation's history. Despite its more than 150 year history, baseball for younger players was fairly uncommon and largely unregulated until the founding of Little League Baseball and Softball in 1939. The first Little League World Series (originally known as the National Little League Tournament) was held in 1947 and was played amongst the nation's seventeen known Little League teams (sixteen of which were in Pennsylvania as well as one from New Jersey).[105] Ever since the very first tournament, games have always been held in Williamsport, Pennsylvania.[106] In 1950, a team of all-stars from Westerly advanced all the way to the Little League World Series, a tournament that today is an international event which draws viewers from across globe.

By 1950, Little League was beginning to expand across the country. Despite the game's growing popularity, there were only two leagues in Rhode Island at the time, one in Westerly and one in Wakefield. That Westerly team has the distinction of being the first from Rhode Island to advance to the Little League World Series. Rhode Island has since sent seven additional teams to the Series, but the next team after the original 1950 squad would not be until 1980.[107]

During the 1950 season of the Westerly Little League, players were required to be between the ages of eight and twelve. The League was composed of four sponsored teams: The Elks, the Sportsmen's Club, the Red Fox Beverage Company team, and the Ashaway Line and Twine team.[108] Each team had their own uniforms and were supported by a farm team from which they could call reserves when needed.[109] Games were played on a field 2/3 the size of a regulation field constructed at the Westerly High School athletic complex, where they often drew crowds of more than five hundred spectators.[110] Players were sometimes traded among the four teams. The first trade of the season took place on June 20, when the Sportsmen's Club traded their pitcher with a 3-0 record to the Red Fox team for a power-hitting outfielder and a reserve infielder.[111]

"Mr. Little League" Johnny Garafolo, 1950
(Photo: Westerly Sun, Westerly Public Library)

While the Westerly Little League had many tremendous players during the course of the 1950 season, including Walter Brown of the Red Fox team who batted .418 and Richard "Dickie" Chipperfield of the Sportsmen's Club, who hit .365, the League's uncrowned Most Valuable Player was undoubtedly pitcher Johnny Garafolo of the Elks, who compiled a record of nine wins to zero losses.[112] Throughout the year, Garafolo contributed significantly to his team's offense, clubbing homeruns on a regular basis. Due in large part to his skillful play, Garafolo's Elks team was eventually named League Champions.[113]

At the conclusion of the regular season, the league's best players were named to an All-Star team coached by Vero Morrone and Hank Manfredi which would represent Rhode Island in the New England regional championship tournament.[114] In order to fund their travel to Pittsfield, Massachusetts to participate in the tournament the team held a highly successful tag sale, raising $1,537.81 to cover the cost of the trip.[115]

Charlie Sposato Hoisted Up by His Teammates after Throwing a No-Hitter, 1950
(Photo: Westerly Sun, Westerly Public Library)

As the regular season drew to a close, the Westerly team traveled to Wakefield to take on the only other Little League team in Rhode Island, the Wakefield All-Stars. Westerly won the game, 12-3, capping off their three game sweep of Wakefield on the season.[116]

After this tune up game, the boys headed off to Pittsfield, where they would face the best competition all of New England. On August 11th, Johnny Garafolo faced off against the Concord (NH) Braves in the opening round of the tournament. Garafolo pitched well through the first two innings, allowing only one run. Westerly quickly got out to a 5-1 lead after two innings, and the coaches made the decision to move Garafolo to the outfield and brought in Charlie Sposato to pitch. Unfortunately, Sposato struggled, allowing three runs in the third inning and putting the tying runner on base before the coaches reversed their decision putting Garafolo back on the mound. The young ace proceeded to shut the Braves down, halting their rally. In addition to his stellar pitching, Garafolo also contributed two hits and scored a run in Westerly's 5-4 victory.[117]

The 1950 Westerly Little League All-Stars
(Photo: Westerly Sun, Westerly Public Library)

The next day, Westerly faced off against the host team, the Pittsfield All-Stars. The winner of that game would advance to the Northeastern United States tournament for the right to play in the Little League World Series. After his near complete game the night before, Johnny Garafolo was given the task of patrolling centerfield while Bobby Payne took the mound for Westerly.[118] In front of approximately 1,500 fans, including Westerly Town Council President Farquhar Smith and more than one hundred others who made their way from Rhode Island, Westerly trounced the hometown Pittsfield team, 10-2.[119]

Bobby Payne pitched a gem in the championship game, striking out four while only giving up a run in the first and last frames. The second inning put Westerly in a position to win early on, after they scored seven runs. In that inning, Johnny Garafolo clubbed a two-run homerun and Bobby Payne followed that up with a homerun of his own on the very next pitch.[120] By the time the game concluded, Westerly had used all fourteen players on their roster. After the game, all players in the tournament were treated to dinner at the New Berkshire Restaurant. The Westerly boys then made their way home where they received an enthusiastic welcome from many who had listened to the game called by Art Borgis on radio station WERI, Westerly.[121]

Six days after their New England championship victory, the Westerly All-Stars were off to Schenectady, New York, where they were set to face off against Wellsville (NY). Initially, Westerly was scheduled to play the team from Port Chester, the New York State Champions, but a polio epidemic led Westchester County Commissioner William A. Holla to cancel the team's trip to the tournament. As a result, Westerly squared off against second-place Wellsville.[122] The two champions clashed in a best of three series, with the winner moving on to Williamsport.

On August 18th, Westerly and Wellsville squared for their first game in the pouring rain. Once again, Johnny Garafolo played the role of hero for Westerly. The left-hander pitched masterfully, striking out seven batters in a weather-shortened five inning game. Coming into the third inning, Westerly was down 1-0 before they picked up three runs on homeruns by Roy Bailey and Johnny Garafolo.[123] They then added five more runs in the fifth inning, putting the game away for good before it was called at the end of that inning with Westerly ahead, 10-2.

The next day, the teams were prepared to meet in their second game, however, it was postponed until the following day due to more rain in the area.[124] When the time came for Westerly to face Wellsville in game two, the boys from Rhode Island were more than ready. As was the theme throughout the post-season, Johnny Garafolo once again came through for Westerly, turning in perhaps his best performance of the season in front of 2,000 spectators. He tossed a one-hit shutout, striking out twelve batters in six innings to shut the door on the series and end Wellsville's dreams of playing in the Little League World Series. Not only did the lefty completely shut down his opponents on the mound, he also provided an offensive spark, driving in four runs on a single and a homerun. Between the two games against Wellsville, Garafolo struck out nineteen batters in eleven innings. With that victory, the team punched their ticket to Williamsport, leading *The Westerly Sun* to refer to the team as the "Cinderella Club" of the Little League World Series.[125]

Unfortunately for Westerly, the clock struck midnight just as the World Series began. On August 24th, they opened up the tournament against a powerful team from Houston, Texas in front of 6,000 fans. Despite putting on multiple displays of offensive firepower on their road to Williamsport, the Westerly All-Stars could not get it going against the Texans. In their only game in the 1950 Little League World Series, Westerly failed to collect a single hit, and only one batter reached base when Charlie Sposato walked in the fifth inning. The team became one of many in a long line of victims for Houston's Billy Martin. Westerly struck out fourteen times in the game and became the second consecutive team to be no-hit by Martin.[126] The no-hitter was nearly broken up when Dickie Chipperfield dropped a bunt down the first base line, but he was ruled out by the first base umpire.[127]

The game also marked the only loss for Johnny Garafolo over the course of the entire 1950 season. Garafolo gave up five hits in total, while his teammates committed four errors in the game, a surprising result, given that the team had played fantastic defense on their journey to Williamsport. One small consolation for the Westerly boys is that the Houston team they fell to were later crowned World Champions upon defeating Bridgeport (CT), 2-1.[128] While the end of their season arrived earlier than they had hoped, the Westerly boys were still able to return home with their heads held high, as they had gone further than so many other teams in America that season.

On August 30th, four days after Houston was crowned the World Series champions in Williamsport, 118 Westerly Little League players were celebrated with a day-long event. The boys were taken to Legion Town Camp in Charlestown, where they swam and played baseball, volleyball, and other sports. That evening, John Gentile, the exalted ruler of the Westerly Elks Lodge, was presented with a trophy on behalf of the league-winning Elks team, led by Johnny Garafolo. All players, coaches, and umpires for the league were presented with special pins commemorating their successful season.[129]

The following year, Westerly proved that their success was not a fluke when they defeated the Bristol Little League All-Star team 1-0 to win the Rhode Island State Championship.[130] Unfortunately, the pint-sized players were unable to replicate their success from 1950, and although they advanced to the regional championship tournament in Stamford, Connecticut, they did not secure a bid to the World Series.

While the 1950 All-Star team had several standout players, it was clear from the very beginning that the team was driven by the play of Johnny Garafolo. In 1956, he was selected as captain of the Westerly High School baseball team and upon graduation, he attended the University of Rhode Island, where he played baseball and basketball. Garafolo was highly touted as a college baseball player and in 1958, he was signed by the Milwaukee Braves organization.[131] He played for five different teams between 1958 and 1962, and in those five seasons, he batted .285 with twenty-three homeruns while driving in 194 runs.[132] Garafolo reached his highest level in 1961 when he was promoted to the Double-A Austin (TX) Senators for eleven games. Ironically, that same season, he also played twenty-one games for the Wellsville (NY) Braves, home to the team Westerly defeated to advance to the Little League World Series eleven years earlier. After retiring from baseball, Garafolo worked as a teacher, first in Washington state, and later in Rhode Island, including a stint as a teacher at Westerly High School.[133]

Since 1950, Rhode Island has sent a representative to the Little League World Series eight times, most recently in 2019 when the Barrington Little League All-Stars achieved a spot in Williamsport. In 1996, the Cranston Western team advanced all the way to the Championship game, where they were defeated by Fu-Shing Little League of Kaohsiung, Taiwan, 13-3.[134] Although they did not win a game in Williamsport, the 1950 Westerly Little League All-Stars will always have the distinction of being the very first to represent the Ocean State on the grand stage.

Dave Stenhouse and Sons: A Baseball Family

"Perhaps the highlight of the 1962 season, at least on a personal level, came on August 5th, which was named 'Dave Stenhouse Day' at Fenway Park, when the Senators took on the Red Sox. Between games of a doubleheader, a ceremony was held honoring the pitcher, which was attended by one thousand fans who traveled north from Westerly. Although Stenhouse did not pitch that day due to a knee injury, he was still celebrated roundly by the crowd. During the event, which Stenhouse called 'The greatest day of my baseball life,' he was made an honorary member of the Westerly Fire Department and received accolades from the University of Rhode Island and the state of Rhode Island."

The legacy of local baseball players runs deep. Perhaps the most well-known baseball player to come out of Westerly is Dave Stenhouse, a stellar pitcher who played over a decade of professional baseball. While Dave Stenhouse's achievements are impressive in their own right, two of his sons, Dave Jr. and Mike, also played professional baseball for many years, developing a strong family legacy in the national pastime.

David Rotchford Stenhouse was born in Westerly on 12 September 1933 to Clarence and Mary G. (Driscoll) Stenhouse.[135] From 1947 to 1951, he attended Westerly High School, and it was there that he acquired a reputation as a standout athlete. Interestingly, it was Stenhouse's ability on the basketball court for the Bulldogs that garnered him the most accolades initially.[136] In his senior year, in addition to playing on the baseball team, Dave was named captain of the basketball team, and in response to his success, he was named the 1951 Rhode Island Athlete of the Year by the Rhode Island Association of Sports Writers.[137]

In the fall of 1951, Stenhouse began attending the University of Rhode Island, where he played on both the baseball and basketball teams for four years. Stenhouse's greatest season on the basketball court came during his junior year when he averaged 17.1 points per game. On the baseball diamond at URI, he compiled a less than stellar record of eleven wins and sixteen losses, but his talent as a pitcher was clear.[138] In 1952, he played in a

Canadian summer league for a team in Grand Falls, New Brunswick, finishing with a record of twelve wins and six losses.[139] The following summer, he played for the Kentville (Nova Scotia) Wildcats, finishing with a record of thirteen wins and six losses. While in college, Stenhouse also participated in ROTC and was nearly inducted into military service before having his service deferred while he was pitching for the Des Moines Demons.[140]

After four seasons with the Rhode Island Rams, Dave Stenhouse gained the attention of several major league clubs, including the Pittsburgh Pirates and Milwaukee Braves. Ultimately, he signed with the Chicago Cubs on 29 June 1955.[141] When interviewed by *The Westerly Sun*, Stenhouse stated "I believe there is more of an opportunity with the Chicago team…this is a terrific contract."[142] As part of his contract, Dave gained permission from the Cubs to leave the team in mid-September to return to URI in order to complete his credits for a degree in engineering.

Stenhouse received attention from other major league teams as well, as Branch Rickey of the Brooklyn Dodgers compiled a scouting report on him. According to this report, "He looks to me like a boy with excellent control and he is intelligent. He has aptitude. He can get a usable change-up [sic] on his fast ball right away." Rickey did note, however, that Stenhouse had very recently suffered a pulled tendon in his throwing elbow and that this resulted in a gamble on his recovery.[143]

In 1956, Stenhouse played for the Class-D Lafayette (LA) Oilers, the 1955 champions of the Evangeline League.[144] The highly touted pitcher performed extremely well, finishing with a record of sixteen wins and four losses and an earned run average of 1.92 over twenty-six games. Although the Oilers finished in first place once again in 1956, the finals were cancelled when franchises were found to be losing money in the face of decreased attendance. Stenhouse then played for the Des Moines (IA) Demons of the Western League. While in Des Moines, Stenhouse set the modern club strikeout record with 182 and led the league in strikeouts that season.[145] While starting for Des Moines, Dave also had bright spots as a batter including a game against Amarillo in which he collected three singles in four at-bats. In 1958, he played for the Fort Worth (TX) Cats briefly before moving up to the Pueblo (CO) Bruins.[146] On 20 June 1958, Stenhouse threw a no-hitter in Topeka, Kansas, striking out eleven batters in a 5-0 victory.[147] He finished the season with a record of sixteen wins and eight losses, making the Western League's All Star Team.[148],[149]

Dave Stenhouse at Fenway Park on Dave Stenhouse Day, 5 August 1962
(Photo: Westerly Sun)

On 2 December 1958, Dave Stenhouse was drafted by the Cincinnati Redlegs out of the Cubs farm system. He was then sent to Seattle, where he started for the Triple-A Rainiers of the Pacific Coast League for the 1959 and 1960 seasons.[150],[151] In 1961, he pitched for the Jersey City Jerseys of the International League.[152] From 1959 through 1961, he pitched to a record of thirty-nine wins and thirty-seven losses. Despite a somewhat lackluster won/lost record, Stenhouse saw a fair amount of success, including being named to *Look Magazine's* All International League Team for 1961. He also pitched a one-hitter and three two-hitters while racking up fourteen wins for the Jerseys. In 1961, the Redlegs had an obvious need for pitchers, however, they did not call up Stenhouse, leading him to express his disappointment to *Look Magazine*.[153]

On 15 December 1961, Dave Stenhouse was traded with Bob Schmidt to the Washington Senators for Johnny Klippstein and Marty Keough.[154] This move provided Stenhouse with a new opportunity, and he made the Senators' Opening Day roster out of spring training. He debuted on 18 April 1962 with two scoreless innings against the Detroit Tigers and then made several relief appearances before being used as a starting pitcher.

Stenhouse did not disappoint when called upon in the major leagues. In his first start, Stenhouse pitched seven innings of three-hit ball against the eventual champions, the New York Yankees. In his next start, he nearly shut out the Orioles. In his third start, Stenhouse pitched a four-hitter against the Chicago White Sox. Through the first half of the 1962 season, Stenhouse had a record of 6-3 and was near the American League lead in ERA. Due to his early-season success, he was selected to play in the 1962 All-Star Game. Despite all of his success, Stenhouse still had to combat with his nerves during the All-Star Game. During his warmups, he accidentally hit a television camera. He ended that season with a record of 11-12 and an ERA of 3.65 in thirty-four games. In 1962, he led the Senators pitchers in wins, games started, complete games, and innings pitched.[155]

Perhaps the highlight of the 1962 season, at least on a personal level, came on August 5th, which was named 'Dave Stenhouse Day' at Fenway Park, when the Senators took on the Red Sox. Between games of a doubleheader, a ceremony was held honoring the pitcher, which was attended by one thousand fans who traveled north from Westerly. Although Stenhouse did not pitch that day due to a knee injury, he was still celebrated roundly by the crowd. During the event, which Stenhouse called "The greatest day of my baseball life," he was made an honorary member of the Westerly Fire Department and received accolades from the University of Rhode Island and the state of Rhode Island. In attendance were his parents, brother Nick, wife Phyllis, and sons Mike and Dave Jr.[156] 5 October 1962 was also proclaimed Dave Stenhouse Day by the Town of Westerly.[157] At the end of the year, Stenhouse was named the Rhode Island Athlete of the Year once again. Despite Stenhouse's strong showing, the Senators finished 1962 in last place with a record of 60-101, thirty-three and a half games behind the first place Yankees and eleven and a half behind the ninth place Athletics.[158]

In spite of high expectations based on his past performance, the subsequent seasons were not nearly as successful for Dave Stenhouse. In

1963, he compiled a record of three wins and nine losses with an ERA of 4.55 in sixteen games.[159] The following year was equally disappointing, as he achieved two wins against seven losses with an ERA of 4.81.

After the 1964 season, Stenhouse would never reach the major leagues again. The 1965 season saw the pitcher play for the Double-A York (PA) White Roses before moving across the country to join the Triple-A Hawaii Islanders.[160] Dave would remain in Honolulu until May 1967, when he was released by the Islanders, at which point he retired from professional baseball.[161] Stenhouse did not stay out of baseball long, however, as he was named varsity baseball coach and assistant basketball coach at Rhode Island College in December 1968, remaining there for several years.[162] In 1981, he took up the coaching position for the Brown University baseball team, a job he held for ten seasons until retiring from coaching at the conclusion of the 1990 season.[163] His 1986 Brown team finished with twenty-three wins, the most in school history.[164]

Dave Stenhouse Receiving His Look Magazine Award, 1961
(Photo: The Westerly Sun)

Dave Stenhouse's love for Rhode Island was apparent. Not only did he return to the Ocean State after his playing career came to an end, but he returned home to work between each season of his professional career.

Dave Stenhouse Sr. was not the only member of his family to find themselves on professional baseball rosters. Both of Dave's sons, Dave Jr. and Mike Stenhouse, spent several years playing professional baseball. Mike Stenhouse was a highly touted outfielder beginning with his career at Cranston East High School, when he was named to the Rhode Island Interscholastic Baseball Team in 1974.[165] Despite fielding offers from high-profile college teams including Arizona State, Mike opted to attend Harvard, where he found great success with the Crimson. In 1977, as a freshman, he was an All-Ivy League player, hitting .475, second best in Division I.[166] In 1979, he was drafted 26th overall by the Oakland Athletics, but chose to return to Harvard after Major League Baseball refused to make him a free agent following a salary dispute. In the next draft in January 1980, he was selected 4th overall by the Montreal Expos, and in 1982, he was called up to the Major League roster.[167] Mike spent much of the 1982, 1983, and 1984 seasons with Triple-A Wichita, where he found significant success, hitting .355 with twenty-five home runs over three seasons.[168]

In 1985, Mike was traded to the Minnesota Twins before the start of the season. It was in Minnesota during the 1985 season where he would see career highs in virtually every category including games played, at-bats, hits, homeruns, runs batted in, stolen bases, walks, and batting average. In December 1985, Mike Stenhouse was dealt to the Boston Red Sox for pitcher Charlie Mitchell.[169] In 1986, he would play in Fenway Park, the same stadium where his father was warmly received by hometown fans in 1962. Unfortunately, Mike's career with the Red Sox was brief, as he collected only two hits in twenty-one at bats. This would prove to be his final major league season. He would later go on to work as an analyst for the Pawtucket Red Sox and an announcer for the Montreal Expos during the 1996 season. Today, he is the CEO of the Rhode Island Center for Freedom and Prosperity, a public policy group.[170]

Mike Stenhouse's brother, Dave Jr. also found himself involved in professional baseball for a number of seasons, spending six years in the minor leagues, three of which were at the Triple-A level. Dave Jr., a catcher, was a fifth-round draft pick for the Toronto Blue Jays in the 1982 amateur draft.[171] He debuted for the Medicine Hat Blue Jays, where he hit .305 with eight home runs in 187 at-bats.[172] In 1983, he was invited to the Blue Jays spring training camp. The following season, he jumped several levels in the minor league system, moving all the way up to the Triple-A Syracuse Chiefs. The next three seasons saw Dave Jr. play mostly in Syracuse, although he never received a call to the Major Leagues. After 1987, Dave Stenhouse Jr. retired from professional baseball, although he did play for the barnstorming Grey Sox team with his brother, Mike.[173]

While the chances of any one person having a career in professional baseball are quite low, the chances of three men from the same family achieving this goal are virtually non-existent. These low odds make the story of the Stenhouse family even more amazing. The legacy of Dave Stenhouse has since become a part of Westerly's lore, and he is still remembered for his beginnings with the Bulldogs.

Bill Collins, Yankee Rogers and Wrestling in the Early 20th Century

"Upon his return to Westerly, Collins set his sights on a battle with a notorious local competitor, Charles "Yankee" Rogers of Fall River. The men had met before, but this time, Rogers indicated that he would agree to fight Collins for a side bet and the entire gate receipts but he did not want to receive a cent of the profit if he could not defeat Collins. On New Years Day, the two men met once again at the Ancient Order of Hibernians Hall in Westerly (currently the Sharah Zedek Synagogue on Union Street), a popular venue for wrestling at the time. The matchup was proclaimed "one of the best wrestling exhibitions seen in Westerly in some time."

When one thinks of professional wrestling as it exists today (of which this author is admittedly a large fan), it usually conjures notions of pageantry, fast-paced action and over the top characters, but it was not always this way. The concept of professional wrestling is one which is centuries old and was rather popular in New England more than one hundred years ago. One facet of professional wrestling as it existed in the 1910's which remains to this day is the concept of "babyfaces" vs. "heels" (fan favorites and villains respectively). At the turn of the century, there were several wrestlers who were well-known to Westerly residents, but two men stood out as the most prolific competitors for many years, Bill Collins, a celebrated competitor and "Yankee" Rogers, a man who stoked the ire of many local fans.

Due to the transient nature of professional wrestling, competitors often moved around and competed in matches across New England throughout the year. Because of this, very little can be found regarding either Bill Collins' early life or his later life. Collins was said to have been born c. 1889 based on a 1913 court statement in which he claimed to be twenty-four years old.[174] The first account of Collins in Westerly comes from a mention that he was to wrestle the popular Abe the Newsboy "within 150 feet of the boundary line" on 27 January 1909, likely a reference to the fact that citizens of Westerly often opposed wrestling matches held locally.[175],[176] The two competitors grappled to a one hour draw much to the delight of the fans in attendance.

Despite being evenly matched in their first bout, local newspapers said that Abe was "looked upon as a winner" in their rematch in March 1909.[177]

(Photo: Westerly Sun)

That same month, there were some in Westerly who began to question the violence of these matches, particularly when another locally-revered competitor, Jack "The Irish Giant" McGrath was barred from wrestling in Westerly because "his style is too strenuous."[178] This claim was particularly interesting when one considers that professional wrestling of this era bore more similarities to modern amateur wrestling than it does today.

Nearly all of the matches during the early twentieth century were contested under two-out-of-three falls rules and in at least some instances wrestlers were not "allowed to use the fingers or thumbs as it might prove serious."[179] Interestingly, however, strangleholds were permitted. There is some uncertainty as to whether the results of these matches were pre-determined, and if so, whether the public was aware of this fact. In several instances, newspaper accounts plainly state that wrestlers "agreed" to throw (or pin) their opponent in a pre-set amount of time, and it was not unusual for a competitor to place wagers on the outcome of their own matches. However, this may have simply meant that the wrestlers agreed to such a wager and not to an actual outcome.[180]

In February 1910, Bill Collins was in the capital city where he signed an agreement to fight strongman Captain Charles Clayton in Providence on March 3rd. However, this match does not appear to have happened, as that same day, he was at Pawcatuck Armory where he filled in for a bout with Jack McGrath when McGrath's scheduled opponent failed to appear. According to one summary of the fight, Collins was "in great condition and put up a strong defense against McGrath" but he was thrown three times in one hour by the mighty Irishman. Collins was also a proficient boxer, and in the summer of 1910, he was even said to have done more boxing than wrestling and he also managed other local wrestlers when he was not competing himself. In a bold move, another local wrestler, Charles Clayton, wrote into a local newspaper to challenge Collins to a third rematch in May 1910.[181]

In the spring of 1911, Collins, previously a Connecticut resident, made a new home in Westerly and took up a position as a mixologist at a café while teaching wrestling on the side as he was recovering from a broken foot suffered during a match with Zeral Olansky. Collins sought revenge against Olansky in a rematch in Holyoke, Massachusetts as well as other bouts in Massachusetts throughout the spring. After taking the summer to rest, Bill Collins made his return to the mat when he challenged Oscar Samson to a match on Labor Day as part of Westerly's holiday celebration.[182] If anyone had questions about Collins' conditioning, these questions were put to rest when he embarked on a tour of Vermont in the autumn 1911. In Newport, Vermont, Collins won two of three falls in a matchup that lasted over an hour. This would pale in comparison, however, to his epic battle with Sandy Dryden when the first fall came after one hour and fifty-two minutes. Prior to his departure for Vermont, Bill Collins dispatched of his opponent, Alex Sandow of Boston, as the headliner of a vaudeville show.[183]

After a lengthy tour which took him across Vermont, Massachusetts, and parts of Canada, Collins returned to Westerly for a short rest after having competed three to four nights every week.[184]

Bill Collins, 1911
(Photo: Westerly Sun)

Upon his return to Westerly, Collins set his sights on a battle with a notorious local competitor, Charles "Yankee" Rogers of Fall River. The men had met before, but this time, Rogers indicated that he would agree to fight Collins for a side bet and the entire gate receipts but he did not want to receive a cent of the profit if he could not defeat Collins.[185] On New Years Day, the two men met once again at the Ancient Order of Hibernians Hall in Westerly (currently the Sharah Zedek Synagogue on Union Street), a popular venue for wrestling at the time. The matchup was proclaimed "one of the best wrestling exhibitions seen in Westerly in some time."[186] The match, described as "fast and clean all the way" with "clever work" resulted in each man getting one fall, leaving the audience pleased and showering the wrestlers with continuous applause.[187] The following month, the two men were set to meet again, in what is thought to have been Rogers' final appearance in Westerly.[188]

In March 1912, an event transpired which led the *Norwich Evening Bulletin* to proclaim that wrestling "is now dead as the proverbial doornail and Charley 'Yankee' Rogers…killed it."[189] Rogers, who had taken up residence in Westerly and made friends with many local men, advertised a wrestling match at Bliven's Opera House between nationally-known wrestler Dr. Ben Roller and John Perelli of Boston.

On the night of the event, Rogers and his friend Harry Parker provided a short exhibition of wrestling and showed films of other matches, but when the main event was set to begin, it was revealed that neither Roller nor Perelli were present and, in fact, they were likely not aware that they were even expected to be at the Opera House. Fans immediately began to demand a refund, but the Opera House proclaimed that they merely rented the space to Rogers for the evening and they had no hand in the entertainment. Rogers would then boldly proclaim that he had been made aware that Roller would not be present but at that time, he had already rented the venue and in order to fund the rental, he advertised Roller regardless. After avoiding a riot in response to his trickery, Rogers boarded the very first train out of Westerly and it was said that he would not be wrestling in Westerly in the future.[190] A week later, it was reported that Rogers had not been seen in town since the incident and it is unlikely that he ever returned.[191]

After the downfall of the local wrestling scene at the hands of Charles Rogers, Bill Collins was to face his own adversity in 1912. In December of that year, Collins was stabbed by a man named Sam Royster and although the prospects for his recovery were said to be good, Collins still suffered immensely, being bed-ridden for several weeks after the incident. In fact, three weeks after the stabbing, Collins was still too weak to appear in court to give his side of the story, although several "men of leisure" appeared in the courthouse to see Collins.[192] Royster was eventually convicted and sentenced to two years in prison.[193]

Amazingly, Collins managed to continue his wrestling career for several years after the Rogers incident. In 1914, he spent the winter in New Hampshire, Vermont, and Massachusetts on a tour of northern New England. Adding to his plight, Collins was struck by an automobile in 1913 and when he brought suit against the driver to recover lost wages as a result of his injuries, the judge awarded Collins no damages.[194] Collins was involved in another incident in September 1917 in which a man named David Helme assaulted him with a knife while shouting "Sam Royster did a poor job, but I'll do a better one!" Two years later, Collins was still displaying his skills on the mat, challenging all comers at a local fair. To win a cash prize in these contests, Collins' opponents only had to last a certain length of time in the match, but his opponents rarely outlasted the clock. The final record of Collins that could be located was a mention that a star wrestler, Al Benham, was injured in a match against Collins at a local carnival.[195] It is clear that for a relatively short span, Bill Collins and Yankee Rogers were two of the biggest names in Westerly's sporting scene and were largely responsible for the rise and fall of professional wrestling in Westerly.

The Legend of Tarzan Brown

"At the marathon's finish line, a contingent of Westerly residents awaited Brown, and upon his approach, performed a "war dance." After his victory, Tarzan Brown was offered congratulations by the Rhode Island State Assembly, as well as from many Indigenous groups across the state. A week after the race, Brown was also commended at a banquet hosted by the Westerly Chamber of Commerce, who had contributed to the fund raising money for his races. Westerly Sun *sports editor Abe Soloveitzik was the man responsible for starting the fund for Brown."*

While numerous athletes who have achieved a great deal of fame in the sports world have come out of Westerly, perhaps none is more revered than Ellison Myers 'Tarzan' Brown, winner of the 1936 and 1939 Boston Marathons. Brown, a member of the Narragansett tribe, was born in Westerly on 22 September 1913, the fifth of eight children born to Byron Otis Brown, a millhand, and his wife Grace Ethel (Babcock) Brown.[196] Although popular lore of the day suggested Tarzan grew up on the Narragansett Reservation, census records show that the family lived on Potter Hill Road between 1915 and 1920, before moving to Pierce Street by 1925.[197] Tarzan Brown dropped out of school in the eighth grade and by the age of sixteen, he was working as a laborer with the railroad in Alton, Rhode Island.[198]

Chief Horatio N. Stanton of the Narragansetts discovered Brown's talent for distance running early on and inspired him to pursue running competitively.[199] While most knew him simply as 'Tarzan,' he was also known to some as 'Deerfoot.'[200] Brown's 'rhythmic foot motion' is said by veteran runners to be 'the most perfect they have ever seen,' a trait which aided his early success.[201]

On 16 April 1935, Tarzan's mother, Grace Brown, passed away and just two days later, her son took part in his third Boston Marathon. At the age of twenty-one, Tarzan Brown had never finished above thirtieth place, however, this time he finished thirteenth overall, showing a strong improvement.[202] Even more impressive was the fact that he completed the final six miles of the race without his shoes, as he was forced to remove them after they caused him pain and difficulty in running.[203\]

Despite his challenges at a young age, Tarzan was not discouraged. His early career was marked by ups and downs, including a victory in a 30 km race in Boston in August 1935, and a suspension by the New England branch of the Amateur Athletic Union. Tarzan's suspension came after he competed in a Labor Day Olympic Marathon in Philadelphia without receiving a travel permit. The issue, however, was quickly resolved and he was reinstated on 8 September 1935, the same day on which he set a new world record in the 20 km race in Newport.[204] In spite of Tarzan's newfound success, by the following year, he was back to working odd jobs in Alton to make ends meet.[205] His luck was about to change.

On 20 April 1936, the legend of Tarzan Brown was born. Running as part of the Tercentenary Athletic Club of Providence, he defeated 183 other competitors in the Boston Marathon, finishing with a final time of two hours, thirty-three minutes and forty seconds, about one minute behind the record.[206] With this win, Brown, at the age of twenty-two, became the youngest winner of the Boston Marathon.[207] After his victory, he was awarded a silver trophy, a diamond-studded gold medal and a laurel crown, as well as an opportunity to make the United States Olympic team competing in Berlin that year. Given his lackluster finishes in past Boston Marathons, Brown was considered a longshot to win with many journalists labeling him as an unknown. A major part of the lore of Tarzan Brown was derived from the way in which he was portrayed by the media in the aftermath of his victory. Brown's hometown *Westerly Sun* claimed that he trained by running in the "wooded trails of Rhode Island" and that he "inherited the traits of his Indian ancestors."[208] Claims were also made that Brown was the first "100% American" to win the marathon since 1907, although it is not clear what this meant.[209]

One of the most well-known features of the Boston Marathon course is the incline near the Newton City Hall which has been dubbed "Heartbreak Hill," a name that was inspired by one of Tarzan Brown's most notorious exploits. It was at this spot during the 1936 race that Tarzan was approached by Johnny Kelley, the most prolific marathon runner in history (he ran in sixty one Boston marathons, winning two and finishing in the top ten in eighteen) when Kelley patted a laboring Brown on the back. Tarzan perceived this as an act of arrogance and used it as motivation to claim first place in the race. Brown pulled ahead and never looked back. After the race, Boston sports editor, Jerry Nasson, went on to coin the term "Heartbreak Hill."[210]

Breaks Record

Tarzan Brown
(Photo: The Westerly Sun)

At the marathon's finish line, a contingent of Westerly residents awaited Brown, and upon his approach, performed a "war dance."[211] After his victory, Tarzan Brown was offered congratulations by the Rhode Island State Assembly, as well as from many Indigenous groups across the state.[212] A week after the race, Brown was also commended at a banquet hosted by the Westerly Chamber of Commerce, who had contributed to the fund raising money for his races. *Westerly Sun* sports editor Abe Soloveitzik was the man responsible for starting the fund for Brown.[213]

Tarzan Brown's impressive victory in the 1936 Marathon was enough to earn him a spot on the United States team for the 1936 Summer Olympics in Berlin. On 12 July 1936, Brown took his first ever boat trip when he traveled from Providence to New York City before departing for Berlin. Brown's travel to the Olympics was largely financed by Westerly residents who hoped for his success.[214] Unfortunately for Brown, he suffered a muscular injury while running in an informal race against an American heel-and-toe runner. Although Brown was able to start the Olympic marathon, he was forced to drop out after the seventeenth mile as a result of his injury.[215] This was the first time in his career that he was unable to complete a race he had started and it was a bitter disappointment for Westerly's Olympian.[216]

Even though his Olympic race did not end as anyone had hoped, Tarzan Brown was victorious in his next seven consecutive races, including four full marathons. Perhaps his most impressive feat occurred between October 11th and 12th, 1936. During that forty-eight-hour span, Brown won a full marathon in Portchester, New York, hitchhiked to Manchester, New Hampshire, and ran another full marathon the following day. All told, Brown traveled over four hundred miles without rest to get to the Manchester marathon. His intense schedule was not without consequences, however. In November, he was forced to take a hiatus from running to undergo surgery for a strangulated inguinal hernia. On 27 November 1936, three days after being discharged from the hospital, Brown married Ethel Mae Wilcox of Charlestown. After his wedding, Brown moved between Charlestown, Westerly, and Bradford, unable to secure permanent employment.[217]

On 8 April 1937, Tarzan Brown reported to *The Westerly Sun* that he intended to begin training to run in the 1937 Boston Marathon, which was only ten days away.[218] Given his short training period for the race, perhaps it is not stunning that he finished in thirty-first place despite being considered a popular favorite going into the event. Brown's health during and after the race were the biggest stories, as he was said to have lost eight pounds over the course of the twenty-six mile circuit and he was forced to slow his speed to a walk a dozen times.[219] Still, Brown defied the odds and ran a ten-mile road race in Norwich the following month.[220]

Tarzan Brown returned to the Boston Marathon in 1938, but his performance was well below what many had come to expect him. Brown finished a full hour after that year's top three competitors and with a time of three hours, thirty-eight minutes and fifty-nine seconds, he was only able to place a disappointing fifty-fourth. [221] While Tarzan Brown may not have been the talk of the running world in 1938, 1939 proved to be an entirely different story.

On 19 April 1939, in front of an estimated five-hundred thousand spectators, Tarzan Brown devastated his competition in winning the Boston Marathon, setting a new record in the process. His final time was two hours, twenty-eight minutes, and 51.8 seconds, three minutes ahead of the previous record. Not only did Brown finish first, he crossed the finish line with his closest competitor nearly a quarter of a mile behind.[222] As with many events in Tarzan Brown's life, his performance in the 1939 Marathon is surrounded by lore, including the story that he arrived at the marathon without officially entering, forcing him to borrow the two dollar entry fee from Walter Brown, a member of the Boston Marathon and Olympic Selection Committee. Another story, this one told by Tarzan himself, claims that Brown wrote to a Boston sportswriter before the race and told him that he would be the winner.[223]

Once again, Tarzan Brown was celebrated by his admirers in Westerly. In order to capitalize on Brown's popularity in town, the Catholic Youth Organization of the Church of the Immaculate Conception sponsored a ten-mile race which concluded in downtown Westerly. It is estimated that between seven and eight thousand spectators lined the course to see the local hero in action. This marked the first time he had run an officially timed race in his birthplace. Tarzan finished with a final time of fifty-two minutes and 27.6 seconds, the fastest recorded time for a ten-mile race.[224] Brown finished more than a full minute ahead of the second-place runner, Pawtucket's Leslie Pawson, a former Boston Marathon winner and Brown's greatest rival throughout the 1930's. At the finish line, prizes were awarded to the first fifteen runners across the finish line by Rhode Island Attorney General Louis

V. Jackvony. There were no other runners from Westerly among the first twenty to finish the race.[225]

Throughout the remainder of 1939, Tarzan Brown continued to participate in races across Rhode Island and Massachusetts, most of which were ten-mile courses. Throughout the year, he ran twenty-five races of nine miles or more, and in twenty of those races, he had the fastest recorded time.[226] Brown would continue to enter the Boston Marathon on a near-yearly basis after 1939, however, he never reached the same heights he achieved in his second victory. His final Boston Marathon was the 1946 contest which saw him finish in twelfth place. The 1946 Boston Marathon served as a sign to Brown that his days as a professional runner were behind him and he did not compete in any major contests outside of occasional local races after that time.[227]

Tarzan Brown's life after his second Boston Marathon victory was marked by a series of personal and financial struggles. After struggling to find steady work which would provide for his family, Brown was forced to sell many of his prizes from the races he won. The 1950's were not kind to Brown, who found himself on the wrong side of the law several times throughout the decade.[228]

In April 1955, a Tarzan Brown victory was in the news once again, this time, it was when the forty-one-year-old Brown came up victorious against twenty-two-year-old Albert T. Jordan in an informal race in Wakefield.[229] The race, which took place on a two-and-a-half-mile course, came about when Jordan insulted 'old-time runners' like Brown. In the end, it was Tarzan Brown who walked away with a win, one last time.

Brown maintained a relatively low profile in the 1960's and in the early 1970's, he was the recipient of several accolades, including induction into the American Indian Hall of Fame in 1973 and being an honoree of a testimonial dinner in November 1974. On 23 August 1975, Ellison M. "Tarzan" Brown passed away after being struck by a van in the parking lot of a Misquamicut Bar. Brown had previously been seen arguing with the assailant, Philip K. Edwards of Middletown, Connecticut, who was charged with several crimes related to the incident.230 Although his professional career was brief, ending by the mid-1940's, Tarzan Brown left behind a legacy of success and was once an inspiration for the entire town of Westerly.

Chapter VI
Politics, Law and Order

Westerly has long been viewed as a relatively pleasant, quiet town with very little in the way of scandal or controversy. That is not to say there has not been the occasional incident that captivated and concerned locals. However, for every major crime committed in Westerly, there has been someone who stepped up and sought to make a positive difference. Whether it was by voting or running for office, Westerly residents have frequently attempted to make their voice heard.

This chapter opens with an analysis of some of the strangest statutes still in effect as of 2021 as part of the Rhode Island General Laws While nearly all of these laws are benign and have little impact on the day-to-day lives of those in Westerly, some are still cited to this day in court cases.

When it comes to political participation, Westerly has often played a significant role in the outcome of local, state, and even national elections. This can be seen through the election of George Herbert Utter, a Westerly resident who served as both the governor and a senator for Rhode Island at the start of the twentieth century.

Westerly's zeal for participation in important elections can also be seen in its turnout for the 1920 Presidential Election which was also the first election locally in which women were granted the right to vote. In the previous chapter, there was an account of the life of the first woman to cast a ballot in Westerly, Anna Thornton Williams.

That very same year, there was also a crime that rocked Westerly when Charles Bailey, a local man, was accused of murdering his brother and fleeing to Maine where he was tracked down and brought to justice by Westerly police officers.

The last story presented in this chapter is notable for several reasons. First, it shows the importance of family history. Secondly, it is quite simply a fascinating look at a still seemingly unresolved mystery with criminal implications. To this day, many questions surrounding the events at the Tin

Tub Saloon remain unanswered and it is quite likely that the true story may never be known.

The narratives in the following chapter tell two very different sides of Westerly's history, one of criminal activity and one of law, order, and politics. While both sides may be vastly different, they are both of very deserving of being told and forever remembered.

Rhode Island's Strangest Laws

"In many cases, these laws exist simply because lawmakers have not bothered to consider repealing them while in other cases, they still remain in use. Although these laws are rarely cited and virtually unknown, they serve as a telling reminder of the past."

Given its colonial roots, it should come as no surprise that the State of Rhode Island has had some laws enacted that are considered both archaic and unnecessary by modern standards. What would likely surprise many Rhode Islanders is just how many of these laws remain effective as part of the Rhode Island General Laws and are still enforced today. Some of these laws have practical applications that might not be apparent to many citizens, but others defy most reasonable explanations.

Rhode Island General Laws § 11-22-11

*"Every person who shall drive any horse over any of the public highways, **for the purpose of racing or trying the speed of the horse**, shall be fined not more than twenty dollars ($20.00) or imprisoned not exceeding ten (10) days."*[1]

This law is perhaps the strangest of all laws still effective in Rhode Island. This statute which appeared in the 1896 Rhode Island General Laws, was an obvious carryover from the period prior to the popularization of automobiles in the United States. Despite the fact that it likely has little practical use today, the law was analyzed and reaffirmed as recently as 1956, long after horses ceased to be used as a major method of transportation in the state. In 2018, this was one of the laws targeted for repeal by House Majority Whip John Edwards who unsuccessfully led a campaign for the removal of several of Rhode Island's more impractical laws.[2]

Rhode Island General Laws Chapter 11-12

*"Every person who shall **voluntarily engage in a duel with any dangerous weapon**, to the hazard of life, shall be imprisoned not exceeding seven (7) years nor less than one year."[3]*

      This act, commonly referred to as Rhode Island's "Dueling Law," was first recorded in the state more than two hundred years ago, and was another that was targeted by Edwards in 2018. To the surprise of many, Edwards' efforts were derailed by the fact that the law is still used on rare occasions. In November 2017, a North Providence woman pled no contest to "aiding a fight by appointment" for encouraging her daughter to fight another girl, an act explicitly prohibited by the dueling law.[4] The portion of the law this woman was charged with violating reads:

"Every person who shall be present at any fight as provided in § 11-12-6 as an aid, second or surgeon, or who shall advise, encourage or promote the fight, shall be imprisoned not more than five (5) years or be fined not exceeding one thousand dollars ($1,000)."[5]

      Despite the seemingly unlikely circumstances that would result in a Rhode Islander being charged under the dueling law, these exact circumstances have come about as recently as 2017.

Rhode Island General Laws § 45-16-1

*"Whoever is legally chosen to the office of town sergeant, and refuses to serve in that office, **shall pay a fine of seven dollars ($7.00)**, to and for the use of the town, to be levied and collected, upon conviction, by warrant of distress issued by any justice of the peace of a town, the warrant to be directed to the division of sheriffs, and no person is obliged to serve in the office more often than once in seven (7) years."[6],[7]*

      This law is intriguing for two reasons. First, this law requires a situation in which an individual would be unwillingly chosen to the office of town sergeant. Second, this law, which was last updated in 2012, calls for an amusingly small fine of only seven dollars. When this law was recorded in 1896, a fine of $7 would be equivalent to just over $222 in 2021, making this fine a bit less puzzling, however, with a revision as recently as 2012, it is unclear why this fine was never increased.[8]

Rhode Island General Laws §§ 15-1-2 and 15-1-4

"No person shall marry his or her sibling, parent, grandparent, child, grandchild, stepparent, grandparents' spouse, spouse's child, spouse's grandchild, sibling's child or parent's sibling."[9]

*"The provisions of §§ 15-1-2 and 15-1-3 **shall not extend to, or in any way affect, any marriage which shall be solemnized among the Jewish people**, within the degrees of affinity or consanguinity allowed by their religion."*[10]

While the initial law seems rather straightforward and is similar to current laws in most states, the provisions set forth in § 15-1-4 add an interesting qualification for marriages among close family. The fact that Rhode Island State Law allows the practice of a particular religion to determine the legality of a certain action makes this law rather unique.

Rhode Island General Laws § 5-2-9

*"Town or city councils or licensing authorities in any city or town may permit licensees operating bowling alleys, or persons paying a tax for the operation of a bowling alley, to operate rooms or places where bowling, playing of billiards, or pocket billiards for a fee or charge may be engaged in by patrons of those rooms or places on the first day of the week .... provided, that no bowling alley or rooms or places where bowling, playing of billiards, or pocket billiards for a fee or charge is **operated on the first day of the week within two hundred feet (200') of a place of public worship used for public worship.**"*[11]

This law, which was first passed in 1923, is another which takes religion into consideration. It is likely that few, if any, people outside of the proprietors of pool halls and bowling alleys, are aware that these facilities cannot be open on Sundays unless they are more than 200 feet from any place of public worship. While billiards are sometimes considered a vice and a game susceptible to gambling, the inclusion of bowling alleys indicates how they were once held in a similar regard among lawmakers. Similarly, according to Rhode Island General Laws § 41-6-6: "No license shall be granted for any area or enclosed ground [for athletic games] within five hundred feet (500') of any church or chapel."[12]

Rhode Island General Laws § 9-6-9

"In every action or proceeding, civil or criminal, for libel or slander, the defendant may, with his or her plea of not guilty or his answer, file a written notice that he or she will prove the truth of the publication charged as libelous, or of the words charged as slanderous, and in such case may, upon the trial, give the truth in evidence, without any special plea of justification or affirmative defense in his or her answer; and the truth, **unless published or uttered from malicious motives***, shall be sufficient defense to the person charged."[13]*

All states have laws against defamation in place, however, the Rhode Island law contains a unique requirement. As the law states: "the truth, unless published or uttered from malicious motives, shall be sufficient defense." In most defamation laws, the truth in evidence alone can be an adequate defense against guilt regardless of motive, however, in Rhode Island, the truth is not a sufficient defense when a statement is made with malicious intent.[14]

Rhode Island General Laws § 44-18-30(29)

"There are exempted from the taxes imposed by this chapter the following gross receipts:"

"(29) Bibles. **[Unconstitutional; see Ahlburn v. Clark, 728 A.2d 449 (R.I. 1999)**; *see Notes to Decisions.] From the sale and from the storage, use, or other consumption in the state of any canonized scriptures of any tax-exempt nonprofit religious organization including, but not limited to, the Old Testament and the New Testament versions."[15]*

This may be one of the only state laws in existence which specifically states that it has been ruled unconstitutional within the text of the law itself. In 1989, the United States Supreme Court found that a sales tax exemption on bibles and religious literature was unconstitutional in the case of *Texas Monthly, Inc. v. Bullock*. This ruling led the Rhode Island Tax Administrator, Gary Clark, to enact a regulation, SU 92-136, "which made bibles and other canonized scriptures subject to state sales tax."[16] This regulation, however, conflicted with the Rhode Island State Law which was reaffirmed in 1956. This confusion left Rhode Island booksellers confused as to how to tax certain literature. Ten years later in 1999, in deciding the case of *Ahlburn v. Clark* the Rhode Island Supreme Court confirmed that Rhode Island General

Law § 44-18-30(29) was unconstitutional.[17] Despite this, the law remains in place.

The State Laws of Rhode Island contain some fascinating provisions which can, at times, lead to more questions than answers. The antiquated nature of several of the statutes highlighted above have relatively minimal applicability to modern society, while others defy reasonable explanation. In many cases, these laws exist simply based on the fact that lawmakers have not bothered to have them stricken from the books and in other cases, they still remain in use. Although these laws are rarely used and virtually unknown, they serve as a telling reminder of the past.

The World is Better for His Life: The Story of George Herbert Utter

"In February 1913, at sessions of both the House of Representatives and the Senate, memorial addresses were delivered in Utter's honor. Although many of these addresses were powerful, perhaps the most poignant words delivered on the floor of the United States Senate describing George H. Utter came from former Rhode Island Governor and then-Senator George P. Wetmore who concluded his address simply: "The world is better for his life."

Despite the pivotal role the town has played in the history of Rhode Island, very few of the state's governors spent any considerable amount of time in Westerly. One exception to this was George Herbert Utter who served as the chief executive of Rhode Island in 1905 and 1906. Although this is the highest office he held during his lifetime, Utter's legacy is so much more than simply his stint as governor. On the state level, he held several notable positions throughout his career but in Westerly, he is perhaps best known for his role as the founder and publisher of *The Westerly Sun*.

George Herbert Utter was born on 24 July 1854 in Plainfield, New Jersey as the only child of George Benjamin Utter and Mary Starr Maxson.[17] The elder George Utter was the founder and printer of *The Sabbath Recorder*, a weekly newspaper for Seventh Day Baptists which he began on 13 June 1854, just a month before his son's birth, and is still in print today. Although the Utter family made their home in Plainfield, the *Recorder* was published at 9 Spruce Street in the heart of Lower Manhattan.[18]

In 1861, George H. Utter came to Westerly with his parents where his father continued to work as a printer and publisher, founding *The Narragansett Weekly* with his brother, J.H. Utter.[19] George H. graduated from Westerly High School and went on to attend Alfred Academy (later Alfred University) in Alfred, New York. This school was likely chosen due to the its affiliation with the Seventh Day Baptist Church, which was incredibly important to the Utter family.[20]

George H. Utter was baptized on 11 April 1874 at the Pawcatuck Seventh Day Baptist Church with which he would remain affiliated for the rest of his life.[21] After two years in western New York at Alfred Academy, George H. Utter completed his college education in Massachusetts, graduating from Amherst College as part of the class of 1877.[22] While at Amherst, he was a member of the Delta Kappa Epsilon fraternity.[23]

After graduating from Amherst, George became associated with his father and uncle in their publication of the *Narragansett Weekly* where the younger Utter was serving as an editor.[24] On 29 May 1883, he was named aide-de-camp (a personal assistant who is also usually a high ranking military officer) to Governor Augustus O. Bourn, and at the same time, he was made a Colonel in the Rhode Island Militia.[25]

This was his first appointed or elected role and would serve as his initial foray in politics. He would fulfill this role until 1885. In 1885, Utter was elected as a representative in the Rhode Island General Assembly, where he would remain until 1888. During his final year, he served as the Speaker of the House.[26] While working to represent the people of Westerly at the State House in Providence, he continued to serve those same citizens in other ways, specifically as a publisher. Upon the death of J.H. Utter in 1886, the younger George Utter was taken into *The Narragansett Weekly* firm with his father.[27]

After serving four years in the House of Representatives, George H. Utter continued his political ascent when he was elected to serve in the Rhode Island Senate from May 1889 to 1891. During that time, he was an active part of the Rhode Island Judiciary Committee, serving as Chairman in 1891.[28] Although he was a lifelong Republican, Utter's political career commanded respect from members of both parties. It was said that "While he was a staunch Republican, he was not the sort of partisan who stood for everything his party did. He went with his party so long as he believed it to be right, at least in a moral sense, and when it ceased to be that he did not follow it."[29]

George Herbert Utter, 1905
(Photo: Library of Congress, Prints & Photographs Division, photograph by Harris & Ewing)

This was especially true in his later years when he was known to oppose the Republican "boss" Charles Brayton, whom he "refused to follow…blindly or otherwise."[30] Such was Brayton's respect for Utter's political acumen that in a letter dated 3 November 1906, in response to Utter having referred to Brayton as a political "boss" (a common suggestion throughout his career), Brayton wrote "I feel whatever you may have said or done with reference to my being a so-called "boss" was from a sense of duty, which has always governed your actions."[31]

The 1890s were a very busy decade for George Herbert Utter, particularly on the political front. In 1891, he was elected to the position of Rhode Island Secretary of State and was re-elected annually for the next four years. In 1894, he stepped down as Secretary of State in response to growing business obligations, likely the result of his father's death in 1892 and the launch of *The Westerly Sun* on 7 August 1893.[32] On 5 August 1894, Utter spoke at the dedication of the Westerly Library and Memorial Building, where he celebrated those who risked their lives during the Civil War.[33]

The Pawcatuck Seventh Day Baptist Church
(Photo: Westerly Historical Society)

Shortly after this event, on 3 September 1894, George Utter was made a deacon of the Seventh Day Baptist Church of Pawcatuck.[34] He also served as the superintendent of the church's Sabbath school for twenty years and filled the role of treasurer of the missionary society.[35] In addition to all of the duties already mentioned, George H. Utter added to his commitments by accepting a position on the board of directors for the Washington Trust Bank in 1898.[36]

George H. Utter's next step on the political ladder in Rhode Island came a decade later in 1904 when he was elected as the state's Lieutenant Governor. He served in this position for only one year before he ran for Governor of Rhode Island.[37] On 8 November 1904, Utter narrowly defeated the incumbent, Democrat Lucius F.C. Garvin. Utter received 33,821 total votes (48.94 percent), only 856 votes more than Garvin, or a margin of 1.23

percent of the total votes cast.[38] After his first year in office, Utter ran for a second term in 1905. Apparently, the citizens of Rhode Island approved of his job in 1905, as Utter faced Garvin once again and this time, he won by 5,495 votes, a margin more than six times of that in 1904.[39]

One of the interesting facets of Utter's tenure was his practice of abstaining from any gubernatorial work on Saturdays. Whenever work on Saturdays could not be avoided, Governor Utter named Lieutenant Governor Frederick Jackson as his delegate.[40] Utter's observance of one of the major tenets of the Seventh Day Baptist faith was reported in many newspapers, especially after he sent his lieutenant to Washington D.C. to participate in the inaugural parade of President Theodore Roosevelt in 1905.[41]

In 1906, Utter once again ran for Governor facing off against Democrat James H. Higgins. This time, he came up on the losing end of the election by 1,318 votes.[42] This is the last time Utter would run for Governor as 1907 saw his former Lieutenant, Frederick Jackson receive the Republican nomination.[43] After the 1906 election, George H. Utter would take a brief respite from politics while still operating The *Westerly Sun* in his adopted hometown. This absence from politics was relatively brief, however.

In November 1910, George H. Utter was elected to serve as the Representative in Congress for Rhode Island's 2nd District. This term extended from 4 March 1911, to 3 November 1912.[44] In May 1912, Utter contributed an article to *The Red Man*, the monthly magazine of the Carlisle Indian School in Carlisle, Pennsylvania, and was a guest at the school's commencement ceremony that year.[45] This article focused heavily on religion, a topic very important to Utter's life.

In the fall of 1912, Utter campaigned to retain his seat in Congress. However, on 3 November 1912, just two days before the election, George Herbert Utter died at his home in Westerly. On October 26th, while in Washington D.C., Utter was taken to the hospital where doctors discovered a malignant tumor on his liver. Upon finding that the tumor could not be removed, he was taken to his home in Westerly where he died less than a week later.[46] The tributes to George H. Utter upon his death were both frequent and heartfelt.

On 6 November 1912, his funeral was held in Westerly and local businesses were closed while schools were given a half-day so that all could celebrate his life.[47] In February 1913, at sessions of both the House of Representatives and the Senate, memorial addresses were delivered in Utter's honor. Although many of these addresses were powerful, perhaps the most poignant words delivered on the floor of the United States Senate describing George H. Utter came from former Rhode Island Governor and then-Senator George P. Wetmore who concluded his address simply: "The world is better for his life."[48]

The First Duty of Every Red-Blooded American: The Election of 1920

"Two nights later on the eve of the election, a meeting for women was held at the Westerly High School Hall to show the first time voters how to complete the ballot properly and to answer any questions that they may have had. In the days leading up to the election, the campaigning by the Republican Party continued, with advertisements claiming that voting the straight Republican ticket was "the First Duty of Every Red-Blooded American."

The 1920 Presidential election was a monumental moment in the history of our nation. For the first time, women were legally allowed to vote in a presidential election after the ratification of the Nineteenth Amendment to the United States Constitution on 18 August 1920. This election offers remarkable insight into the views of many Westerly voters at the start of the Roaring Twenties.

Nationally, the 1920 elections represented a shift in American politics, as the Republican Party's candidate, Warren G. Harding, won handily after receiving 60.3% of the vote. Harding's opponent, James M. Cox, received only 34.1% of the national vote.[49] This result signaled renewed support for the Republican Party after Woodrow Wilson, a Democrat, was elected to the presidency with ease in 1912 and was re-elected by a much smaller margin in 1916.[50] Between 1900 and 1932, a Republican won six of the eight presidential elections.

THE FIRST DUTY

of

Every Red-Blooded American

on

Tuesday Next

Is to go to the polls as early as possible and vote the straight REPUBLICAN ticket, thereby assuring the election of

HARDING and COOLIDGE

AND OUR REPUBLICAN REPRESENTATIVE

WALTER R. STINESS

Advertisement for the 1920 Election
(Photo: Westerly Sun)

This Republican domination was quite apparent in Rhode Island, where Harding's 107,463 votes were more than twice the 55,062 received by Cox.[51] To date, this is the final election in which a Republican received more than 60% of the vote in Rhode Island. The cause for this domination becomes clearer upon a closer look at the days leading up to the election, as well as the results in Westerly.

Three months before the election, on 26 August 1920, the headline spanning the front page of the *Westerly Sun* read "Proclamation That Suffrage Has Been Ratified Is Signed by Secretary Colby."[52] This news confirmed to residents of Westerly that the Nineteenth Amendment had been ratified and consequently, women were now free to vote in all elections. Over the next several months, the election season began ramping up across America, a fact that was quite apparent across southern Rhode Island.

Those who hoped to vote in the elections on November 2nd were required to pay the Westerly Poll Tax (a practice that was not abolished until the passing of the Twenty-Fourth Amendment in 1964) of one dollar by October 30th if they wished to vote. Aside from precluding a citizen from voting, failure to pay the poll tax could also result in jail time according to Rhode Island law, a portion of which was published in the *Sun*.[53]

Women were not required to pay the Poll Tax for 1920. In order to aid citizens in ensuring they were prepared to vote, on October 26th the Westerly Town Council met and served as a board of canvassers, allowing men and women to come in and register to vote. This was promoted as the final opportunity for eligible citizens to register as they were required to be added to the voting list prior to Election Day.[54] *The Westerly Sun* implored citizens "It is the duty of every would-be voter to make certain that his or her name is on the voting list."[55]

Prior to the advent of television, newspapers were among the most common forms of media used to present political advertisements. On October 27th, nearly one third of an entire page was devoted to a message from Walter R. Stiness, the Republican candidate for Rhode Island's Second Congressional District. Perhaps the most intriguing accolade bestowed on Stiness that was highlighted in this advertisement was an endorsement by the National Security League for having been "one hundred percent American because of his vote on war matters."[56]

That same day, just six days before the election, a "rally of all voters of the town of Westerly" was held at the town hall.[57] Although the announcement of this event specifically mentions that it is for "all voters," it was quite clear that this referred to those who intended to vote for Republicans. This was made abundantly clear by the statement that "Republican issues will be discussed" and attendees would be able to "hear the Republican side of the story."[58] It is also mentioned that women were invited to attend and it was hoped that they would "turn out in large numbers."[59]

At this rally, the Democratic opponent of Stiness, Luigi De Pasquale, was roundly criticized for supposedly using his position as a member of the Rhode Island General Assembly to avoid being drafted in World War I despite being a single man and only twenty-five years old.[60] Italian-American men from Westerly who died in the war were referenced by name as a means of further admonishing what the opposition perceived to be De Pasquale's decision.[61]

Three days later on October 30th, Democratic candidates and supporters held a rally of their own. However, the sentiment towards the Democratic Party in Westerly was readily apparent from the tone of the announcement which began "Democratic spellbinders are to waste their time by holding a rally in republican Westerly…"[62]

The time and location of this rally were never provided. Two nights later on the eve of the election, a meeting for women was held at the Westerly High School Hall to show the first-time voters how to complete the ballot properly and to answer any questions that they may have had.[63] In the days leading up to the election, the campaigning by the Republican Party continued, with advertisements claiming that voting the straight Republican ticket was "the First Duty of Every Red-Blooded American."[64] The sponsor of these advertisements was listed simply as "a Westerly Citizen Who Believes in Republican Principles."[65]

On 2 November 1920, Americans made their way to their local polling places and cast their ballots. The first person to place their vote in Westerly was Anna Thornton Williams.[66] [For more about Mrs. Williams see page 136.] For the first time in history, the election results were conveyed to *The Westerly Sun* by telephone.

The *Sun* served as the pre-eminent source for voting returns across the town, as they installed a stereopticon across the street from their offices to broadcast the results and offered their facilities as a base for those interested in following the local and national races.[67] The Colonial Club of Westerly also presented real-time results, as they ran telegraph wires from the Westerly Library to the Post Office where the club was headquartered.[68]

As was expected, Westerly residents overwhelmingly chose Warren G. Harding as their selection to be the next United States President. The combination of Harding and Calvin Coolidge received 2,070 votes in Westerly to 490 votes for Democrat James M. Cox and his running mate, Franklin Delano Roosevelt.[69] Westerly's proportion of voters supporting Harding (78.63%) was much larger than the State of Rhode Island as a whole (63.97%).[70]

Four other candidates received at least one vote in Westerly, including Robert Colvin Macauley of the Single Tax Party who received one lone vote in town and only 5,750 nationally.[71] Harding was not the only Republican to win big in Westerly. Walter R. Stiness crushed Luigi De Pasquale 1930 to 646 and Emery J. San Souci, the Republican candidate for Governor of Rhode Island vanquished his opponent, Edward M. Sullivan, by a tally of 2045 to 510.[72]

In addition to contributing significantly to the overall Republican victory, Westerly also sent three local men to the Rhode Island Legislature: Senator Abraham P. Datson and Representatives Samuel H. Davis and Joseph T. Murphy.[73] All three of these men were members of the Republican Party and received an overwhelming share of the votes coming out of Westerly.[74]

After serving less than three years of his term, Warren G. Harding died in office and was succeeded by his Vice President, Calvin Coolidge. It is likely that Westerly voters approved of the work done by the men they supported so fervently in 1920, as they voted to re-elect Coolidge by a margin of more than 42% in 1924.[75] Although the 1920 presidential election in Westerly was not a particularly close or contentious race, it remains a significant historical landmark both locally and in America as a whole.

Charles E. Bailey: The Man Behind Westerly's 1920 Murder Trial

"Upon seeing the officers approach the boarding house, Bailey took off towards the nearby woods. As their man tried to make a getaway, the officers fired in Bailey's direction, eliciting his surrender. After giving himself up to the police, Charles Bailey was held overnight in jail in Portland, Maine and the following morning, he departed with the officers for Westerly."

"I'm shot!" Edgar Bailey cried out. "I'm sorry; get a doctor, quick!" replied Edgar's brother, Charles, as he ran from the scene.[76] This is the commotion that played out in a house on Boylston Street in Westerly on 23 October 1920. The events that took place over the next several months would result in an interstate manhunt and the first murder trial in Westerly in several decades.

Charles E. Bailey was born on 18 May 1862, to William W. and Julia (Jones) Bailey in the small town of Durham, Maine, just twenty-five miles outside of Portland.[77] Four years later, a second son, Edgar A. Bailey, was born.[78] When the boys were young, Julia and William were divorced. Interestingly, however, Julia, Charles, and Edgar were living with William Bailey's parents in Parkman, Maine in 1870 and 1880.[79] It is unclear precisely where Charles lived for many years after 1880, but one later account described Charles as "addicted to strong drink and of a roving disposition," suggesting he likely lived a somewhat nomadic lifestyle.[80]

Between 1915 and 1918, Bailey found work in fertilizer mills in Bowdoinham, Maine.[81] It was also said that Charles E. Bailey lived in Portland, Maine for much of his early life, however, the next known record of Charles Bailey was dated to 1919 when he was living with his mother and brother on Boylston Street in Westerly while he worked as a laborer.[82] All that is known about Bailey's life in Maine is that he was "a well-known horse trader" and was also known throughout the state as a lumberman and iceman.[83] In 1920, he was still living with Julia and Edgar, this time described more specifically as a farm laborer.[84] In statements portraying Charles from

1920, he was depicted as "spare build, active and wiry and wears a heavy gray-tinged moustache."[85]

The night of 23 October 1920 was the night that changed the Bailey family forever and resulted in a wild chain of events that rocked Westerly. Accounts of the evening vary slightly depending on the source, however, it is known for certain that on the evening of October 23rd, Charles E. Bailey returned home (possibly intoxicated, as reported by at least one source,[86]) and spent time with his brother and mother. At about 9:30 p.m., Charles left the room where Edgar and Julia sat and went upstairs to retrieve a revolver from his bedroom. Charles then re-entered the room and shot Edgar in the abdomen. It was at that time that Edgar announced that he had been shot and Charles replied: "I'm sorry; get a doctor, quick!"[87]

Edgar A. Bailey was rushed by the Westerly Sanitary Corps to Lawrence Hospital in New London.[88] At 12:20 a.m. Edgar was admitted to the hospital where doctors discovered that the bullet passed through his intestines. It was originally hoped that he would survive the ordeal.[89] According to the medical examiner's report of Edgar's death, shortly after being admitted to the hospital, he was operated on by Drs. Lee and Douglas and it was found that he had multiple injuries to the intestinal tract and omentum and to make matters worse, Edgar was hemorrhaging. Still, he hung on for more than two days. According to Medical Examiner Harold H. Heyer, at 4:05 p.m. on 26 October 1920, Edgar A. Bailey "came to death due to violence."[90]

Shockingly, despite the shooting happening at 9:30 p.m., Westerly Police were not informed of the incident until after midnight, when Edgar's doctor placed a call to them, by which time Charles was able to make an escape. As a result, the police were not able to track the suspect down immediately.[91] When questioned about the incident, the boys' mother claimed the shooting was accidental.[92] While Edgar fought for his life in a hospital bed, Charles E. Bailey escaped to the woods in Westerly to evade police detection. The following day, October 25th, Charles came out of the woods on Post Road in Westerly and was able to get a ride to Providence on a truck. Once in Providence, Charles took a train to Boston and then from Boston to Brunswick, Maine. Once in Brunswick, Charles walked to Bowdoinham, just nine miles away.[93]

On October 28th, the funeral of Edgar Bailey was held in Westerly and he was interred in River Bend Cemetery.[94] Over the next several days, Westerly Police officers followed all leads and searched diligently for Charles E. Bailey. On 1 November 1920, a private session of the Westerly Town Council was held so that Police Chief Thomas E. Brown could brief the council on the status of the case.[95] At that time, Brown indicated that he believed Bailey was in the vicinity of Portland, Maine, where he had spent much of his life. Upon hearing this, the council authorized a reward of $100 for Bailey's capture and recommended that Brown travel to Maine to locate Bailey.[96] A rumor in town initially led many to believe Charles Bailey had committed suicide due to the fact that a man matching his description was seen running into the woods just before a gunshot was heard, however, this was disproven relatively quickly.[97]

On Friday, November 5th, Police Chief Brown and Constable Max Reithel departed for Maine in search of their fugitive.[98] By Sunday afternoon, the officers had a strong lead on Bailey. After unsuccessfully searching for their man at local stables due in large part to his reputation as a horse trader, the Westerly officers inquired with the local police.[99] At 3 p.m., Brown and Reithel, along with Yarmouth (Maine) Deputy Sherriff George W. Gerow, located Bailey at a boarding house in Bowdoinham.[100]

Upon seeing the officers approach the boarding house, Bailey took off towards the nearby woods. As their man tried to make a getaway, the officers fired in Bailey's direction, causing him to surrender.[101] After giving himself up to the police, Charles Bailey was held overnight in jail in Portland, Maine and the following morning, he departed with the officers for Westerly.[102]

On the morning of Monday, November 8th, Charles E. Bailey returned to Westerly in police custody where he was temporarily held while awaiting trial. The following morning, he was brought to the Third District Court in Kingston where he plead not guilty to the charge of murder.[103] On Friday November 12th, Bailey returned to the court for a preliminary hearing, at which time he claimed he had no money to pay for an attorney. The defendant was then reminded that he had $143 ($1,900 in 2021) in his possession at the time of his arrest. Bailey countered this claim by stating the money was owed to his mother, although she denied that was the case.[104] Bailey was eventually assigned A.T.L. Ledwidge as his attorney.[105] The hearing was adjourned and it was proclaimed that the trial would begin at the Superior Court of Washington County in Westerly the following Monday.

Charles Bailey (Second from Right) and His Captors, 1920
(Photo: Norwich Bulletin)

Although Bailey never denied shooting his brother, he did consistently maintain that the shooting was accidental, hence his plea of not guilty to the charge of murder. Julia, the matriarch of the Bailey family, and the only other living eyewitness to the incident, was also steadfast in her belief that the shooting was unintentional.[106] Another witness, John J. Gilcrist, was called to testify during the trial. Gilcrist claimed that prior to the shooting, he had been with Charles who had "a couple glasses of cider" on their trip into the country.[107] Gilchrist also revealed that after the shooting, Charles came to his house and said he had something to tell him, however, Gilchrist did not listen, closed the door, and went to bed.[108]

According to the statement given by the accused to Chief Brown, Bailey was holding the revolver that he intended to take "into the country to trade off" when he started clicking the revolver which inadvertently fired.[109] Chief Brown then testified that Charles told him "Edgar acted as if he did not want [him] around the house and [he] did all the chores. He never felt a [sic] Welcome at home."[110] This statement was particularly damning, as it established a possible motive, which had been lacking up to that point.

After hearing from the Westerly Police Chief, Charles Bailey was brought to the stand to testify. According to Bailey, he purchased the revolver about two years prior from a man named Will Whitmore who lived on Wells Street in Westerly. At the time of the purchase, there were three cartridges in the revolver. Whitmore fired one of the cartridges while Bailey fired the other and Bailey testified that the third cartridge had remained in the gun unused for so long that he had forgotten about it.[111] Bailey further claimed he had never purchased any shells for the gun and none were ever given to him. When asked about the incident, Bailey testified that there was no trouble in the house that evening and there were no problematic discussions.[112] Bailey also told of his journey to Maine and indicated that he did not communicate with anyone while in Westerly after the shooting and he told no one of the incident while in Maine.[113]

The trial took place over the course of two days between November 29th and 30th, 1920 and the overall time from opening statements to the start of jury deliberation was seven hours and thirty minutes.[114] After just over three hours of discussion and consideration, the jury declared Bailey guilty of manslaughter.[115] The first ballot delivered by the twelve members of the jury revealed that seven jurors supported a guilty verdict while the remaining five favored an acquittal.[116] In order to provide more context, the jurors had been taken to the scene of the murder.[117] Over the course of the two day trial, the jurors were required to stay together and were put in the custody of the sheriff to ensure this. Several months after being declared guilty, Bailey was sentenced to twelve years in prison.[118]

Bailey served his sentence at the Rhode Island State Prison in Cranston where his incarceration was recorded in 1925.[119] On 15 June 1926, Charles E. Bailey escaped from the State Prison at 9:45 a.m. but he was returned to the prison on the same day. Bailey was paroled on 29 October 1928. It is unknown where he resided upon his release, but it is known that by 1939, he had returned to Westerly, where he lived on the town farm off of Bradford Road.[120] In 1940, records indicate that Bailey was an inmate on the town farm, but it is uncertain as to whether he was simply living on the farm or serving another sentence.[121] On 29 January 1942, Charles Bailey died on the Westerly Town Farm where he had been working as a gardener.[122] Bailey left no surviving family, and although he was interred in River Bend Cemetery, he was not buried with his mother and brother. For a brief period at the end of 1920, the actions of Charles E. Bailey led to the one of the few murder trials in Westerly's long history.

Court Cases, Dynamite, and Liquor: The Story of the Tin Tub Saloon

"While the legal battles over the ownership of the Canal Street property continued on, Natale Bonvenuto faced more immediate problems for his business. On 4 April 1913, an unknown assailant set off a stick of dynamite under the saloon building at midnight. Thankfully, no damage resulted from the attempt aside from a small trash fire. Upon seeing the small blaze, the fire department was called in, but little effort was required."

Being a genealogist by trade and having spent countless hours poring over records of thousands of my ancestors, I thought I knew everything I could possibly learn about many of my forebears, especially ones as recent as four generations ago. For this reason, I was surprised to learn of a series of incidents involving my great[2] grandparents that led me to uncover a series of fascinating events from Westerly's past.

Natale Bonvenuto, my great[2] grandfather was born in Acri, Calabria, Italy on 11 December 1864 to Angelo, a farmer, and Teresa (Morrone) Bonvenuto.[123] On 1 March 1889, he arrived from Calabria at the port of New York and made his way to Rhode Island.[124] Little is known about his early life in America, but he is presumed to have arrived in Westerly by 1895, because it was in this year that he married Christina Falcone, who had herself been born in Acri and arrived on 8 December 1894.[125] For several years after arriving in the United States, Natale worked as a general laborer, most often finding himself as quarryman, like so many of his fellow Italian immigrants.[126] After several years of laboring in the granite quarries, Natale sought a different way to support his wife and four children. However, Natale's initial attempts at moneymaking found him on the wrong side of the law.

On Christmas Eve 1908, police visited Natale's home at 75 Pierce Street and seized four half-barrels of ale, ten gallons of whiske-y, and a gallon of wine, likely the product of an illegal saloon being run out of his home.[127] On 13 January 1909, on the orders of the Third District Court of Rhode Island, the Westerly Police dumped all the seized liquor down the gutter. According to the *Norwich Daily Bulletin*, "there was beer flowing down the gutters of Cookey Hill" and "an early morning opening saloon smell pervaded the vicinity."[128] On January 15, Natale and Christina stood before the Third District Court, having been charged with keeping liquor with intent to sell. They both pled *nolo contendere*, accepting the conviction without admitting guilt. *The Norwich Daily Bulletin* noted that Christina, being the mother of three children including a two-year-old, had her case suspended for three months and was placed on probation. [In actuality, Christina and Natale were the parents of four children with the youngest being four years old at the time.] Natale, however, contended that his wife was the only one who had violated the law, as she was the only one to have sold liquor that evening. Despite his questionable defense, the judge imposed the full penalty, ten days in jail plus a twenty dollar fine, upon Natale. Natale appealed to have the jail sentence withdrawn in exchange for a higher fine, but the court was bound by statute and had no say in the sentence.[129]

Natale and Christina remained in the good graces of local law enforcement after their initial troubles. In March 1911, a man by the name of John Carney petitioned to transfer the liquor license from his Canal Street bar to Natale.[130] At some point before February 1912, Natale's petition was accepted allowing him to transfer the license. The location of the saloon Natale took over was in the path of planned expansions being undertaken by the New York, New Haven, and Hartford Railroad, and at the request of the railroad, he moved the building onto a piece of land on the opposite side of Canal Street.[131] When the building was relocated, the land where it was moved to was believed to be owned by the railroad. This supposition was questioned by Concertino Grills the owner of the land directly adjacent to the saloon. Grills argued that the saloon was located partly on his property and brought a lawsuit against both the railroad and Natale Bonvenuto. Lawyers for Grills argued that the improper location of the saloon made the liquor license illegal.[132]

In February 1912, Grills constructed a fence blocking the main entrance to the saloon. Patrons could still enter the building through the rear, but it was judged that the fence must be removed.[133] Although the license to sell liquor was challenged by lawyers for Grills, health officers chose not to order the saloon closed. At that time, the court also ruled that Natale could continue to operate his saloon at the same location until the title of ownership was determined.[134] There would be many more claims in this case which would continue on for several more years. In the meantime, however,

Natale continued to operate his saloon, which had since come to be known as the Tin Tub.

While the legal battles over the ownership of the Canal Street property continued on, Natale Bonvenuto faced more immediate problems for his business. On 4 April 1913, an unknown assailant set off a stick of dynamite under the saloon building at midnight. Thankfully, no damage resulted from the attempt aside from a small trash fire. Upon seeing the small blaze, the fire department was called in, but little effort was required.[135] Detectives were unsuccessful at finding the culprit and Natale offered a fifty dollar reward for discovering the attacker(s). This attempt would be the first of many at destroying the saloon over the following months.

Less than two weeks later, early in the morning on 17 April 1913, Engineer Walter Pendleton at the Westerly Light and Power Company's plant called in a fire alarm when he found the rear end of the Tin Tub Saloon ablaze. According to one account of the fire, the flames had "burned through the floor and inside [the saloon's] contents were badly burned and blistered as a result of the excessive heat. Some of the bottles that were behind the bar burst and a number of barrels of liquor in the basement were destroyed. The stock and fixtures were damaged beyond repair, but the bar can be repaired at considerable expense, however." The article noted that insurance would party cover the losses. When investigators entered the building after the fire had been extinguished, the found evidence that kerosene had been spread on the floor, indicating that the fire was likely set intentionally. The newspaper coverage of the fire described Natale as "a quiet, peaceable man" and stated that he was "at a loss to know why the guilty party or parties are committing such outrages upon his property."[136]

As if the damage caused by the fire were not enough, on 8 August 1913, a second attempt was made to blow the saloon up with dynamite.[137] This marked the third time since April of that year that someone had attempted to destroy the building. For the first time, a possible motive for the crimes was presented. According to *The Westerly Sun*: "The police believe that these attempts at destruction are prompted by jealousy, as Benvenuti [sic] seems to be doing a profitable business in his little place, while more pretentious saloons are hardly able to meet expenses."[138]

Still, Natale persisted with his business, as he was granted a new liquor license in November 1913. That same month, another saloon was attacked. This time, the culprit, possibly the same as from the other incidents, attempted to dynamite an establishment owned by Joseph S. Grills.[139] As with the crimes against Natale's saloon, a culprit was not identified.

Trouble continued to find its way to the Tin Tub Saloon over the next several years. On 10 February 1914, a man by the name of Pasquale Salameno, a former police officer, shot a patron, Charles Brown, at the saloon. Brown survived the shooting and Salameno faced charges of assault with intent to kill and carrying a concealed weapon.[140] Brown was wearing a coat, a sweater, a vest, and two shirts, and as a result, the bullet did not penetrate all of the clothing and was uninjured.[141]

In April 1914, the Rhode Island Supreme Court heard the case of *Grills vs. the NYNHH Railroad and Natale Bonvenuto*. Ultimately, the court decided in favor of Grills and determined that "the building must be removed or mutual arrangement made to the contrary."[142] The court cases continued on through the following year, as Natale brought a suit against Joseph S. Grills at the Westerly Superior Court in May 1915.[143] On Independence Day 1915, the Tin Tub Saloon *once again* escaped serious harm when the building next to it (described by *The Westerly Sun* as being within three feet) was destroyed in a fire. Despite the close proximity of the saloon to the burning building, Natale's saloon suffered only a scorched wall facing the burned building.[144]

As for the court cases Natale was involved in, it appears they were quietly resolved. In November, the case against Joseph S. Grills was assigned for trial in Westerly.[145] On 2 December 1915, Judge John W. Sweeney of the Rhode Island Superior Court was a witness in the case, as he was Natale's attorney before being appointed a judge. This is the last known reference to the case made in local newspapers, suggesting that the case may have been resolved and was not challenged further.

In November 1916, Natale was denied a liquor license, marking the end of his career as a saloon owner.[146] By 1917, he is once again recorded as a laborer, suggesting he likely returned to his career as a quarryman.[147] Meanwhile, Joseph S. Grills, who had begun operating a saloon on Canal Street some years earlier, continued running his bar for several years after the Tin Tub closed.

Natale Bonvenuto died in Westerly on 7 January 1927 at the age of 62.[148] It is unlikely that he ever discovered the perpetrator who attempted to destroy his business on multiple occasions, as there does not seem to have been a resolution to the investigation. Despite several attempts to take away his livelihood, my great-great-grandfather, Natale Bonvenuto, persisted, continuing to operate his saloon in the face of danger.

Chapter VII
Local Institutions: The Beating Heart of the Community

As the name of this chapter suggests, the institutions that have served Westerly throughout its three and a half centuries of history have been the life force of the town, providing citizens with places to gather, learn, and communicate with one another.

One of the most critical of these organizations is the Westerly Ambulance Corps (originally known as the Westerly Sanitary Corps) which formed just prior to the outbreak of the Influenza Epidemic of 1918. [For more on this epidemic, see page 126.] This timing allowed them to fulfill a desperate need to a community in crisis. Also in this chapter is the story of the Martin House, one of the most recognizable buildings in downtown Westerly and the site of many well-known businesses.

Education has long been a pillar of society in Westerly, as evidenced by the long history of local public schools. This also applies quite well to the Westerly Business College where many residents received training and learned necessary career skills.

In the following chapter, there is also a comprehensive history of the Washington Trust Company spanning more than two centuries. The bank's story could (and has) easily filled an entire volume on its own. Local journalism has also responded to a great need in the community through the distribution of newspapers, a topic which is discussed at length in the following pages.

This chapter also provides the history of a structure which would have fundamentally changed Westerly as a community, the Orient Point Bridge. This proposed bridge to Long Island would have made transportation between Westerly and New York easier than ever before but at a great cost to the town as a whole.

There have been many institutions, both real and imagined, that have played a major part in serving the town of Westerly and these very same establishments have been a cornerstone of the town both past and present.

The Westerly Ambulance Corps: Assisting Those in Need Since 1917

"Prior to the construction of Westerly Hospital in 1925, the Sanitary Corps took patients to New London, New Haven, Providence, and Boston. In the 1920s, roadway systems were not nearly as comprehensive and direct as they were in later decades, and as a result, it took six hours to get from Westerly to Boston."

For over one hundred years, the Westerly Ambulance Corps has been valiantly serving the community in its times of greatest need, proving to be one of the town's most essential organizations.

On 26 July 1917, the Westerly Red Cross Sanitary Corps was formed as a "detachment for war work." At the founding meeting, the following positions were selected: Thomas Perry, President, Dr. Frank I. Payne, Medical Director, and Timothy O'Connors of Barbour's Pharmacy, Pharmaceutical Director. It was also decided at this time that a course of study to join the Corps would be developed which would take eighteen months to complete.[1] In forming an organization, the Sanitary Corps of Westerly became the first such group in the State of Rhode Island.[2] In December 1917, the Sanitary Corps was called upon for its first major mission when they were summoned to Boston. There they would await a call to provide aid after the infamous Halifax Explosion which claimed two thousand lives.[3] Twenty-four members of the Sanitary Corps traveled to Boston, but were never requested to provide aid.[4]

The following year, in March 1918, the Corps was invited to join the State Sanitary Organization and uniforms were ordered for the group.[5] Then, disaster struck the United States as an outbreak of influenza gripped the nation beginning in 1918. Westerly was not spared, and the Corps took immediate action, setting up a fifty bed hospital in the Beach Street School, where they treated up to 460 patients in December 1919 alone.[6] [For more on the 1918-1920 influenza epidemic, see page 126.] That same year, funds were raised to purchase an motorized ambulance to take patients to Wakefield, as Westerly did not have a hospital at the time.[7] Prior to the construction of

Westerly Hospital in 1925, the Sanitary Corps took patients to New London, New Haven, Providence, and Boston. In the 1920s, roadway systems were not nearly as comprehensive and direct as they were in later decades, and as a result, it took six hours to get from Westerly to Boston.[8]

For several years in the Ambulance Corps' infancy, they were granted use of the state armory in Westerly for meetings, drills, and lectures. In February 1920, however, they were informed by the Quartermaster General that they were required to vacate the space by April 1st, forcing the organization to seek a new facilities.[9] While the unit was initially developed as a non-profit organization, by 1920, appeals for donations were necessary to maintain a high level of service. In addition, these funds were used to develop a potential headquarters on land they had purchased on Main Street.[10] In 1925, they were granted an additional plot of land on Main Street by Courtland B. Bliven, but this property was transferred to Henry R. Segar in 1944.[11],[12]

Dr. Payne was a consistent presence during the Sanitary Corps' early years when he served as a mentor and guide to those who joined the Corps. In 1926, at the fourth annual Sanitary Corps Dinner, the group presented a testimonial to the dedication and hard work of Payne, who had been ill for several months. According to their speech, Payne was "the founder and organizer of the Westerly Sanitary Corps, instituted August 1917, [and] he has constantly been its leading spirit, guide, and adviser."[13]

By the 1930s, the Corps was soliciting donations on a yearly basis through the collection of membership dues. These membership drives were promoted locally through the *Westerly Sun* which ran endorsements by members, including one piece in 1931, in which a man explains how his annual membership fee of $2.50 ultimately saved his family $307.[14] The price of subscription service remained low for many years, only being raised to $3 in 1959. By 1992, the fee was $25 per year, keeping pace with inflation, as a $2.50 fee in 1931 would be worth about $23 in 1992.[15] In the early 1930s, the Sanitary Corps was headquartered in the Clyde Mills where they remained until 1934, at which time they opened new rooms in the Price Building on Main Street.[16]

The work of the Westerly Sanitary Corps was incomparable in September 1938, when Westerly was struck by a hurricane, the single greatest crisis to hit the town. In the aftermath of the hurricane, the *Westerly Sun* lauded the efforts of the Sanitary Corps' workers, noting that they "rendered invaluable humanitarian service in Westerly and vicinity" and noted that "many members remained on duty for hours without sleep or rest."[17]

In 1938, the Corps had two ambulances in its fleet, and in the days after the hurricane struck on September 21st, one ambulance was used to provide first aid around the beaches and the other was used to render emergency services in all other stricken areas.[18] Having two ambulances in their employ was viewed as a necessity for the Corps after the opening of Westerly Hospital in 1925.[19] By the 1940s, the ambulances in service with the Corps were replaced frequently, as older ambulances dropped in value as soon as newer models were introduced. Despite the frequent need for replacement, Westerly taxpayers were never asked to fund these purchases, as was often the case for most towns at the time. Instead, the Sanitary Corps would hold drives to help fund the ambulances.

In August 1950, the Westerly Sanitary Corps was deeded two buildings at the Westerly State Airport which were initially constructed in 1942 by the United States Navy and were transferred to the State of Rhode Island in 1947. The Corps was permitted use of these buildings as "an emergency hospital in times of disaster and for other purposes deemed essential to the public interests of said Corps."[20] Another caveat of this transfer was that the Corps could never sell the property to "any corporation, firm, or person."[21] In October of that same year, the Sanitary Corps purchased the plot of land on Chestnut Street where their first headquarters were to be built.[22]

The 1950s were productive for the Westerly Sanitary Corps, as it saw several major changes by the middle of the decade. In 1955, the Rescue Squad was formed, and shortly thereafter it became an essential branch of the Corps service.[23] Also in 1955, the Chestnut Street headquarters were completed and these facilities would serve as the base of operations for the Corps for nearly fifty years.

On 13 January 1956, the Westerly Sanitary Corps officially adopted a revision to their charter which stated that after more than thirty-eight years under the original name, they would henceforth be known as the Westerly Ambulance Corps Inc.[24] At the start of the 1960s, the Corps fleet included two ambulances, a surf boat, a rescue jeep, and a fully-equipped rescue truck.[25]

In 1967, the Corps celebrated their fiftieth anniversary, and in September of that year, they held several events including an old timers' night, a banquet for all active members, and an open house at their Chestnut Street building. It was noted that in the organization's first fifty years, they took more than twenty-four thousand calls in Westerly and the surrounding communities.[26] In 1981, a garage was built to house the Corps' three ambulances, three rescue trucks, and two boats. By the time of their seventy-fifth anniversary in 1992, the Corps' received an average of eleven calls a day or about three thousand eight hundred per year. In 1991, they also expanded their capabilities by adding an advanced life support unit, expanding the resources of the Corps. The seventy-fifth anniversary was also celebrated in grand fashion, including a three hundred person parade, a demonstration of their LifeStar helicopter at St. Pius X school, and an open house.[27]

2002 was another banner year for the Corps, as they began operating out of a new headquarters building on Chestnut Street, across the street from their former facility. The $2 million complex houses all their equipment, vehicles, and dispatching facilities.[28] Over the last one hundred years, the Westerly Ambulance Corps has provided incredible service to the community, and has truly lived up to their mission statement:[29]

"The Westerly Ambulance Corps is committed to provide quality emergency medical and dispatch services through our compassionate and caring volunteers and employees to the community and surrounding areas. Our service-oriented professionals strive for excellence through training and education. Our organization will continue its tradition of community service through public education, providing special event coverage and giving assistance to other emergency services when called upon. The Corps followed this vision since 1917 and will continue to assist those in need."

The Westerly-Pawcatuck YMCA: Ninety Years and Counting

"The philosophies behind the YMCA's ideals appealed to many in smaller communities, including Westerly, where after the Civil War, a group of local men started an organization they called a YMCA. The group established a reading room stocked with papers and magazines from their files, held daily prayer meetings, and provided Sunday school services. Eventually, the group's Secretary and Missionary, Thomas C. Crocker, resigned and in 1876, the organization folded due to diminished funding and the absence of a permanent home."

Since 1928, the Westerly-Pawcatuck YMCA has been bringing the community closer together. Ask any of your friends, family members, or coworkers, and chances are, a majority of them learned to swim, took a class, or played in sports leagues at the Y. Their importance to the community is immense, and the organization is one complete with rich and noteworthy history.

While the Westerly-Pawcatuck YMCA in its current incarnation traces its roots back to 1928, the story of the YMCA in Westerly began much earlier. On 6 June 1844, a twenty-two-year-old dry goods clerk in London named George Williams formed an organization which he named the Young Men's Christian Association. Seven years later, in 1851, the first YMCA in America opened in Boston.[30] The philosophies behind the YMCA's ideals appealed to many in smaller communities, including Westerly, where after the Civil War, a group of local men started an organization they called a YMCA. The group established a reading room stocked with papers and magazines from their files, held daily prayer meetings, and provided Sunday school services. Eventually, the group's Secretary and Missionary, Thomas C. Crocker, resigned and in 1876, the organization folded due to diminished funding and the absence of a permanent home.[31]

While the earliest YMCA in Westerly met an unceremonious end, efforts were initiated once again in 1894 to form a similar group. On April 7 of that year, thirty-seven young men gathered at First Baptist Church, where they agreed to form a 'society for young men.'[32] They called the newly formed entity the Young Men's Christian Association of Westerly. Membership in the Association was limited to males over the age of sixteen. Active members were required to be a member in good standing of any evangelical church in town. Associate members, however, could be any male 'of good moral standing.'[33] This ambitious idea was abandoned on 7 September 1894, when members determined that the funds necessary to begin could not be raised. The organization was also hindered when the Memorial Building could not provide the space for free as had been promised. Remaining funds were donated to the People's Mission.[34] [For more on the People's Mission, see page 318.] After yet another failed attempt to begin a YMCA in Westerly in 1906, the idea lay dormant for more than two decades.

In 1918, with the country immersed in World War I, classes were held in Westerly as part of the Extension Division of the United YMCA Schools, beginning a relationship between the Association and the town.[35] Finally, a decade later, on 7 March 1928, the Westerly YMCA was incorporated as the organization that still exists today. In May 1928, a committee was elected, and D. Harold Rogers, the coach of the Westerly High School football team, was named as the group's first President. At the second annual meeting on 22 May 1929, a gift of $10,000 from Charles Perry was announced, as was the news that women were thenceforth permitted to become members, a relative rarity among YMCAs.[36]

While the all-important first steps in developing a local YMCA had been completed and the organization flourished, the need for a permanent home still loomed overhead. It was not until 1937, nine years after its founding, that the YMCA secured the property of Dr. Edwin Ransome Lewis at 95 High Street, which they purchased for $10,000 from the Westerly Hospital.[37] Although they now owned the necessary property, it would be fifteen years before a new building that served their needs was completed. The outbreak of World War II in 1941 led to a restriction on building supplies, significantly slowing the process of constructing a home for the YMCA. In 1942, an agreement was reached between the Board of Directors and the Red Cross. According to this agreement, the Red Cross would pay one half of the taxes and all interior expenses in exchange for use of the 95 High Street building. The board also voted in favor of making all vacant rooms available for use by servicemen and designated a special servicemen's lounge.[38]

In late 1943, the building at 95 High Street was officially dedicated exclusively as a YMCA building. At the time, there was no gymnasium in the building, and therefore, the library's facilities were used. Shortly thereafter, the Association created a junior basketball league which had nearly ninety members. As the war was drawing closer to an end, a new push for a proper building was put into motion and by July 1944, $222,700 had been pledged towards this goal.[39]

An important day in the history of the Westerly-Pawcatuck YMCA was 16 July 1945, as this was the beginning of the day-camping program. From 1945 through the 1947 season, camp was held at Burlingame State Park. In 1948, the Y received a thirty-three acre tract of land adjacent to Burlingame, which was donated by Miss Katherine Foster. Until 1960, the site was used almost exclusively for camping and would later be known as Camp Watchaug.[40]

In September 1950, a contract for the new YMCA headquarters was awarded to the F. Samuel Nardone Company. Shortly thereafter, the old house at 95 High Street was razed and the Y's headquarters were moved to the Old Town Hall temporarily. Throughout 1950, the YMCA offered a variety of activities, including: baseball leagues, a girls' basketball league, Saturday morning gym classes, industrial golf leagues, a photography club, a bridge club, and painting and toleware classes, among many others.[41]

In June 1951, a cornerstone laying ceremony for the new building was held, and less than a year later, in May 1952, the YMCA's new building was dedicated and opened to the public. At the time of the building's opening, the Y had nearly six hundred members over the age of twenty-one.[42] This number would continue to grow over the next several years, reaching 1,250 members in total by 1955.[43]

It was only four years after the completion of the new building before another facility was deemed necessary: a swimming pool. Before the pool was completed in 1959, the nearest for YMCA use were in Norwich and New London.[44] The 1960s saw multiple important additions to Y properties. In 1960, the arts and crafts building was constructed at Camp Watchaug, and in 1966, the camp saw the construction of a boathouse, an important asset.

That same year, expanded membership led to the opening of a new parking lot, allowing more people than ever to access the Y's increasing amenities. This year was important to the history of the YMCA for another reason. In 1966, the bylaws were amended, allowing the organization to install the first female president, Grace Panciera.[45]

As the 1960's progressed, expansions continued on the YMCA's facilities. In 1969, the Atlantic Fleet Seabees constructed a new, modern lodge at Camp Watchaug, which helped the camp in their goal of promoting interest in ecology and conservation. Renovations to the YMCA's facilities were soon to follow when the basement was converted to add a physical fitness center, locker rooms and shower space, as well as a sauna and lounge area.[46] Over the years, the YMCA has hosted many community events, including The Westerly Library Book Fair, Radio auctions, and Antiques Shows.[47] Growth to the organization continued through the decades, and forty years after the 1973 renovations, the YMCA received a massive upgrade, as nearly $10 million dollars was invested in refurbishments providing the property with a much needed overhaul.[48]

As the YMCA continues to build on over ninety years of history in Westerly, the words written in the 1928 Articles of Association regarding the YMCA's purpose: "Said corporation is constituted for the purpose of the improvement of the spiritual, mental, and physical condition of young men and of young women and of boys and girls," remain true today.[49]

The Many Lives of the Martin House

"On May 3rd of that year [1897], the hotel found itself on the wrong side of the law for the first (but not the last) time. That day, the Granite City Hotel was raided by the police who seized a large quantity of liquor. According one account, the reason for this raid was that Westerly is a no-license town, "but liquor has been openly sold here during the last few months." The police apparently felt it was time to crack down on the illegal practice and the hotel was targeted."

In March 2016, the Savoy Bookshop and Café opened in downtown Westerly, completing the long-awaited and much-needed facelift of the Martin House, a building that has been a fixture on Canal Street for over 125 years.[50] Over the course of its history, the Martin House has been the site of a wide array of businesses including hotels, pharmacies, and restaurants. Today, after extensive renovations, the building is considered by many to be a gem of the downtown area.

The Martin House was constructed in 1888 by Captain Michael F. Martin, an Irish immigrant and the owner of the Steamboat Hotel in Stonington.[51] Martin had owned the land since purchasing it from Horatio N. Campbell on 18 November 1880,[52] and Campbell had purchased the land from Pardon Lewis on 9 December 1863.[53] It is said that the hotel's construction began in 1882, but Martin ran out of funds and returned to seafaring for a period before completing the building six years later.[54] The hotel officially opened for business on 19 September 1889, when Michael Martin invited the public to view the property, while offering cigars to all who wished to partake.[55]

According to an 1892 advertisement, the hotel was new and "just opened." The advertisement also noted that the hotel had forty-two bedrooms, large parlors and a billiard room. A room at the Martin House would cost a guest $2.00 (approximately $59.00 in 2021), while dinner would run them fifty cents (approximately $15 in 2021). Interestingly, the hotel offered special rates for 'dramatic companies,' suggesting the prevalence of acting troupes arriving in Westerly.[56]

By 1895, Martin began leasing out the building and it became known as the Foster House.[57] During these early years, a man named John Linden owned and operated the Foster House Pharmacy on the building's first floor, while the remainder of the building continued to serve as a hotel.[58] The hotel's proprietors at this time were John Henry Carley and David Carley. A brief review of the hotel made note of their high-quality service as well as cuisine which compared positively to any other fine hotel. The building's location across from the train depot was often cited as an advantage.[59]

1892 Advertisement for the Martin House from a Town Directory

An advertisement for the Foster House Hotel published in 1896 claimed that for either $2.00 or $2.50, you could rent a room ($64 and $80 respectively in 2021) which was heated by steam and lit by gas.[60] Despite only being eight years old, the rooms were advertised as "lately renovated and refurnished."[61] While staying at the hotel, one could easily contact David Carley, the hotel's proprietor, as rooms were equipped with electric return call bells.[62]

By 1897, the hotel had already undergone the second of its many name changes, when it was doing business as the Granite City Hotel. On May 3rd of that year, the hotel found itself on the wrong side of the law for the first (but not the last) time. That day, the Granite City Hotel was raided by the police who seized a large quantity of liquor. According one account, the reason for this raid was that Westerly was a no-license town, "but liquor has been openly sold here during the last few months." The police apparently felt it was time to crack down on the illegal practice and the hotel was targeted.[63] Altogether, twenty men were arrested and four hundred dollars (approximately $12,900 in 2021) was seized from the hotel. The raiding party was led by Dr. B.L. Lewis, a member of the Westerly Town Council. This caused a scandal as the hotel's landlord, Frank B. Cook, was also a councilman in Westerly.[64] Cook resigned the following morning at the Town Council's monthly meeting,[65] and in October 1897, Cook sold all of his right and title in the property to F.C. Sheldon of Providence.[66]

After just two years of ownership, Sheldon determined that there was not enough financial incentive to continue operation of the Granite City Hotel and on 12 August 1899, he closed the doors for the final time. After shutting down the hotel, Sheldon continued to use the building as a lodging house for men only, with rooms available by the day or week.[67] Shortly thereafter, the lease was given up to a Thomas Gaffney of New London. Gaffney then arranged for Mrs. Mary F. Martin, widow of Michael F. Martin, to reopen the hotel on 1 October 1899.[68] Martin contracted a Boston hotel manager to run the reopened Martin House and placed the hotel's offices in the space that was then being used by the Westerly Drug Company.[69]

Over the course of its history, the hotel experienced its share of fires, most of which caused little to no damage. In August 1898, a small fire was discovered at the hotel and "caused much excitement during the night among the guests in the house." The damage, however, was minimal.[70] On 7 May 1911, a fire was discovered in the hotel's barroom after a lit cigarette was thrown on the sawdust covered floor, however, a timely discovery prevented any notable damage.[71]

The building's most notable fire, however, took place on 1 August 1951. At about noon on that day, a fire was ignited when some kindling in the basement became engulfed in flames. The fire quickly climbed the elevator shaft, and three people had to be removed from the third and fourth floors by ladder. More than one thousand people gathered on Canal Street to watch as the guests were extracted from the building. The damage to the structure was assessed at $10,000 and the businesses on the first floor, including the Jack and Harry Store, the Mansfield Bar and Grill, and Spaghetti and Chip House also incurred losses.[72]

From 1910 to 1919, Andrew J. Martin, son of Michael F. and Mary Martin, operated the hotel until control was once again ceded to his mother, Mary Graf, formerly Martin, who served as proprietor until 1933, when Andrew took over one final time.[73]

The Martin House Hotel, 1913
(Photo: Westerly Historical Society)

On 20 October 1939, Andrew J. Martin officially closed the Hotel Martin with the bar and grill room having closed the day prior. At the time of its closing, the fifty-room hotel had been continuously serving as such since its construction in 1888. The hotel had been owned by Mrs. Mary Graf until her death in February 1939. While the death of Mary Graf certainly played a role in the hotel's closing, Andrew J. Martin claimed that the shutdown of the hotel was "for none of the usual reasons." When the *Westerly Sun* reported on the closing, they noted that the Hotel Martin "catered to middle class families and held a good reputation in Rhode Island hotel circles."[74]

The building's vacancy was relatively short lived, however, as the Martin House was purchased by Emanuel Mandel of Norwich on 21 January 1943. At one time, Mandel had operated a hotel in Miami, Florida, and was therefore accustomed with the business. The building was sold for $22,500 ($347,300 in 2021) and upon reopening, it was christened the Hotel Delman, a name Mandel chose by reversing the syllables in his surname. The resurrection of the hotel was lauded, due to a housing shortage in Westerly at the time.[75]

It was not long after its opening when the Hotel Delman ran afoul of the law. On 31 May 1943, Westerly police raided the hotel "looking for tangible evidence that would back up the reputation the place has gained."[76] In the aftermath of the raid, Mandel was charged with "maintaining a common nuisance."[77] Overall, ten people were arrested, six of whom were released after questioning. The four who were held, included Mandel, William McGrane, a night clerk charged with "receiving certain persons in the Delman Hotel for lewd and indecent acts," and two women who pled not guilty to "moral charges."[78] The raid was conducted by plainclothes officers and was assisted by Rhode Island State Police, shore patrol officers, and military police from Niantic, Connecticut.[79]

Mandel's ownership of the property was relatively brief, ending when he sold the property to Maria Rose Mastrandrea on 3 May 1945, after just over two years in operation.[80] While Mastrandrea initially maintained the Hotel Delman name, it was announced on 2 July 1945 that the business would operate under the name Hotel Westerly and would be managed by Maria's son, John.[81] Early on, business was quite good for the hotel, as John Mastrandrea recalled in a 1993 interview "I remember times when we [the owners] would turn 300 people away for the weekend."[82]

In 1954, the Hotel Westerly advertised rooms at a rate of $2.00 and $3.00 (approximately $20 and $30 in 2021), which included those "with and without bath." The hotel also boasted 'fine food' and that they were the "only hotel in town with elevator service."[83] On 16 May 1955, the hotel underwent its final name change when it was rechristened the Hotel Savoy.[84] The explanation for the change was that it was to preserve the hotel's reputation. There was often confusion when reporters mentioned that tourists who caused trouble were "customers of a Westerly hotel," leading many to incorrectly assume this meant the Hotel Westerly.[85] At the time of the change, the hotel contained forty night rooms and four apartments.[86] The new name was chosen by Maria Mastrandrea as a tribute to the royal family of Italy in the years prior to World War I, specifically, King Victor Emmanuel who was the head of the House of Savoy.[87]

The Mastrandrea family continued to own and operate the hotel for many years. Through a series of transactions, the Martin House eventually came into the possession of neurologist Carlo Brogna and his Downtown Group LLC which purchased the property in 2000 for $325,000. In 2007, Brogna announced that after renovations to the building, high-end housing units would be made available for purchase.[88] In 2013, the group 10 Canal Street LLC, headed by local philanthropist Charles M. Royce, purchased Units 10A and 10B from the Downtown Group,[89] and in April 2016, the centerpiece of the renovated Martin House, Savoy Bookshop and Café, was officially opened for business. The bookstore has since been visited by several notable individuals including Bill and Hillary Clinton and Governor Daniel McKee.

Despite its history filled with both ups and downs, the Martin House remains one of Westerly's most remarkable buildings and stands as a monument to the town's history as a travel destination. Today, the building is also a major part of the efforts to revitalize downtown Westerly and has become a great example of a modern space in a historic venue.

The Westerly Business College: Practical Business Training Without Leaving Home

"Students under the commercial department were taught "single and double entry bookkeeping, how to handle commercial paper, and making accurate and rapid computations."[99] In addition to the above, students were also taught spelling, business correspondence, and punctuation. In order to graduate, students were required to write at a rate of one hundred words per minute in Pitman shorthand, transcribe five dictated letters "almost accurately" at a rate of twenty-five words per minute, and type-write at a rate of forty words per minute for half an hour."

On 21 January 1898, an announcement was published in the *Westerly Sun* which proclaimed that Professors C.W. Wales and H.L. Gifford of Easton, Pennsylvania had decided to open a business college in downtown Westerly.[90] According to the newspaper, "this is a branch of education that will be greatly appreciated by many of our young people and will give them an opportunity to get a practical business training without leaving home." Amazingly, the school was scheduled to open just two weeks later on 7 February 1898 with classes being held in the Barber Memorial Building on High Street.[91]

Two days after the school's initial announcement, C.W. Wales provided more details about the institution to the *Sun*'s reporters. Wales indicated that the courses of study would include all types of bookkeeping, shorthand writing, and English studies, which would be divided into three separate departments. Tuition was set at $60 for one year of day classes and $30 for one year of night classes (approximately $1,930 and $965 respectively in 2021). After a delay of one week, the school began operations on 14 February 1898.[92] Shortly after its opening, the school outgrew its space in the Barber building and began operating out of the Wells Block on Broad Street.[93]

During the 1899 school year, the *Westerly Sun* extolled the work of the school, claiming that they graduated many talented bookkeepers, stenographers, and typists.[94] At first, the school occupied only the third floor of the Wells Block, but after increased enrollment in 1899, expansion into the second floor was necessary. The college held a celebration marking its first anniversary on 13 February 1899, and it was attended by more than one hundred fifty people. Entertainment for the evening was provided by the college's orchestra.[95]

In July 1902, after more than four years as the proprietor of the Westerly Business College, C.W. Wales retired and sold the college to professor George LaMunyon of Norwich. Under Wales' leadership, the school once had fifty-two students enrolled at one time and more than one hundred students had graduated from the college during his tenure. LaMunyon was a graduate of the Lincoln Normal School in Lincoln, Nebraska, and went on to teach at Eastman's College in Poughkeepsie, New York until 1900, when he took a position as a professor at the Norwich Business College. It was noted that LaMunyon would be assisted in his work at the Westerly college by his wife, who also had several years of teaching experience.[96] LaMunyon planned to offer courses in stenography, typewriting, and English, as well as shorthand writing, with the choice of Pitman or Gregg style.

LaMunyon's management of the College continued until the Fall of 1907, when the school was purchased by a man named C.H. Young of Ontario, Canada. Young was identified as a "staunch supporter of Isaac Pitman shorthand," which he believed took six to eight months of course work to master. Young was also president of the Westerly Methodist Sunday School, but resigned in response to the increased work involved in operating the college.[97]

Under Young's guidance, students in shorthand courses were taught "how to operate single and double keyboard typewriters, how to use a letterpress, mimeograph and tabulator, and general principles of filing."[98] Students in the commercial department were taught "single and double entry bookkeeping, how to handle commercial paper, and making accurate and rapid computations."[99] In addition to the above, students were also taught spelling, business correspondence, and punctuation. In order to graduate, students were required to write at a rate of one hundred words per minute in Pitman Shorthand, transcribe five dictated letters "almost accurately" at a rate of twenty-five words per minute, and type-write at a rate of forty words per minute for half an hour.[100]

Westerly Business College, 1909
(Photo: Westerly Historical Society)

The College's growth in the first decade of the twentieth century was apparent based on the establishment of several societies, including a literary and debating society which was introduced in February 1908.[101] In March 1910, Jacob Seidner, son of the famed mayonnaise entrepreneur, Otto Seidner, and a student at the college, entered a blindfolded contest in 'touch-typing.' According to an account of the event, "the students showed excellent training under Prof. and Mrs. Hinman."[102] Later that same year, an entry in the *Norwich Bulletin*, indicated that "a large number of young people of the borough [of Stonington] are attending the Westerly Business College."[103] The following year, two students, Daisy Coon and Phyllis Horn, gave an exhibition of their skill in shorthand and typewriting. Daisy was able to record one hundred eighty words per minute in short hand, while Phyllis typed seventy-six words per minute while blindfolded.[104] Due in large part to significant growth, Rev. John M. Collins was appointed as the field representative for the New London, Norwich, and Westerly business colleges.[105] Another sign of the school's progress was the introduction of athletic teams. In June 1914, "the Westerly Business College nine" played the Old Mystic Young Men's Association baseball team.[106]

C.H. Young operated the school until some time before May 1916, at which point Walter Edwin Canfield was cited as the school's proprietor. Canfield was also the owner and operator of business colleges in Norwich and New London.[107] The last known reference which describes the school as actively operating is the 1922 *College and Private School Directory of the United States*, which indicates that Canfield was still serving as Principal.[108] Despite its unknown fate, it is clear that the Westerly Business College had an impact on the community, as it graduated many students who went on to serve in positions both in Westerly and throughout the country.

An Equal Right and Privilege: The Roots of Education in Westerly

"The most widely accepted date for the establishment of a school whose history and location are known is 1792 when "the red schoolhouse" was established by the Pawcatuck Schoolhouse Company on what is today Union Street (where Congregation Sharah Zedek stands today). The schoolhouse, which came to be known as the Pawcatuck Academy, was named for Pawcatuck, a village of Westerly, that formed a portion of downtown."

"Every inhabitant of this town, whether they be free of the town or not, shall have an equal right and privilege of sending their own children, and the children of others…under their care, for instruction and bringing up."

In 1767, the above quote accompanied a vote in Westerly which resulted in the construction of four schoolhouses, three for small children, and one for "youth."[109] After 1767, the history of public education in this town is somewhat ambiguous until the nineteenth century, when several schools were established.

The most widely accepted date for the establishment of a school whose history and location are known is 1792 when "the red schoolhouse" was established by the Pawcatuck Schoolhouse Company on what is today Union Street (where Congregation Sharah Zedek stands today). The schoolhouse, which came to be known as the Pawcatuck Academy, was named for Pawcatuck, a village of Westerly, that formed a portion of downtown.[110] The Academy was officially chartered by the State of Rhode Island in May 1800.[111] Despite the 1767 quotation mentioning "every inhabitant," the Pawcatuck Academy served as an elementary school for boys only, where they learned reading, writing, arithmetic and religion. Any education a girl received at that time came exclusively in their home or in one of the several small private schools run by women in their own homes.[112] The Academy amended their charter in June 1832 and continued to operate until 1835, when it closed its doors.[113]

In June 1799, "An Act to Establish Free Schools" was passed in Rhode Island. This act stipulated how many schools each town in the state was required to form and maintain and for how many months each year. The act stated that Westerly must establish the equivalent of three free schools for a total of four months each year.[114] The location and the fate of these free public schools is not known.

The Pawcatuck Academy
(Photo: Westerly Historical Society)

The Pawcatuck Academy remained Westerly's only private, independent school until 1816, when Union Academy was established.[115] This school was also situated on Union Street, where the Fire Station now stands.[116] According to the Academy's charter, a committee of three shareholders would be formed to oversee operations and to perform checks on the quality of the instruction. This resulted in the formation of Westerly's first known school committee. The charter also stipulated that the headmaster was to receive an annual salary of $400 (approximately $7,600 in 2021). The school's first headmaster, Charles P. Otis, performed so well, however, that his salary was increased to $500 annually and he remained with the Academy until 1824.

After Otis' departure, the committee amended their charter, eliminating the headmaster's salary. Instead, teachers were required to pay rent for the use of the facilities as well as a tax of twenty-five cents per student quarterly. Despite these changes, suitable teachers were still found, and it was considered an honor to teach at the Academy.[117] The Union Academy building outlasted Pawcatuck Academy by one year, closing their doors in 1836. The building was later relocated to 27 Granite Street where it still stands today.[118]

In 1820, the state granted Westerly $143.98 for the funding of the town's schools.[119] At some point during that decade, school districts were created with one public school catering to older children, and one elementary school in each district.[120] In 1828, there were six schoolhouses (as well as the two academies) in Westerly which were open year-round and each school was limited to thirty scholars.[121]

In 1835, Margaret Alcorn opened a school that was entirely free, serving those who could not pay regular school fees. The terms at this school lasted for twelve weeks, during which time students were taught to read, write, and do basic arithmetic. It is not known when Miss Alcorn's school ceased operation, but the last known teacher, Miss Maria Burlingame, served the school through at least 1841, when she paid $30 to rent the building where classes were held and for the windows that the students broke.[122]

The following year, the location originally occupied by the Union Academy became the site of another school, the Westerly Institute (commonly referred to as 'the Academy' locally). On the site, a new building was constructed at a cost of $2,800, which was funded by the Pawcatuck Academy Association. The school was constructed and owned by Westerly School District No. 1 and an intermediate school was housed in the basement. The building's first floor was a high school until 1856, when the people of Westerly voted to discontinue "that grade."[123] One teacher at the institute was John A. Goodwin, who would later go on to be Speaker of the House of Representatives in Massachusetts.[124] The Westerly Institute continued to operate at the same location until 1870, when it was closed. The building was then occupied by the Pawcatuck Library, which was demolished in 1893 to make room for the fire station.[125]

In 1846, yet another primary schoolhouse was erected in Westerly. This facility was equipped with several educational amenities, including a blackboard spanning the entire length of the schoolhouse, slates for the children on which to practice their work, and a spacious playground. This schoolhouse accommodated sixty students with thirty desks. In 1849, a report of the town's public schools noted that in addition to this schoolhouse, one other in Westerly educated the young children, while older children attended an 'intermediate department' and the local high school. It was said that "these schools, as at present organized and managed, meet the educational wants of the village."[126]

1853 saw the construction of American Hall on High Street where the Barber Memorial Building now stands. The hall was built by P. and J. Barber for the original purpose of hosting events including lectures, balls and concerts. By 1858, the hall was home to the Westerly High School, where a man by the name of A.J. Foster served as principal. Foster was assisted by a trio of teachers who educated the school's one hundred eighty pupils, an increase of thirty students from the previous year. The school-year was divided into four terms of eleven weeks, beginning in September, November, February and May. Each term concluded with an examination, similar to today's high school system. The school's stated purpose was to educate students for college, as well as to prepare teachers and accountants. The students were divided into three major classifications: Common English (reading, spelling, arithmetic, geography, grammar, analysis, United States history and bookkeeping), Higher English (ancient and modern history, physiology, botany, algebra, geometry, surveying, navigation, and bookkeeping), and Languages (Latin, Greek, German, French, Italian, and Spanish). The fees for Common English were $4.50, while High English was $5.00 and Languages were $6.00 (approximately $146, $163, and $195 respectively in 2021).[127] As for free services, lectures open to the public were often held at the school. Unfortunately, reduced enrollment during the Civil War resulted in the school's closure in 1862. Total school enrollment in Westerly went from 240 in 1857 to just 77 in 1863.[128]

1870 was a pivotal year for the history of education in Westerly. The year saw the closing of one school, the Westerly Institute, while also witnessing the opening of another, the Elm Street School. The Elm Street School, which later came to be known simply as the Westerly High School (and later became the site of St. Pius X School), was considered a much-needed establishment. At the school's dedication, several prominent local men spoke highly of the virtues of public education, extolling its importance to the growth of young children.[129]

It was apparent by the 1870's that the belief in the value of education was proliferating. In 1875, Westerly's school expenditures were $18,667.69 (approximately $453,190 in 2021), the most of any town in Washington County. That same year, 1,026 pupils were counted, representing only 2.6% of all students in Rhode Island.[130]

Interior of the Elm Street School
(Photo: Westerly Historical Society)

After thirty-three years, those in Westerly believed there was a need for a new high school in the town. In 1903, a new building was opened at the corner of Broad and Granite Streets in downtown Westerly, part of what is now Wilcox Park, next to the Westerly Library and Memorial Building. The land where this school was built was donated by Harriet Wilcox, who, along with her husband, Stephen, were local benefactors who helped to shape the landscape of the downtown area. [for more on the Wilcoxes, see page 48.] By the 1930's, further growth of the student body required the construction of a larger building. As a result, Ward Senior High School was erected, and is still in use today.[131]

For more than two hundred fifty years, Westerly has been actively advancing its educational standards, while supporting growth and development of its educational system. From humble beginnings in one and two room buildings, schools in Westerly have grown to accommodate a much larger number of students (Westerly High School currently has an enrollment just under 1,000 students).[132] Despite the rapid growth of Westerly's pupil population, the efforts of the town have kept pace with this growth, providing today's students with a high-quality education which looks toward the future with great hope.

"The selection of Charles Perry as the bank's cashier in 1826 was a bold decision because he was just sixteen years old at the time of his ascension to the post, which was what allowed him to serve the institution for such a long period of time. Charles Perry Sr. was later chosen as President in 1881, opening up the cashier position which was then filled by his son, Charles Perry Jr. Charles Jr. would follow in the footsteps of his father, acting first as Vice President from 1904 to 1906 before a tenure as President which lasted from 1906 to 1929. Charles Perry Jr. was only the third in a long line of Perrys working for the Washington Trust Company."

Two hundred and twenty years. That is the length of time that the Washington Trust Company has been serving the people of southern New England. For more than two centuries, through forty-five presidential administrations and the addition of thirty-four states to the union, Westerly's oldest bank has continued to be a community institution.

In 1800, the Washington Bank was founded in Westerly with a total of $50,000 in capital in preparation to serve the citizens of Westerly.[133] The bank was just the fourth incorporated in the State of Rhode Island, less than a decade after Providence Bank became the first when it was established on 3 October 1791.[134] On 21 June 1800, the bank selected their first Directors, with Rowse Babcock being named President and Arnold Clarke of Stonington chosen as the Cashier.[135] Two months later on August 22nd, the bank opened its doors to the public operating from a room at the lower front of the Paul Rhodes Hotel on Broad Street at the site which would later be occupied by the Dixon House.[136] This site would serve as the home of the bank for the next thirty-six years.

In the days before they began operation, the bank's directors contracted an engraver out of New Haven named Amos Doolittle to develop the plates for the bank's very first notes.[137] Doolittle provided three plates, one with four $1 bills, another with a $10 bill and three $5 bills, and a third with three $3 bills and a $25 bill.[138] The notes of the Washington Bank were historic as they were the first with an image of George Washington's face printed on them.[139] Although he was a skilled engraver when it came to lettering and scrolls, Doolittle's lack of experience in portraiture was not given consideration when he was contracted, resulting in some less than flattering depictions.

On 13 June 1801, less than one year after the bank opened for business, President Rowse Babcock died at the age of fifty-five and was replaced shortly thereafter by board member Thomas Noyes, a distinguished officer during the Revolutionary War.[140] One notable event of Babcock's brief presidency occurred on George Washington's Birthday (February 22) 1801, when the Washington Bank issued its first dividend.[141] On 28 December 1805, the bank's founding Cashier, Arnold Clarke, died leaving a vacancy at the important post. Until the beginning of the twentieth century, the role of President was considered largely ceremonial in nature and the day-to-day maintenance of the bank was the responsibility of the Cashier.[142] The position was not vacant for long, as it was filled shortly thereafter by Thomas Perry, a schoolmaster from Charlestown and cousin of war hero Commodore Oliver Hazard Perry.[143]

Perry's selection was historic due in large part to the fact that it was the beginning two centuries of Perry men serving as Officers for the bank. Thomas Perry was Cashier of the Washington Bank for twenty-one years before being succeeded in 1826 by his son, Charles Perry Sr., who would go on to serve the bank in various capacities until his death in 1890. The selection of Charles Perry as the bank's cashier in 1826 was a bold decision because he was just sixteen years old at the time of his ascension to the post, which was what allowed him to serve the institution for such a long period of time.[144] Charles Perry Sr. was later chosen as President in 1881, opening up the cashier position which was then filled by his son, Charles Perry Jr. Charles Jr. would follow in the footsteps of his father, acting first as Vice President from 1904 to 1906 before a tenure as President which lasted from 1906 to 1929. Charles Perry Jr. was only the third in a long line of Perrys working for the Washington Trust Company. Charles Jr.'s son, Arthur L. Perry, held several officer positions before succeeding his father as President in 1929 and Arthur's son, Robert B. "Bob" Perry was also named President in 1963.[145] Robert Perry's son, Harvey C. Perry, also served as an Officer at the bank, representing the sixth generation of Perrys, as he was the great-great-great grandson of Thomas Perry.[146]

The Washington Trust Building
(Photo: Westerly Historical Society)

Several other men would hold the role of President of Washington Bank before Charles Perry Sr.'s nomination in 1881. Jeremiah Thurston replaced Thomas Noyes upon the latter's death in 1819, serving until 1830. Thurston, who served as Lieutenant Governor of Rhode Island from 1816 to 1817, represented the first in a line of several prominent politicians to be named President of the bank.[147] Thurston's successor was Nathan Fellows Dixon, who served the bank while also fulfilling his duties as a United States Senator representing Rhode Island from 1839 until his death in 1842.[148]

As was the case with the Perry family, the Dixon family would also become a significant clan in the history of the Washington Bank. Nathan F. Dixon (I)'s son, Nathan Jr., held the ship steady for nearly four decades during his time as President of the bank from 1842 until his death in 1881.[149] While Nathan Jr. was among the longest serving Presidents in the history of the bank, he also embarked on a career in politics that provided him with a front row seat to several of the century's most notable historical events. Dixon held a seat in the Rhode Island House of Representatives for four non-concurrent terms totaling twenty-one years between 1841 and 1877. Early into his first term, Dixon was a member of the Governor's Council which helped guide Samuel Ward King through the Dorr Rebellion. He also served in the United States House of Representatives from 1863 to 1871 upon being elected by the citizens of Rhode Island to represent their interests while America was engaged in the Civil War. Dixon Jr.'s presidency was followed by that of Charles Perry Sr. who then passed the torch in 1890 to Nathan F. Dixon III, also a United States Senator representing Rhode Island much like his grandfather was before him.[150]

For many years, the history of the Washington Bank was relatively typical as operations were both successful and remarkably consistent. It was during the presidency of Dixon Sr. that the most noteworthy change in the bank's early history took place. In 1836, a building was constructed, providing the bank with their own facilities for the first time. The doric-style Greek temple was built of Westerly granite and was located facing Broad Street where the current bank building now stands.[151] The "Greek temple" as the structure was known, stood until 1924 when it was dismantled and replaced.

Many banks have come and gone throughout Washington Trust's history and few local institutions have offered sustained competition. The Westerly Savings Bank was one of the rare institutions which had long-lasting success, surviving for half a century alongside the Washington Bank. By the 1850s, a new class of workers was appearing in New England and more and more people were looking to save their hard-earned wages, opening the door for the Westerly Savings Bank.[152] The Westerly Savings Bank was incorporated in 1854 and carried out its business throughout its entire history out of the Washington Bank building. The Washington Bank and the Westerly Savings Bank were closely associated with one another with many ties between the two as both establishments shared several board members. In 1904, after a long period of growth, the two banks merged, forming the Washington Trust Company.[153]

Arthur L. Perry, Charles Perry, Arthur Perry, and Thomas Perry Inside the Washington Trust Building, 1925 (Photo: Westerly Historical Society)

The 1860s brought about another major change for the Washington Bank. On 23 February 1863, the National Bank Act of 1863 was passed, creating a system of national banks while levying a significant tax on state-chartered banks that did not receive a national charter. In response to this law, the Washington Bank was granted a national charter and was rechristened Washington National Bank.[154]

Over the course of the nineteenth century, there was only one known attempt at robbing the Washington National Bank. On 28 December 1870, at just around one in the morning, Captain Jonathan Crandall, a bank watchman, was seriously wounded in his effort to apprehend would-be robbers.[155] Initially, it was believed that Crandall, who was shot in the head, would not survive leading several news outlets to report the crime as a murder. It was later said that he was expected to survive after several months in recovery.[156] The four banks in Westerly at the time offered a $5,000 reward for the capture of the assailants but it is not known if the robbers were ever found.[157]

The Washington National Bank persevered through national economic crises in 1873 and 1893, never faltering despite widespread repercussions for other banks across the country, allowing them to remain a mainstay of the local economy as it began its second century in 1900.

As the Washington National Bank started its second century serving the citizens of Westerly, operations remained steady despite an increasingly crowded field. In 1900, there were eight banks operating in Westerly, but this absolute abundance was not to last. By 1904, only three of those banks were still in operation,[158] and by 1911, only Washington Trust remained.[159]

At the turn of the century, Albert L. Chester was serving as the President of the bank, a position he held until 1906.[160] During his presidency, the entire interior of the bank was remodeled, updating several of the facilities to meet the needs of an ever-changing world.[161] These updates were necessary due in part to the increased demand. At the start of the twentieth century, there were three thousand saving accounts open with the bank with a total of $1.7 million invested.[162]

In 1901, Washington National Bank played a significant role in the consolidation of banks in Westerly when they purchased the Phenix Bank which had been in operation since 1818.[163] To obtain the bank's assets, Washington National outbid the Industrial Trust Company and the Manufacturer's Trust Company with an offer of $68.25 per share.[164] Three years after the acquisition of the Phenix Bank, the Washington National Bank made perhaps the biggest move in its history to that point, merging with the Westerly Savings Bank. In doing so, the bank became a state institution and organized as a trust company, allowing it to take on the name Washington Trust Company.[165]

On the 100th anniversary of Thomas Perry being named the bank's cashier, his grandson, Charles Perry, was named the President of Washington Trust, continuing the legacy of Perry men serving at the bank.[166] While the early twentieth century was certainly a prosperous time for the bank as a whole, this period was not without its challenges. In 1907, a financial crisis struck the nation, and many state and local banks were drawn into bankruptcy. Washington Trust, however, was able to pay all of its customers in full and on demand, reflecting the bank's financial stability.[167] This healthy financial outlook was also reflected in the 5,455 savings accounts open with the bank in 1910, nearly twice the 3,000 that were open in 1900. This was evidence of both the bank's success as well as changes in the ways that

Americans used their money.[168] The following year, the bank had assets totaling $4.7 million, also more than twice as much as in 1900.[169]

Washington Trust continued its practice of acquiring local banks with their purchase of the First National Bank of Hopkinton in 1914. The First National Bank, which opened its doors in 1865, was the only national bank in the state that did not accept the provisions of the national reserve banking system. The institution subsequently went into liquidation and Washington Trust took over all accounts on 26 April 1914.[170] This move allowed Washington Trust to open a branch in Hope Valley, expanding their reach locally.[171]

In April 1917, the United States entered World War I and shortly thereafter, Washington Trust took part in the war effort by selling war bonds. Westerly residents purchased $2,398,450 worth of these bonds from the bank in 1917.[172] By the end of the decade, the Washington Trust Company had tripled the number of accounts it held just twenty years before.[173]

The 1920s were financially prosperous for many Americans, a fact which was evident in the significant changes at Washington Trust over the course of the decade. In 1920, greater business necessitated the construction of a temporary wooden building which was used until a new building was completed on the same site.[174] In November 1922, the "little Greek temple" building, which was to be torn down, was purchased by Frank Sullivan of the Sullivan Granite Company, likely so that the granite components of the building could be reused for other projects.[175] The dismantling of the original Washington Trust Building was completed in 1924, allowing the new building to be constructed on the same site on the corner of Broad and Main Streets.[176] The vault from the previous building was retained with the new building being built around it. According to one account: "Graced by a main banking room of striking proportions and equipped with every modern facility for the conduct of business, it provides a worthy setting for an institution which has progressed without faltering."[177] On 1 January 1925, the new Washington Trust Building officially opened for public viewing.[178]

Just as the 1920s were marked by great financial gains, the 1930s brought about hard times for many in America. Washington Trust persevered through the Great Depression much as they had during several other economic crises. In 1931, to help locals to weather the storm, the bank opened a small loan department. Conservative policies throughout the 1920's allowed Washington Trust to remain open throughout the Depression including the 1933 Bank Holiday during which many banks closed their doors for good.[179]

The success of the small loan department made it clear to those in power at Washington Trust that an expansion of customer services would be beneficial. Between 1941 and 1945 while the country was in the midst of the second World War, the bank launched consumer loan and money management services.[180] Just as it had immediately after World War I, America encountered a decade of economic success in the 1950's. According to a history of the bank published in 1950: "The last five years have brought brisk business, an expanding resumption of resort activities, [and] extensive building operations. While looking to the past with fond regard, Westerly looks to the future with enthusiastic faith."[181]

After more than one hundred fifty years of performing tabulations and calculations by hand, Washington Trust purchased their first electric calculator in 1959, greatly expediting the work of many bankers.[182] Technological advances were a frequent occurrence in the second half of the twenty century. In 1965, the bank opened its first two drive-through windows in an effort to provide customers with a quicker and more convenient method of banking.[183]

The future was rapidly approaching, as evidenced by the installation of a Honeywell 1250, the bank's first computer in 1970. This computer, which was the size of a full room, was the cutting edge of technology at the time despite the fact that it possessed only 16 K of memory.[184] That same year, the computer system was put to further use when a new building was constructed in Richmond and linked by computer to the main office in Westerly.[185] Six years later, a new computer system was installed which allowed the branches in Westerly and Hope Valley to work together.[186] Shortly thereafter, the bank introduced one of its most innovative concepts to date, the "One Account." This account combined "the convenience of savings, checking, and loan account all in one."[187]

In the 1980's, Washington Trust continued to expand both in Westerly and throughout Rhode Island. One hundred eighty-two years after the opening of the first location in downtown Westerly, the bank opened the Franklin Street facility in its hometown. Two years later, the first, and so far only, offshore building was opened on Block Island. As the 1980's came to a close, two additional branches were founded with the Charlestown branch opening in 1988 and the Narragansett branch following a year later.[188]

As the new millennium approached, Washington Trust began to invest in new public-facing technology which would significantly improve the user experience for account holders. These improvements were likely among the reasons that *Money* magazine named Washington Trust the best bank in Rhode Island in 1996. In 1999, the bank launched its website and the following August, online banking was available for the first time. On 22 August 2000, Washington Trust celebrated its two hundredth anniversary. Banking from the convenience of one's own home would never have been dreamed of when the bank first opened its doors to the public two centuries prior.[189] In the twenty-one years since the bank celebrated its two hundredth anniversary, it has continued to innovate while providing dependable service to its account holders.

"License to Do No Wrong": Newspapers in Westerly, 1825-1919

"During the late nineteenth century, a number of specialized newspapers intending to promote a specific ideology or lifestyle were started in Westerly. Perhaps the most successful of these was the Westerly Daily Tribune *which was published from 6 September 1888 to 19 May 1898. This newspaper, which briefly operated under the name* The Daily Tribune *from 1889 to 1890, claimed to be "The First Prohibition Daily Newspaper Established in the World." Given the fleeting nature of some short-lived publications, this claim is difficult to verify; however, it is known that it was the preeminent source of news for the prohibition cause in Westerly."*

For the last 128 years, *The Westerly Sun* has served as the primary source for local news, and for much of this time, Westerly was a one-newspaper town. This was not always the case, however. At the peak of newspaper production in Westerly from 1893 to 1896, there were as many as five newspapers in publication.

"No Party, No Sect": The Literary Echo

The history of newspapers in southern Rhode Island is believed to have begun in 1825 when fifteen-year-old Charles Perry published *The Bung Town Patriot*, widely regarded as the first newspaper published in Washington County. The paper did not last particularly long and ceased printing before the decade came to an end.[190]

The Literary Echo.

G. H. PARDEE, PROPRIETOR.	Literature, Science and Art.—no Party—no Sect.	TERMS, $1.00, IN ADVANCE.
VOLUME I.	WESTERLY, R I, AUGUST 21, 1851.	NUMBER 21

It was not until more than two decades later that another notable and long-lasting newspaper began publication in Westerly. In April 1851, *The Literary Echo* started its run as the sole source of news in town.[191] After less than six months, the *Echo* saw its first major change when, on 21 August 1851, it was renamed *The Literary Echo and Pawcatuck Advertiser*, a name which would last for nearly five years. *The Echo* was owned by George H. Babcock and edited by a man named H.G. Champlin. *The Echo* focused its content on "Literature, Science and Art" and they strove to remain independent politically and religiously. This independence was championed by the newspaper's motto "Literature, Science and Art, 'No Party, No Sect.'"[192]

The Narragansett Weekly.

x 2.   WESTERLY, R. I., THURSDAY, MAY 6, 1858. $1

Once again, a name change was in the cards, and on 22 June 1856, the newspaper was renamed *The Westerly Echo and Pawcatuck Advertiser*. In 1858, the paper was taken over by the Utter family with George Benjamin and J.H. Utter becoming its proprietors. On 29 April 1858, the paper was first published under its most well-known name: *The Narragansett Weekly*.[193] Under the ownership of the Utters, the paper had its offices at 56 Main Street in downtown Westerly.[194] The newspaper retained the same title for two full decades before it was renamed a final time, beginning publication on 28 March 1878, as *The Westerly Narragansett Weekly*. The newspaper's forty-eight year run was ended on 16 March 1899 when it was formally absorbed by *The Westerly Sun*.[195]

STILLMAN'S IDEA.

Printed and Published Every Other Week.

VOL. I.   WESTERLY, R. I., JULY 22, 1885.   NO. 11

The News and The Tribune: The Peak of Newspaper Publication in Westerly

During *The Narragansett Weekly's* run in the second half of the nineteenth century, several other newspapers were launched in Westerly. Of these competing newspapers, two, *The News* and *Stillman's Idea* were published by E.A. Stillman. *The News*, which began on 25 August 1873, was published irregularly with a large gap in publication that ended on 12 November 1896.[196] When the newspaper returned in 1896, it was labeled as a new Volume One, Number One and there was more news coverage than the previous incarnation. *Stillman's Idea* first appeared in the summer of 1885 and was a bi-weekly publication. It is uncertain when or why either of these newspapers folded, however, copies maintained by the Westerly Public Library are available for dates up to 1897.[197]

THE NEWS.

VOL. 1.   WESTERLY, R. I., AUGUST 25, 1873.   No. 1.

During the late nineteenth century, a number of specialized newspapers intending to promote a specific ideology or lifestyle were started in Westerly. Perhaps the most successful of these was *The Westerly Daily Tribune* which was published from 6 September 1888 to 19 May 1898.[198] This newspaper, which briefly operated under the name *The Daily Tribune* from 1889 to 1890, claimed to be "The First Prohibition Daily Newspaper Established in the World."[199] Given the fleeting nature of some short-lived publications, this claim is difficult to verify; however, it is known that it was the preeminent source of news for the prohibition cause in Westerly. During the periods leading up to elections, the paper would publish information regarding candidates on the Prohibition Party ticket.[200] In addition to the daily edition, the *Tribune* also published two weeklies: *The Westerly Journal* and *The Weekly Tribune*.[201]

The *Tribune* carried the "Latest News By Wire from All Over the World," providing citizens in southern Rhode Island with a means of accessing stories from across the globe. The *Tribune* cost only one cent (equivalent to just twenty-eight cents in 2021), making it an affordable way for Westerly residents to read about the goings-on in the world around them.[202] Local news was also important to the *Tribune* as they noted that their offices, located at the Foster House Block on Canal Street, were "in telephonic communication with all parts of Washington and New London Counties."[203] Over the course of its history, the *Tribune* claimed to have an ever-growing readership.

In 1889, the *Tribune* claimed to have a daily circulation of 2,500, and the following year, that number grew to 2,700 subscribers.[204] By 1896, the daily circulation of *The Westerly Tribune* was claimed to be over 3,500. By the time the newspaper was in its final year, subscribers could have the paper delivered daily for three dollars annually ($97.30 in 2021, or approximately twenty-seven cents per day in today's money). [205] For the last four years of its existence, the *Westerly Daily Tribune* was one of at least five newspapers in town, which may have led to difficulty in maintaining their readership base. On 19 May 1898, *The Westerly Daily Tribune* published its final edition, ending a nearly decade-long run as one of the town's most important news sources.[206]

Watch Hill Life: Newspapers in Watch Hill

Nearly all the newspapers printed in Westerly during the nineteenth century spread the focus of their local news stories across the town's many villages and neighborhoods. However, there were some which covered a more specific area and catered to a particular segment of the population.

Westerly newspapers often dedicated a portion of their coverage to the happenings in Watch Hill, but as the popularity of the village increased in the final two decades of the nineteenth century, it became apparent that a news source dedicated to the area was needed. Out of this need, *Watch Hill Surf* was born. In June 1888, the five-cent newspaper began its brief run. This newspaper contained information on arrivals and departures of guests, social news, and advertisements. The 31 August 1888 edition contained a formal farewell from the staff, and it is unclear when the paper officially folded or why publication ceased.[207]

Six years after *Watch Hill Surf* broke ground as the first known newspaper dedicated exclusively to the booming village, another publication sprung up to serve both locals and visitors. On 12 July 1894, *Watch Hill Life* began as a semi-weekly endeavor with a five-cent price tag.[208] Much like its predecessor, *Watch Hill Life* focused on the happenings in the area, including news from the Watch Hill Chapel, an electric car schedule, and hotel news.[209] The newspaper was published during the summer from July to September by a Turkish oriental rug dealer and printer named John C. Kebabian.[210] A decade after the start of *Watch Hill Life*, a third newspaper began in Watch Hill. In the summer of 1904, *Watch Hill Topics* began as a weekly seasonal newspaper and the following summer, it became *Seaside Topics*, a popular newspaper among residents of Watch Hill.[211]

The Sun, The Times, and The Westerly News

At the height of the newspaper boom in Westerly, one periodical would emerge which would outlast all others: *The Westerly Sun*. In 1893, the *Sun* began its service to the town of Westerly and 128 years later (as of this writing), it is still going strong. This is not to say that it was without competition in the twentieth century, however. In 1901, *The Westerly Times* joined the market. The *Times* was published every Saturday and could be purchased for just two cents or one dollar for a full year.[212] The newspaper was headquartered at 16 Chestnut Street in Westerly and claimed to have the largest circulation of any weekly newspaper in Rhode Island.[213] Despite this popularity, the *Times* would eventually come to an end in 1916.

The Westerly Sun Composing Room, 1898
(Photo: Westerly Historical Society)

The lapse in competition for the *Sun* did not last long, though. The same year that the *Times* folded, *The Westerly News* emerged to fill the weekly newspaper void in Westerly. However, the *News* was different, as they claimed "this paper has enlisted with the government in the cause of America for the period of the war."[214] Although it was said that the paper was "for the period of the war" they continued to publish every Friday from their office at Main and Broad Streets through at least September 1919, after World War I had come to an end.[215] It is not clear exactly when the *News* stopped publishing in Westerly; however, it is clear that *The Westerly Sun* was the preferred paper throughout town, as they have remained the primary purveyors of local news for more than a century.

During the most prolific period, Westerly was home to as many as five local newspapers, providing a variety of perspectives. Each newspaper that has come and gone over the last two centuries offered something different to readers. Since 1851, the presses have never stopped rolling, and there has always been at least one newspaper serving the citizens of Westerly.

A Bridge is a Sound Idea: The History of the Orient Point Bridge That Never Was

"According to the New York Times, at a total length of 23.4 miles, the proposed bridge would be "the second longest bridge of its kind in the United States," only 0.4 miles shorter than the Lake Pontchartrain Causeway in Louisiana."

Anyone who has driven down the east coast of the United States will tell you, if there were a way to avoid traffic in New York City, they would take it in a heartbeat. Several times over the last eighty years, this nearly became a reality, and in the process, Westerly almost became the end point of what would have been the second longest over-water bridge in the world at the time.[216]

Despite being just six miles further from Westerly than Block Island, the shortest route to eastern Long Island from Westerly by car is 224 miles. Due in large part to the lack of a direct route as well as the need to alleviate the traffic through New York City, a bridge connecting eastern Long Island to New England was proposed multiple times. The first such proposal came in 1938 from the desk of Senator Royal Copeland of New York, who was also the Chairman of the State Commerce Committee. Copeland went as far as ordering engineering surveys to determine the viability of a bridge crossing Long Island Sound and terminating in either Groton, Connecticut or Watch Hill. Unfortunately, Copeland died on 17 June 1938, and with that, his idea was shelved. It has also been suggested that the United States' entry into World War II in late 1941 contributed to the lack of interest in the bridge for many years after Copeland's death.[217]

It was not until nearly twenty years later, in the wake of post-war prosperity and the rise of suburbanization, that a bridge from Long Island to Rhode Island was pitched again. In 1957, Charles H. Sells, former New York State Department of Public Works Superintendent and Port Authority Commissioner proposed a two bridge plan with one of the bridges extending between Orient Point, New York and Watch Hill.[218] In response to this proposal, a group of Long Island land developers met with the Westerly-

Pawcatuck Chamber of Commerce. This group indicated that they intended to develop the eastern end of Long Island and sought to give residents an exit route which did not involve travel through the city. The meeting was held in Watch Hill overlooking the proposed approach area on Napatree Point. The Chamber's stance on the bridge at that time was one of firm opposition, a stance they held through every subsequent proposal.[219] The 1957 plan, however, was canceled by New York Governor W. Averell Harriman, due to its high cost and low traffic predictions.[220]

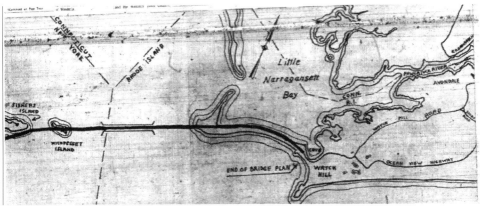

Proposed Plan for the Bridge that Appeared in the Westerly Sun, 1963
(Photo: Westerly Sun, Westerly Public Library)

In 1963, in spite of the inauspicious ends to the previous plans for a bridge crossing Long Island Sound, the most ambitious and promising plan was put forth and made the span appear as a very real possibility. By July 1963, planning truly began when a financial and engineering study was published by famed construction engineer E. Lionel Pavlo.[221] That same month, the Tri-State Bridge Committee held a meeting at the Mohican Hotel in New London, Connecticut.[222]

In October of that year, the *Westerly Sun* obtained a copy of Pavlo's study and subsequently published many details about a proposed bridge extending from Orient Point to Watch Hill.[223] According to the *Sun*'s report on the study, the proposed bridge would terminate on Fort Road in Watch Hill, approaching Napatree Point from the southeast from Fisher's Island via Wicopesset Island. It was also noted that the bridge was likely to be four lanes wide to accommodate the anticipated traffic. As a result, any state roadway leading to the bridge would also need to be four lanes wide and would require new roadways connecting to Route 1, which it was hoped the State of Rhode Island would fund. The most oft-quoted price tag for the bridge was $250 million (approximately $2.2 billion in 2021) which would be financed by forty-year bonds.[224] Because the bridge would be a toll bridge, it could not be subsidized by the federal government.[225] According to the *New York Times*, at a total length of 23.4 miles, the proposed bridge would be "the second longest bridge of its kind in the United States," only 0.4 miles shorter than the Lake Pontchartrain Causeway in Louisiana.[226] While the Pavlo study was encouraging to those who supported the idea of a bridge to Watch Hill, it was noted that construction would take six years.[227]

There were many who enthusiastically supported the idea that a bridge from Long Island would be beneficial for all parties. New York City Traffic Chief Henry A. Barnes was among the pro-bridge advocates, as he believed it would alleviate congestion through New York City, as it was estimated that approximately 8,700 vehicles would use the bridge daily. [228],[229] Another strong proponent of the bridge was Mrs. Eleanor F. Slater, a Rhode Island State Representative from Warwick, who formed and chaired a subcommittee as part of the larger Tri-State Bridge Committee.[230]

While there were several who supported the potential crossing, there were just as many who opposed the notion. Rhode Island Governor John H. Chaffee was on record several times voicing his opposition to any bridge across Long Island Sound which would terminate in Rhode Island. The Fisher's Island Development Corporation also vehemently disagreed with the plans, believing it would have a negative impact on the landscape of the island.[231] Additionally, in October 1963, the Westerly Chamber of Commerce once again voiced their disapproval.[232]

The most vocal opponent to a bridge terminating in Watch Hill, however, was Mrs. Philip B. Eaton, the head of the Watch Hill Improvement Society. Mrs. Eaton's opposition group included members from the Misquamicut Club and the Watch Hill Yacht Club. Resistance was so strong that some seasonal Watch Hill residents threatened to leave the community if a bridge was constructed. The *Westerly Sun* noted that this would have significant negative consequences for the town, as many summer residents of Watch Hill paid a full-year's worth of taxes on their homes despite not using many public services, particularly local schools. In spite of all this, some

Westerly residents felt that the benefits to the local economy of a bridge outweighed the loss of Watch Hill residents.[233]

The 1963 proposal also designated Groton Long Point as an alternate terminus giving the bridge two potential New England entryways.[234] One hindrance to the bridge's potential was that a thirty mile extension of the Long Island Expressway would be necessary, adding to the already significant price tag.[235] While there were several potential hang-ups that threatened to derail plans for a bridge over Long Island Sound, the project continued to move forward in 1963. On October 9th, the *Sun* published an article about the proposal, and with it, a map showing the prospective route.[236] The following month, the newspaper claimed there was significant discussion locally about the pros and cons of the plan with the bridge issue being covered by all types of media including newspapers, radio and television. On 26 November 1963, Dr. Pavlo met with the Governors of New York, Connecticut and Rhode Island to start laying plans for financing the bridge.[237]

By February 1964, as opposition to the bridge grew, Mrs. Eaton offered what appeared to be a somewhat tenuous plan for Westbrook, Connecticut to serve as an alternative terminus for the bridge. Eaton and her group, now known as the Watch Hill Bridge Rejection Committee, claimed that they had an engineer (whose name they failed to provide) check the feasibility of using Westbrook as an endpoint and the engineer declared the notion sound.[238] That same month, Groton Marine Conductor Clarence B. Sharp suggested a tunnel under Long Island Sound as an alternative to the costly bridge. The tunnel would extend from Orient Point to Rocky Neck, Connecticut. At only ten miles long, the tunnel would ultimately cost about one third of the projected price of the over-water bridge.[239]

Issues with the bridge proposition began to come to light in May 1964, when a three-man committee headed by real estate investor Edward McGowan was formed. McGowan claimed "previous engineering feasibility studies, conducted on speculation by private consultants, were 'superficial' and had not covered many vital areas of engineering."[240] In June of that year, the Rhode Island Legislative Study Commission endorsed a proposal by the State of New York for the examination of the engineering and economic problems associated with building the bridge.[241] The study was slated to take eighteen months and was funded by the State of New York.[242]

As this examination got underway, the New York and Rhode Island Commissions took a boat tour across the 23.4 mile route which the bridge was to cover. In August 1964, the Rhode Island Commission was informed by engineer Bertram D. Tallamy that the bridge would be "completely feasible." It was also suggested, however, that five to ten years of legislative and engineering work could be required before construction could begin.[243] By late 1964, references to the proposed bridge tapered off and aside from a mention on 29 December 1964 that the New York State Department had awarded two contracts totaling $88,000 for studies concerning the feasibility of the bridge, little mention was made of the project for several years.[244] While the exact cause of the proposal's failure is not known, it was likely a combination of waning support, high price estimates, and questions regarding the structural integrity of such a project that led to its abandonment.

The defeat of the 1963-64 endeavor was not the end. In 1979, a new proposal appeared in the State of New York which considered five prospective bridges across Long Island Sound. One of these bridges was a new Orient Point-Watch Hill span. The project, initiated by New York Governor Hugh Carey, was projected to cost $1.4 billion (approximately $5.19 billion in 2021) and would provide employment for 18,000 people. It was also estimated by one study that by 1990, the tolls from the bridge would generate between $22 and $27 billion in net revenue less than the bond financing.[245] While this may have been cause for celebration for the pro-bridge camp, the prospects were still bleak. In June 1979, the *Sun* noted that of the five proposed bridges, the Watch Hill crossing was the least favorable. Following in the footsteps of Governor Chafee before him, Rhode Island Governor J. Joseph Garrahy openly opposed the bridge, citing the cost and lack of interest from Rhode Islanders as his primary reasons. Although originally projected to cost $1.4 billion, by June, the estimate had ballooned to $1.7 billion. A random survey of Rhode Island residents found that 70% supported the bridge proposal, however, the procedure for conducting this survey was called into question, and it was largely felt that there was much less support in the state.[246] By September 1979, the project was expected to cost $2 billion. Shortly after this, *The Westerly Sun* reported that the possibility of the bridge's construction was extremely unlikely.[247] Ultimately, it was found that a ferry would more advantageous than a bridge. The Cross Sound Ferry began service in 1975, however, service was not extended to Watch Hill.[248]

Since 1979, the concept of a bridge crossing Long Island Sound has resurfaced from time to time. No proposal over the last forty years has advanced quite as far as the 1963 effort, and although technological advances have made the construction of such a bridge more feasible, it is unlikely that a span across the Sound will come into existence any time in the near future. Despite this, there was a time, fifty-five years ago, when the project was considered a very real possibility.

Public Service and the People's Mission

"While providing aid to those in need was always given as the primary goal of the People's Mission, they also took great pride in their evangelical work, as indicated by a 1908 journal entry by a member which states "a young man, Harry Perry, sends cheque [sic] for $10, but best of all he expresses a desire to give himself up to service which is better than money."

The following article originally appeared in Westerly's Witness, the monthly newsletter of the Westerly Historical Society. Much of the information in this piece was derived from records of the People's Mission, a benevolent society that provided aid in Westerly for many years, which are held by the Society.

Very little is known about the earliest history of the People's Mission. The obituary of its long-time superintendent, Mrs. Dagmar Smith, suggests the Mission was founded in 1892; however, a summary of the Mission's second anniversary meeting was published by the *Westerly Sun* in 1907. [249] While it is possible that there was an earlier mission which was formed in 1892, the subject of this piece is the People's Mission which was formed in 1905. According to their constitution which was approved on 11 March 1911, the Mission's purpose was "engaging in religious and charitable work of conducting religious services and of receiving, collecting, and distributing funds, clothing, food, fuel, and other necessities and supplies among the needy families and individuals of the community."[250] The Mission also claimed that the religious work was evangelical and was conducted under "undenominational" lines. Still, membership in the Mission required one to be "a believer in the Lord Jesus Christ and [to have been] born again."[251]

Records of the Mission's earliest years are limited, however, there were frequent descriptions of the Mission's work published in the *Westerly Sun*. In 1907, the Mission's offerings totaled $380.93 (equivalent to approximately $10,800 in 2021), a relatively small budget given the amount of work the Mission was able to do.[252] That same year, meetings were held four times a week with an average of thirty people in attendance. There were also twelve weeks in which a meeting was held every night, showing the strong commitment of members to their cause.[253] The Mission was headquartered in a wooden house on West Broad Street, just over the bridge in Pawcatuck, from 1913 until 1940.[254]

In their annual report published by the *Sun* in 1907, the Mission presented a summary of their work, which indicated: "During the year very many drunkards and tramps have been into our meetings, some of course for financial aid and others really desiring spiritual help; some of them have been provided with food and many with a night's lodging and breakfast." Another story tells of two boys who had run away from their home in Chelsea, Massachusetts and after finding the boys boarding and providing them with clothes, "they were in the meetings every night."[255]

While the Mission's work focused mainly on helping those in need throughout Westerly and the surrounding area, they also provided aid across the globe, with one worker having sent two barrels of clothes to missionaries in Barbados.[256] Money was also given to missionary workers in Africa and Central America.[257] The Mission also hosted a wide range of speakers, including those who performed missionary work overseas. In 1908, they hosted Reverend William Franklin, who served as a missionary in India for more than fifteen years. Franklin provided details about the circumstances in India at the time, including some rhetoric which would be considered inaccurate and offensive today, and appealed to the audience by proclaiming "Christian mothers, what do you think of this?"[258]

While providing aid to those in need was always given as the primary goal of the People's Mission, they also took great pride in their evangelical work, as indicated by a 1908 journal entry by a member which states "a young man, Harry Perry, sends cheque [sic] for $10, but best of all he expresses a desire to give himself up to service which is better than money."[259] The 1908 annual report shows an even larger increase in services provided by the Mission, including holding over four hundred meetings in Westerly and vicinity over the year (more than one every day).[260] The Sunday school run by the Mission also had a student body numbering about seventy.[261] Meetings were often held throughout Westerly, including four months in White Rock Hall, several weeks in Potter Hill, and Thursday evening meetings in the homes of families who requested them.[262]

In October 1909, it was announced that the Mission's founder, Alexander Smith, for whom the position 'City Missionary' was created, was leaving to work as an evangelistic worker for the Baptist Churches of Rhode Island.[263] His wife, Mrs. Dagmar Smith, however, stayed until 1914, and later returned until the Mission closed its doors in 1947.[264] At the time of his departure, the Mission was still operating very successfully. In September 1909 alone, the Mission made 126 calls upon the dying, the sick, and the needy, and also gave out 300 garments and ten pairs of shoes.[265]

The amount of work completed by the Mission steadily increased over the ensuing years. Between the years 1915 and 1935 (the only period for which records appear to exist), the Mission gave out 71,104 garments, spent $27,773.80 (nearly $550,000 in 2021), and made 9,851 house calls (an average of 492 per year).[266] While the available records serve as a great indicator of the sheer immensity of the work performed by the Mission, they also show a steady shift in the Mission's goals. For instance, house calls saw a 63.4% drop from 1915 to 1935, while garments given out increased almost 400% between 1919 and 1932.[267] The records also paint an interesting picture of the impact of the work done by the Mission. For instance, in May 1944, the Mission gave out cash to a 'Mrs. R. Carter' with the reason given as 'husband's death,' and they also provided cash to Ellison 'Tarzan' Brown, the former Boston Marathon winner and Olympian, who was out of work.[268] [For more on Tarzan Brown, see page 225.]

The People's Mission was also well-known for their annual donation of Christmas and Thanksgiving baskets to those in need throughout the community.[269] Once again, the later years proved to be the organization's strongest, as they gave out 200 Christmas baskets in 1935, compared to the eighteen they were able to provide in 1919.[270]

The People's Mission closed its doors for good in 1948, although the final records available date to March 1946, suggesting a decreased role in the community prior to their dissolution.[271] The incredible impact of the People's Mission on the town of Westerly in the first half of the twentieth century is a tradition which should be remembered fondly.

Chapter VIII
Passing Time in Westerly

What is a town without entertainment? Westerly has long been a hub of leisure and fun for both residents and visitors alike.

Ever since it was first settled by seasonal homeowners in the 1880's, Watch Hill, perhaps Westerly's most popular village, has been at the forefront of entertainment with a wide array of activities to pass the hours during the summer season. Watch Hill's status as a premier location for spending the summertime reached an all-time high during the "Gay Nineties" when leisurely activities were fashionable among the masses.

On the other side of town, those who would spend the entire year in Westerly were frequenting Bliven's Opera House for their fill of popular entertainment. The Opera House, which was located in the heart of downtown Westerly, was a venue for nearly every type of show one could imagine for several decades.

The sources of entertainment have varied significantly over the decades since the Opera House burned down in 1925, as shown in the Walking Tour of Downtown Westerly in 1962, which can be found later in this chapter. This piece is much different from anything else in this volume in that it seeks to transport the reader to a different time entirely, telling stories from the point of view of a Westerly resident in 1962.

This chapter closes with an account of the evening when one of rock n' roll's most skilled guitarists, Stevie Ray Vaughan, performed locally before he became internationally-renowned in the musical world.

Entertainment has always been a defining feature of Westerly as a community and the stories that follow seek to show that not only does Westerly work hard, it plays hard too.

Social Event of the Season: Watch Hill in the 1890's

"Upon arrival, attendees were treated to a well-decorated room dressed with pink bunting and potted plants and music which was provided by the Langstaff Orchestra of Providence. As someone in attendance noted it was not late into the evening before "the floor was very quickly filled with the graceful figure of gay dancers." Concerts were also held annually by the Larkin House Minstrel Company which provided music, comedy sketches, and a cake walk."

For over one hundred and eighty years, Watch Hill has served as a (relatively) quiet, unspoiled summer resort. Watch Hill's status as a premiere summer locale can be traced back to 1883 when a Cincinnati syndicate purchased a 160-acre land tract and divided it into numerous home lots. However, the following decade, just before the turn of the century, was truly the village's boom period.[1]

As is still the case today, the population of Watch Hill was largely seasonal during the 1890's. According to one account from 1893: "the summer population of the point is from 1,500 to 2,000" which they contrast to the population of thirty-six winter residents, only fishermen.[2] After the 1883 land sale, the seasonal population seemed to increase annually.

The growing number of summer residents resulted in a building surge throughout the village, as homes began to spring up seemingly overnight, with dozens built during the decade. Those who did not have their own home or chose not to rent a house could stay at one of the hotels known collectively as the eight great houses: the Columbia House (built in 1890, destroyed by fire in 1916), the Plimpton House (built in 1865, demolished in 1906), the Narragansett House (1844, now the Watch Hill Inn), the Bay View House (built in 1870), the Atlantic House (built in 1855-1856, destroyed by fire in 1916), the Larkin House (built in 1868, demolished in 1906), the Watch Hill House (built in 1835, destroyed by fire in 1916), and the Ocean House (built in 1868, demolished in 2005, was rebuilt and reopened in 2010).[3]

Bay Street, Watch Hill
(Photo: Westerly Historical Society)

During the 1890's, Watch Hill was exceptionally fashionable among the wealthy from cities across the eastern United States, especially New York City. Because of the 1883 land deal with the Cincinnati syndicate, the entire north end of Watch Hill was populated by Cincinnatians. Another notable homeowner in Watch Hill during the earliest period was former Rhode Island Governor Henry Howard.[4]

In addition to the stately, picturesque homes, Watch Hill also boasted numerous other sites worthy of attention including the Shore Dinner House (known for its daily clam bakes) The Misquamicut Golf Club, and the Watch Hill Billiard Room and Bowling Alley, which was for the exclusive use of hotel guests and cottagers.[5] Residents and visitors alike could also spend time at one of Watch Hill's beaches, known as the surf beach and the bathing beach.[6]

While certainly typical for the upper classes of the 1890's, the outfits sported by the men, women, and children of Watch Hill would be considered highly distinctive compared to modern fashion. As an account from 1893 noted: "the young girls dress with perfect simplicity in dainty gingham and outing flannels."[7] As for the ladies: "Diamonds and other precious stones decked the hands of the fair dames."[8] Men were also known to sport bright red golf jackets to formal occasions.[9] Numerous events even awarded prizes for the "smartest dressed."[10]

Despite being removed from downtown Westerly and other hubs including Norwich, New London, and Providence, there was no shortage of transportation options for visitors. For those coming from locations further away, there were steamships including the *Martha* which sailed to and from Mystic on Mondays and Fridays and the *Block Island* which made trips to and from its namesake island. There was also the *Watch Hill*, which went to and from Stonington, where a connecting ship to New York could be caught, and the *Ella* which departed from Norwich.[11] Trains could also be taken from as far away as Boston and New York as part of the New York, New Haven, and Hartford Railroad.[12]

Once guests arrived in Watch Hill, they could participate in numerous activities for all ages. Dances, often referred to as 'full dress hops,' were popular, such as the one on Thursday, 25 July 1895 that was hosted in the music room of the Ocean House.[13] Hops were also held at the beginning of the summer season at many of the local hotels, including the Ocean House's Red Golf Coat Hop.[14]

To celebrate the opening of their newest dining hall, the Ocean House hosted "a grand ball" which was described as "the social event of the season."[15] For this gathering, invitations were sent to cottagers and guests at the hotel. Upon arrival, attendees were treated to a well-decorated room dressed with pink bunting and potted plants and music which was provided by the Langstaff Orchestra of Providence. As someone in attendance noted it was not late into the evening before "the floor was very quickly filled with the graceful figure of gay dancers."[16] Concerts were also held annually by the Larkin House Minstrel Company which provided music, comedy sketches, and a cake walk.[17]

The Ocean House
(Photo: Westerly Historical Society)

Sports were also a popular pastime for guests and residents alike. Golf, in particular, was widespread throughout the village. Some celebrated the Fourth of July in 1895 by attending the opening of the Misquamicut Golf Club, which often hosted mixed foursome tournaments followed by tea.[18] During one summer, it was also said that there were enough tennis players in Watch Hill to host a tournament.[19] On several occasions, there were published accounts of baseball games played between the guests of the Ocean House and the Watch Hill House, a testament to the game's growing popularity.[20]

The most popular activity, without a doubt, however, was bicycling, which saw its first heyday in the 1890's. It was said that a Watch Hill bicycle fete was "a scene of unusual brilliancy and animation."[21] The fete was attended by "hosts of people in bright summer costumes, with a number of brilliant red golf coats scattered throughout the crowd."[22] This particular fete began with a parade beginning shortly after three in the afternoon, which featured bicycles which were "brightly and tastefully decorated."[23] The event also featured a 'slow race,' as well as a trick riding exhibition held by many younger riders, and an egg-and-spoon race.[24] When cycling, the women of Watch Hill were said to have worn outfits which were "particularly tasteful." One article even went as far as to state "It is gratifying to note in this connection that the New York style of ladies' bicycling habit has few or no admirers here." This was almost certainly a reference to the practice of women in New York wearing skirts to ride bicycles.[25]

The 1890's, the first full decade in which Watch Hill was viewed as a true resort destination, was a decade of both progress and tradition. Those lucky enough to live in Watch Hill, or even to have visited, would have seen a booming village with beautiful homes, activities to keep them busy for weeks on end, and above all else, family and friends to spend the season with each and every year.

Bliven's Opera House: A Premier Entertainment Venue

"In 1886 and 1887, the Opera House also hosted 'the People's Lecture Course,' a series of lectures on various topics. Sporting events were also popular at the Opera House, and it served as the setting for several polo games between the local crew and teams from around the state throughout the 1880's and 1890's. While lectures, sporting events, and comedy shows were often featured at Bliven's Opera House, the building was most frequently used as a space for musicians and opera singers."

In the 1880's, decades before the days of digital media and home entertainment, and long before the rise of motion pictures, the most popular forms of recreation were live music and theater. From 1884 to 1925, Bliven's Opera House served as the premier entertainment venue in Westerly, hosting a wide variety of performances throughout its history. Over the span of four decades and two buildings, from the original building's construction in 1884, through a rebuild in 1904, and ending in tragedy as the result of a fire in January 1925, the Opera House was one of Westerly's most notable and popular sites.

Courtland Bradford Bliven was born in Westerly on 16 March 1851 to Bradford Bliven and his wife, Anna J. Barber. C.B. Bliven, as he came to be known, was a prominent man in Westerly, engaging in a wide range of interests, including seafood sales, the sewing machine business, and a financial stake in an insurance company.[26] In 1884, he built the original opera house at what is now 98 Main Street. The building came to be identified with its founder and was subsequently known as Bliven's Opera House.[27] Initially, the opera house served as a skating rink and featured a number of renowned roller skaters, hosting the likes of Professor R.J. Aginton, known as "the Scientific Skater" in January 1885 and Miss Jennie Houghton, "Champion Lady Skater" in February of that same year. Tickets for these skating exhibitions cost fifteen cents for general admission and twenty-five cents for reserved seats.[28]

Bliven's Opera House
(Photo: Westerly Historical Society)

The first performance in what was billed as the "New Opera House," however, was a concert by "the Famous Hungarian Band," a full orchestra performing the "weird and fascinating music of Hungary" which was held on 23 December 1884. Throughout 1885, the building played host to social hops, ice cream parties, and skating performances by 'the midgets' (children aged six to eight years). On some occasions, shows were held specifically for the enjoyment of ladies and children. In late 1885, the Opera House was converted from a skating rink into a vaudeville house and performance stage. After the conversion, performances by Edwin R. Lang's Brilliant Comedy Company and Gorton's Original New Orleans Minstrel Company were held.[29]

In 1886 and 1887, the Opera House also hosted 'the People's Lecture Course,' a series of lectures on various topics. Sporting events were also popular at the Opera House, and it served as the setting for several polo games between the local crew and teams from around the state throughout the 1880's and 1890's. While lectures, sporting events, and comedy shows were often featured at Bliven's Opera House, the building was most frequently used as a space for musicians and opera singers. Throughout the last decade of the nineteenth century, concerts were regularly held and widely attended at the venue.[30]

In 1905, the C.B. Bliven Opera House Company was formed, and shortly thereafter, extensive improvements were made to the facilities.[31] The building, which held 1,200 patrons became a popular site for events requiring larger accommodations, including the heavily attended memorial service of George H. Utter in December 1912 and the graduation ceremonies for Westerly High School.[32]

In the early twentieth century, films grew massively in popularity, and they became a frequent occurrence at the Opera House. In 1916, for example, a twenty minute film, "The Worst of Friends" was shown with tickets going for five and ten cents for a matinee and ten and twenty cents for evening shows.[33] At the height of the 1918 Flu Epidemic, the Opera House became one of the many buildings to be closed in Westerly, when Frank Vennette, the building's manager, made the decision to cancel planned films to prevent further spread of the sickness.[34] [For more on the 1918 Influenza Epidemic, see page 126.]

A Big Griffith Production

Helen Ware and Courtnay Foote in **"Cross Currents"**

This is the production Miss Ware enjoyed such a long run with in New York.

A Five Reel Interesting Feature.

A Sennett Comedy Production
WEBER & FIELDS IN
"The Worst of Friends"
A Three Reeler

The last time you saw these clever comedians was in "The Best of Enemies." This new feature is a scream.

Our Matinees start at 2.15 sharp.   Prices 5c and 10c
Our Evening Shows at 7 and 8.40.   Prices 10c and 20c

In October 1919, the Opera House was host to former baseball player turned nationally-renowned evangelist, Billy Sunday, who delivered one of his impassioned anti-alcohol speeches, which had drawn large audiences across the country among the pro-temperance crowd.[35] In September 1924, David Novogrod purchased the Opera House from the C.B. Bliven Opera House Company.[36] Novogrod's tenure as owner of the building would be short-lived, however, as tragedy struck just months after the purchase.

An Unidentified Group Inside the Opera House
(Photo: Westerly Historical Society)

Just after midnight on 3 January 1925, only hours after a vaudeville and motion picture show had come to an end, the Bliven Opera House was the scene of a devastating fire. At 12:30 a.m., Arthur Fraser of Main Street discovered the fire in the basement of the building and it was determined quickly that the blaze posed a significant threat to downtown Westerly if it was not immediately combatted. The fire ignited several nearby homes, however, all but a few were saved.[37]

The magnitude of the inferno was considerable and was later considered to be the worst fire the town had seen to that point. It was said that the flames reached as high as eighty-five feet in the air and the reflection of them on the sky could be seen up to twenty miles away. Because of the sheer size of the disaster, eight fire companies were called in to assist in extinguishing the blaze which required all available fire hydrants in the area and twenty-seven lines of fire hose.[38] Units arrived from Watch Hill, Stonington, Mystic and New London and they spent the next several hours battling the flames before finally being dismissed at 4:00 a.m., three and a half hours after the fire was first reported.[39]

Once the fire was completely extinguished, the damage assessment began. At the south end of the building, a confectionery and fruit store had its plate glass windows blown out and it suffered irreparable damage. The Opera House itself was estimated to have suffered $60,000 worth of damage (nearly $923,000 in 2021) by owner David Novogrod (who was in New York at the time of the disaster). Part of the damage was covered by insurance. The group that had performed on the night before the fire, the Musical Spillers Act, lost several valuable instruments and incurred a loss of close to $2,000 (approximately $31,000 in 2021).[40] The damage done to the Bliven Opera House was considerable, and as a result, the building never reopened. Despite its unfortunate end, the Bliven Opera House had a significant impact on Westerly as it served as the town's premier entertainment venue for more than forty years.

"Just beyond the bank is perhaps the most well-known local spot, Vars Brothers Druggist and Stationers. Vars, which bills itself as 'the drug store with more' has been operating at this very spot for more than forty years. Another of their famous taglines, 'Meet me at Vars' is rather appropriate, as the store's lunch counter has been described by locals as 'bustling' and is the perfect place to stop by for a toasted egg sandwich and a Cherry Coke. In addition to their popular food service, Vars also sold typical pharmacy fare including medicines, photographic supplies, toilet goods and even typewriter rentals."

The date is 27 April 1962, and it is a Friday afternoon in late spring, the perfect time to travel up and down the streets of Westerly. Much like sixty years from now, Broad, High, and Canal Streets are lined with a wide array of shops and restaurants where people from all walks of life often spend hours socializing. Today, we will take a walk up and down these very same streets as they are in 1962, stopping at several locations along the way.

Broad Street

It is now just after 4:00 p.m. when the tour begins on the steps of the Westerly Town Hall. As we walk down Broad Street crossing over Union Street we will pass the Sears Roebuck Department Store at 41 Broad Street where many in town both young and old shop for their clothes.[41]

Next door to Sears is a long-standing local institution, Hoxsie Buick Automobile Dealers. Currently, Buick is among the largest automobile producers in the country with more than 400,000 cars produced in 1962 alone. At Hoxsie's, those with a family to transport may want to invest in an Invicta station wagon while those looking for more adventure can purchase a Skylark convertible which was just introduced for the 1962 model year.[42]

Those seeking a gift for a loved one should look no further than Woodmansee's Gift Shop, which has been in operation for several decades and was previously run by Leclede Woodmansee as early as 1923.[43] Nine years from now, Woodmansee's will move a few doors down, where it will continue to operate into the twenty-first century. Just beyond Woodmansee's, we find the entrance to the Dixon Square Building at 31 Broad Street. At the top of the stairs in Room 207 is a large beauty shop named Tina's which is run by Tina and her husband.[44]

Down the hall, you will find lawyers, doctors, and even the employment service for the State of Rhode Island which has helped local workers find jobs for more than twenty years. Continuing our way down Broad Street, you'll find Culley Hardware and the Plantation Bank of Rhode Island before we arrive at our next stop, the Singer Sewing Center, where you can purchase a brand new machine for your home sewing projects and even bring in a broken machine for repairs.[45]

The Washington Trust Building is far and away the most noticeable building on Broad Street and will be our next destination. In addition to serving as the base of operations for the bank which first opened its doors on 22 August 1800, the building is also home to insurance agents, barbers, dentists, financial planners, and a local bureau of the *Providence Journal*, just to name a few.

On the fourth floor, you will find Skarrow's, another beauty shop serving the community that is owned and operated by Mrs. Mary Skarrow and her sister, Camille.[46] After departing the Washington Trust building, we will cross Broad Street where we will arrive at the entrance to McCormick's Department Store.

At McCormick's, you will find just about anything you could need, ranging from shoes to perfumes, and dry goods to men's and women's apparel.[47] After taking the time to peruse the shelves at McCormick's to find the perfect pair of two-tone Mary Jane shoes, we will find ourselves back on Broad Street where we can then round the corner and make our way up High Street to continue our tour.[48]

High Street

As we begin our trip up High Street, to your right, you will notice the Westerly Post Office while on your left, you will see the People's Savings Banks, a branch of the Providence-based bank which has helped many in town take out mortgages on their homes.

Just beyond the bank is perhaps the most well-known local spot, Vars Brothers Druggist and Stationers.[49] Vars, which bills itself as "the drug store with more" has been operating at this very spot for more than forty years.[50] Another of their famous taglines, "Meet me at Vars" is rather appropriate, as the store's lunch counter has been described by locals as "bustling"[51] and is the perfect place to stop by for a toasted egg sandwich and a Cherry Coke.[52] In addition to their popular food service, Vars also sold typical pharmacy fare including "medicines, photographic supplies, toilet goods" and even typewriter rentals.[53]

As we make our way across High Street diagonally beyond the Post Office, let us make a brief stop at 25 High Street, home of the Mayflower Tea Room. This restaurant is owned and operated by George "the Greek" Tsouris and his wife, Kailope.[54] The Tea Room is quite popular with sailors from Charlestown as George is known to give the men food on credit until their payday under one condition: that they listen to him play his mandolin.[55]

Crossing back over High Street, we will come across another mainstay of the clothing market in Westerly, Kenyon's Men and Boys Shop, where many a young man stops in with their parents to purchase formalwear. Two doors down from Kenyon's is McLellan's 5 Cent to $1 Store which occupies three storefronts.[56] McLellan's is the place where you can go to find just about anything you could ever need with its rows and rows of racks and glass cases displaying various wares.[57] To put it quite simply, there is a very good reason why their motto is "Try McLellan's First."[58]

Next to McLellan's is a shop better suited to parents than to children. Formed in 1902, the C.W. Willard Hardware store is in its sixth decade serving the homeowners and workers of Westerly. On top of their large selection of kitchen furnishings, farm and garden tools, paints, and even mill supplies, Willard's is also the place to go to for all your radio needs.[59]

While parents explore all that Willard's has to offer, children will find more entertainment two doors down at Nash's newsstand which specializes in toys, stationery, and novelties.[60] As we cross back over High Street once more, we will see Tiny Town, which features clothing for children from infants to pre-teens.[61] Tiny Town is a relatively new arrival in this location, having been further up High Street just six years ago.[62]

The penultimate stop on High Street during our tour will be a one-stop-shop for all your sporting good essentials, the Thomas J. Burdick Sporting Goods Store at 49 High Street. Here, shoppers can purchase Bata Bullets sneakers, the very same worn by the NBA's Baltimore Bullets, as well as the latest from U.S. Keds for the whole family.[63] On top of shoes and athletic gear, Burdick's is also the place to go for toys, especially as Christmas rolls around.

For our last stop on High Street, we will be visiting Morrone's Dairy Bar and Restaurant at the intersection with Canal Street for a bite to eat. At Morrone's, you can get both lunch and dinner, and it is a popular hangout where students are known to congregate after the school day comes to an end. According to one of these students, Morrone's is the place to go for a hamburger, fries, and a vanilla Coke.[64]

Canal Street

Right around the corner on Canal Street, we'll first make our way in front of Thom McAn's shoe store, where each foot is meticulously measured. It is the perfect shoe store as long as you aren't in a hurry![65] Just beyond McAn's is Bannon's Pharmacy which has been serving Westerly since before the first World War. The pharmacy has been advertising free delivery as of late, a service that is sure to appeal to many. While Bannon's is not far from Vars Brother's Pharmacy, the two institutions certainly have their differences. According to at least one person I have spoken to, Bannon's is considerably "more austere."[66]

(Photo: Westerly Sun)

On the other side of Canal Street, you'll see the United Theater, the best place in town to catch a movie. Next door to the United is Limelight Record Shoppe, a newer establishment, but certainly a welcome one. At Limelight, you can pick up some of today's hottest singles, including "Telstar" by the Tornadoes, "Twistin' the Night Away" by Sam Cooke, and an album I highly recommend: "Surfin' Safari" by the Beach Boys.[67]

(Photo: Westerly Sun)

After digging through the crates at Limelight, we'll make our way down to the next shop on Canal Street, Montgomery Ward and Co. Department Store. The yellow brick building is notable for the distinct company logo emblazoned at the top. The building was constructed in 1928 and has been the home of the department store ever since.[68] Montgomery Ward and Co., much like McCormick's, is a great place to find just about anything you're looking for, and their appliance section is top-notch.[69]

A bit further down Canal Street, we'll see Smith's Flower Shop, which has been the go-to spot for all your flower needs from massive arrangements to small bouquets for more than thirty years. Now, we will safely cross Canal Street one last time so that we can make just a couple more stops. At 28 High Street is Brophy's News and Music Store, a great spot to browse some of today's best records while grabbing a copy of the *Westerly Sun*. A few doors down, you'll find Sound-craft Appliances, which specializes in stereos and color televisions, which are gaining traction and growing more and more popular.[70]

With that, our tour of downtown Westerly has come to an end. We hope you enjoyed spending time with us taking a walk down memory lane.

"Double Trouble opened their set with "True Love is Gone" a hard-hitting blues number which showcased Stevie's talent from the very first note. Midway through the set, the band jammed through "The Sky is Crying" a blues standard that would become a posthumous hit for Vaughan in 1991. Joining Double Trouble on stage that night was singer Lou Ann Barton, who later that night, quit Double Trouble and joined Roomful of Blues. The show was released by Dandelion Records in 1998 as part of the set "We Are Double Trouble!" serving as evidence of the show's quality and importance."

On Thanksgiving night 1979, many families all across Westerly gathered around the dinner table as they had for many years and would for many years to come. On this night, however, dedicated music fans excused themselves from the table and made their way down to the Knickerbocker where they gathered in the Cascade Room to hear a classic show by local band Roomful of Blues. While 'Roomful' as they are known to passionate fans, have been a mainstay of the blues scene for over four decades, their opening act that night would go on to be known as one of the most talented and influential guitarists of his era, Stevie Ray Vaughan.

An ad placed in the *Westerly Sun* days before the show listed the opening act that night as "Double Trouble" (interestingly claiming they were from 'Austen,' Texas).[71] After their leader achieved a degree of fame, they came to be known as 'Stevie Ray Vaughan and Double Trouble,' reflecting the guitar virtuoso's drawing power. Double Trouble opened their set with "True Love is Gone" a hard-hitting blues number which showcased Stevie's talent from the very first note.[72] Midway through the set, the band jammed through "The Sky is Crying" a blues standard that would become a posthumous hit for Vaughan in 1991.[73] Joining Double Trouble on stage was singer Lou Ann Barton, who later that night, quit Double Trouble and joined Roomful of Blues.[74] The show was released by Dandelion Records in 1998 as part of the set "We Are Double Trouble!" serving as evidence of the show's quality and importance.[75]

After that Thanksgiving night, Stevie Ray Vaughan spent the next four years building a reputation as one of the best blues guitarists of his era, returning to play the Knickerbocker several times until 1983, when he received his big break. After playing the Montreux Jazz Festival in 1980, he met David Bowie, who later called on him to play on his album *Let's Dance*, bringing Vaughan into the spotlight.[76] Vaughan's stock continued to rise throughout the 1980's until his untimely death in a helicopter crash on 27 August 1990.[77] He was remembered fondly by titans of the blues scene, including B.B. King who said "Stevie Ray Vaughan was like one of my children. The loss is a great loss for blues music and all fans of music around the world. He was just beginning to be appreciated and develop his potential."[78]

Vaughan's connections to Westerly run deeper than his performances at the Knickerbocker. Westerly born drummer Fran Christina, formerly a member of Roomful of Blues, played with Jimmie Vaughan, brother of Stevie Ray Vaughan, in the Fabulous Thunderbirds from 1980 to 1989.[79] When Stevie came back to Rhode Island, he was often supported by local acts including Duke Robillard and Roomful of Blues.

Stevie Ray Vaughan's performances in Westerly serve as a reminder that on any given night, at any given venue, it is possible that you could be seeing a star on the rise.

Sources

Chapter I

1. Buisseret, David, *The Oxford Companion to World Exploration: M-Z*, Topical Outline of Entries, Directory of Contributors, Index, Volume 2, (2007), pg. 332.

2. Morison, Samuel Eliot, *The European Discovery of America: the Northern Voyages, A.D. 500-1600*, (New York, NY, 1971), pgs. 260-261.

3. Ladurie, Emmanuel Le Roy, *The Royal French State, 1460-1610*, (Oxford,UK, 1987), pg. 127.

4. Shaw, Edward R., *Discoverers and Explorers*, (New York, NY, 1900), pg. 103.

5. The Maritime Museum of Rouen, "Reconstructing La Dauphine," https://web.archive.org/web/20071012164148/http://www.musee-maritime-rouen.asso.fr/LANGUES/angleterre.html.

6. The Mariners' Museum, *Exploration Through the Ages*, "Giovanni da Verrazzano," https://web.archive.org/web/20071019184158/http://www.mariner.org/exploratio n/index.php?type=explorer&id=22.

7. National Humanities Center, "Giovanni da Verrazzano, Letter to King Francis 1 of France, 8 July 1524, reporting on his voyage to the New World, http://nationalhumanitiescenter.org/pds/amerbegin/contact/text4/verrazzano.pdf.

8. Ibid.

9. Morison, 303.

10. Letter to King Francis 1 of France, 8 July 1524.

11. Morison, 303.

12. Letter to King Francis 1 of France, 8 July 1524.

13. Ibid.

14. Ibid.

15. Morison, 307.

16. Letter to King Francis 1 of France, 8 July 1524.

17. Ibid.

18. Ibid.

19. Deyo, Simeon L., *History of Barnstable County, Massachusetts, 1620-1637-1686-1890*, (New York, NY, 1890), pg. 952.

20. Wroth, Lawrence C., *The Voyages of Giovanni da Verrazzano, 1524-1528*, (New Haven, CT, 1970), pg. 237.

21. Murphy, Henry Cruse, *The Voyage of Verrazzano: a Chapter in the Early History of Maritime Discovery in America*, (Albany, NY, 1875), pg. 149.

22. Rhode Island General Laws, 25-2-17. Dauphine Day, http://webserver.rilin.state.ri.us/Statutes/TITLE25/25-2/25-2-17.HTM.

23. Huden, John Charles, *Indian Place Names of New England*, (1962).

24. "Notes and Queries" *The Rhode Island Historical Magazine*, Vol. 6, pg. 313.

25. Jarvinen, Brian R., *Storm Tides in Twelve Tropical Cyclones (including Four Intense New England Hurricanes)*, (2006), pg. 6-12.

26. Denison, Rev. Frederic, *Westerly (Rhode Island) and Its Witnesses: For Two Hundred and Fifty Years, 1626-1876*, (1878), pgs. 48.

27. Larkin, William Harrison, *Chronicle of the Larkin family of the town of Westerlie and colony of Rhoad Island in New England*, [sic] (LaPorte, IN, 1908), pg. 3.

28. Illustrated Description, *History and Directory of Pleasant View Beach*, 2nd Edition, (1915), pg. 11.

29. Ibid.

30. Gentile, Donald L., "Pleasant View Has a New Name," Booklet Courtesy of the Westerly Historical Society.

31. *Atlas of Surveys*, Southern Rhode Island, 1895.

32. *Illustrated Description, History and Directory of Pleasant View Beach*, pg. 11.

33. Ibid, 11-12.

34. "Misquamicut Hotel has a 54-year-old History" *Westerly Sun*, 26 August 1957, pg. 10.

35. Gentile, Donald L., "Pleasant View Has a New Name," Booklet Courtesy of the Westerly Historical Society.

36. Mermet, R.E., "The Shore Line Electric Railway" *The Marker*, vol. 5, No. 3.

37. *The Gray Book or "What You Want to Know" of Pleasant View, R.I. for Season of 1922*; The Shore Line Electric Railway Company Schedule.

38. *Illustrated Description, History and Directory of Pleasant View Beach*, 13.

39. Ibid.

40. Ibid.

41. "Pleasant View Has a New Name"

42. *Illustrated Description, History and Directory of Pleasant View Beach*, 14.

43. "Pleasant View Cottages Wrecked by Wind and Tides" *Westerly Sun*, 2 March 1914.

44. The Gray Book or "What You Want to Know" of Pleasant View, R.I. for Season of 1922, Business Guide.

45. "Pleasant View Has a New Name," and Misquamicut Fire District Charter and By-Laws, 2019.

46. Ibid and "Pleasant View, R.I., Now Misquamicut Beach" *Brooklyn Daily Eagle*, 30 June 1929.

47. "Pleasant View Has a New Name,"

48. "To Dedicate a Chapel at Misquamicut" *Westerly Sun*, 8 August 1940.

49. "Martial Law Declared in Rhode Island, Five Known Dead, Millions in Damages" *Boston Herald*, 1 September 1954.

50. "Misquamicut Evacuees Lug Their Belongings on Their Backs" *Springfield Union*, 1 September 1954.

51. "Damage at R.I. Beach Exceeds that of 1938" *Springfield Union*, 1 September 1954.

52. "Many Property Owners Will be Affected in Beach Work" *Westerly Sun*, 18 December 1958.

53. "Ground Officially Broken for New Beach" *Westerly Sun*, 11 May 1959.

54. U.S. Army Engineer Division, North Atlantic, National Shoreline Study, Regional Inventory Report, vol. I, pg. 75.

55. 1960 Press Photo Tanker P.W. Thirtle spills fuel Into Narragansett Bay, RI, photo caption; and "Council Meeting Called; Black Scum Coats Shore" *Newport Daily News*, 6 September 1960.

56. U.S. Army Engineer Division, North Atlantic, National Shoreline Study, Regional Inventory Report, vol. I, pg. 29.

57. Peter Pan Bus Lines Advertisement, *Hartford Courant*, 2 June 1981.

58. Catlin, Roger, "Clegg and Savuka Step Out from Behind Chapman's Shadow" *Hartford Courant*, 11 October 1990.

59. "Early Settlers of Westerly, R.I." *New England Genealogical and Historic Register*, vol. 14, pg. 25.

60. Gifford, Paul M., "The Probable Origins and Ancestry of John Crandall, of Westerly, Rhode Island (1618-1676)," *Rhode Island Roots*, December 2006, pg. 183.

61. Gifford, pg. 168.

62. Gifford, pg. 169.

63. Gifford, pg. 165-184.

64. Domesday Book, Entry for Pucklechurch, courtesy of OpenDomesday, http://opendomesday.org/place/ST6976/pucklechurch/.

65. Rudge, Thomas, *The History of the County of Gloucester: Compressed and Brought Down to the Year 1803*, Volume 2, (1803), pg. 305.

66. Mills, Patrick, "Statement of Significance – St James the Great, Westerleigh" http://www.stjameswesterleigh.uk/pdf/stjames_statement_of_significance_27may2015.pdf.

67. Plaster, Andrew, "Westerleigh" Bristol and Avon Family History Society Journal 151, http://www.bafhs.org.uk/our-parishes/other-parishes/456-westerleigh.

68. Ibid.

69. Ibid.

70. Ibid

71. National Register of Historic Places Registration Form, Lewis-Card-Perry House, NRHP Reference No. 05001152, Section No. 8, pg. 8.

72. Rhode Island Historical Preservation Commission, State of Rhode Island and Providence Plantations Preliminary Survey Report, March 1978, pg. 44.

73. National Register of Historic Places Registration Form, Section No. 8, pg. 10.

74. Public Archaeology Lab, "National Register of Historic Places Consensus Determination of Eligibility: Margin Street Historic District" November 2005, pg. 25.

75. Westerly Land Deeds, Book 22, pg. 41, Mary A. Gavitt to William Card, 29 February 1868.

76. National Register of Historic Places Registration Form, Section No. 8, pg. 8.

77. Perry Homestead Historic District, Living Places, online website.

78. National Register of Historic Places Registration Form, Section No. 8, pg. 8.

79. Ibid, 9.

80. Ibid, 9-10.

81. Ibid, 10.

82. Ibid.

Chapter II

1. William D. Warner, *Architects and Planners*, "Historical Evaluation Report: Westerly Train Station, Westerly, Rhode Island" (1995), pg. 2.

2. Ibid.

3. Ibid.

4. Ibid; and *The Westerly Daily Tribune*, Railroad Tables, 27 June 1890.

5. Ibid, pg. 9.

6. Ibid, pg. 2.

7. Ibid,

8. Ibid.

9. Rhode Island Historic Resources Archive, West Street Railroad Bridge, RIHRA No. WESY-0005, pg. 4.

10. Ibid.

11. Ibid.

12. Ibid, pg. 11.

13. Ibid, pg. 12.

14. Ibid, pg. 13.

15. Ibid, pg. 13-14.

16. "History" The Knickerbocker Music Center Website, https://knickmusic.com/knick-info/.

17. New York Central Railroad, The Knickerbocker, Schedule, 1946, http://www.streamlinerschedules.com/concourse/track3/knickerbocker194603.html.

18. New York, New Haven, and Hartford Railroad, The Merchants Limited, 1936, http://www.streamlinerschedules.com/concourse/track3/merchantsltd193302.html.

19. "History" The Knickerbocker Music Center Website, https://knickmusic.com/knick-info/.

20. Roomful of Blues Official Website, https://www.roomful.com/.

21. "History" The Knickerbocker Music Center Website, https://knickmusic.com/knick-info/.

22. Tipaldi, Art, *Children of the Blues: 49 Musicians Shaping a New Blues Tradition*, (2002), pg. 212.

23. Ibid.

24. "History" The Knickerbocker Music Center Website, https://knickmusic.com/knick-info/.

25. "J.A. Barber Died This Morning" *Westerly Sun*, 26 June 1925.

26. United States War Department, Medal of Honor Certificate, No. 36, James A. Barber, 19 May 1916.

27. "J.A. Barber Died This Morning"

28. Ibid

29. *Westerly Sun*, 26 July 1925, Transcript from the Collections of the Westerly Historical Society.

30. United States War Department, Medal of Honor Certificate, No. 36, James A. Barber, 19 May 1916.

31. "J.A. Barber Died This Morning"

32. Ibid.

33. Ibid and *Norwich Bulletin*, 2 October 1916, pg. 6.

34. Return of a Death, State of Rhode Island, James Albert Barber, 26 June 1925.

35. "Hero of Civil War is Dead" *Westerly Sun*, 7 February 1926; Household of Marcus Naylor, Vernon, Tolland, Connecticut, 1850 United States Census, Roll: 50; Page: 302b; Household of Mark Naylor, Enfield, Hartford, Connecticut, 1860 United States Census, Page: 803; and Manchester, England, Church of England Births and Baptisms, 1813-1915, Mark Nailor, Leigh, Lancashire, England, GB127.L211/1/3/2.

36. Congressional Medal of Honor Certificate, David Johnson Naylor.

37. 1890 United States Veteran Census, Enumeration District No. 200, Line 5, David Johnson Naylor.

38. *Rhode Island, Vital Extracts, 1636-1899*, vol. 11, pg. 193.

39. Ibid, 33.

40. "Funeral Service of Civil War Veteran" *Westerly Sun*, February 1926.

41. Household of David Nayler, Stonington, New London, Connecticut, 1870 United States Census, Roll: M593_114; Page: 769B; Family History Library Film: 545613.

42. Return of a Death, State of Rhode Island, David Johnson Naylor, 7 February 1926, Registered No. 220.

43. Household of David Naylor, Hopkinton, Washington, Rhode Island, 1880 United States Census, Roll: 1210; Family History Film: 1255210; Page: 325A; Enumeration District: 154.

44. Household of David Naylor, Hopkinton, Washington, Rhode Island, 1910 United States Census, Roll: T624_1445; Page: 18A; Enumeration District: 0301; FHL microfilm: 1375458; David J. Naylor, Hopkinton, Washington, Rhode Island, 1915 Rhode Island State Census, District No. 430, Household 120; "Local Laconics" *Norwich Bulletin*, 27 June 1913; "Westerly Has Medal of Honor Man" *Norwich Bulletin*, 3 May 1916; and "Memorial Day Committee" *Norwich Bulletin*, 6 May 1916.

45. "Funeral Service of Civil War Veteran"

46. "Hero of Civil War is Dead"

47. Best, Mary Agnes, *The Town That Saved a State: Westerly*, (Westerly, RI, 1943), pg. 97.

48. Ibid.

49. Barns, Everett, *History of the Pawcatuck River Steamboats*, (Westerly, RI, 1932), pg. 17.

50. Ibid, 19.

51. Best, 97.

52. Ibid, 98.

53. Ibid, 99.

54. Ibid, 98.

55. Ibid, 98-99.

56. Ibid, 99.

57. *The Marker*, vol. 5, No. 3, December 1946.

58. Ibid.

59. *The Watch Hill Life*, July 12, 1894.

60. *Westerly Sun*, June 9, 1901.

61. *The Marker*.

62. Ibid.

63. Cummings, O.R. & Munger, Charles F., *The Shore Line Electric Railway Company: Predecessor Companies*, 13.2, (Warehouse Point, CT: August 1961).

64. *The Marker*.

65. *Westerly Sun*, June 29, 1908.

66. *The Marker*.

67. Ibid.

68. Ibid.

69. Cummings.

70. Hilton, George W. and Due, John Fitzgerald, *The Electric Interurban Railways in America*, (Stanford, CA, 1960).

71. *The Marker*.

72. Ibid.

73. Ibid.

74. State of Rhode Island Death Record, John Champlin, 27 November 1938, Record No. 38-210, No. 9.

75. U.S. City Directories, 1822-1995, Westerly, Rhode Island, 1930, pg. 117.

76. "No Hello Girl" *Westerly Sun*, 19 October 1902.

77.   Best, 182-183.

78.   Advertisement, Westerly Automatic Telephone Company, *Westerly Sun*, 28 March 1902.

79.   Advertisement, 28 March 1902.

80.   "Hearing Tomorrow" *Westerly Sun*, 17 February 1902.

81.   "No Hello Girl"

82.   "Officers Chosen" *Westerly Sun*, 3 April 1902.

83.   "The Westerly Exchange" *Westerly Sun*, 4 April 1902.

84.   "The Westerly Exchange"

85.   Best, 182-183.

86.   "Automatic Telephones" *Westerly Sun*, 24 July 1902.

87.   "One Exchange" *Westerly Sun*, 2 October 1904.

88.   Best, 183.

89.   Ibid.

90.   Gravestone of Harriet A. (Hoxie) Wilcox, River Bend Cemetery, Westerly, Rhode Island, and "Death of Mrs. Harriet H. Wilcox" Westerly Sun, 1 September 1901.

91.   "Death of Mrs. Harriet H. Wilcox" *Westerly Sun*, 1 September 1901.

92.   *Representative Men and Old Families of Rhode Island: Genealogical Records and Historical Sketches of Prominent and Representative Citizens and of Many of the Old Families*, (1908), pg. 109.

93.   "Wilcox, The Inventor" *Westerly Sun*, 20 April 1894.

94.   "Death of Mrs. Harriet H. Wilcox"

95.   Ibid.

96.   "Westerly's Park. Why Does Westerly Need a Park?" *Westerly Sun*, 19 July 1898.

97.   "Westerly Should Have a Park." *Westerly Sun*, 24 July 1898.

98.   "A Park for Westerly" *Westerly Sun*, 21 August 1898.

99.   Ibid.

100. Historic American Landscapes Survey, Wilcox Park, HALS No. RI-1, "Significance"

101. "Babcock House Sold" *Westerly Sun*, 4 April 1899.

102. "The Gift Accepted." *Westerly Sun*, 28 June 1899.

103. "Death of Mrs. Harriet H. Wilcox"

104. "A Tribute." *Westerly Sun*, 8 September 1901.

105. "A Memorial Sermon." *Westerly Sun*, 9 September 1901.

106. New York, Wills and Probate Records, 1659-1999, New York County, Wills, Vol 0675-0676, 1901-1903, pgs. 147-162.

107. "Will Light Wilcox Park" *Westerly Sun*, 13 July 1902; and "Band Stand in the Park" *Westerly Sun*, 17 July 1902.

108. "A Larger Park" *Westerly Sun*, 14 November 1906.

109. "More Park Land." *Westerly Sun*, 21 April 1907.

110. Chick, Larry, "Westerly and Its Bands" (1982), pg. 1. Courtesy of the Westerly Historical Society, pg. 2.

111. Ibid.

112. Ibid.

113. Ibid, 3.

114. Ibid, 1.

115. Ibid, 3.

116. Westerly Band Webpage, History, http://westerlyband-gov.doodlekit.com/home/history.

117. Chick, 3.

118. "Local Singers Will Resume" *Westerly Sun*, 11 January 1946.

119. "Singers to Give Concert" *Westerly Sun*, 4 April 1946.

120. "Choral Club Has Rehearsal" *Westerly Sun*, 5 February 1946.

121. Chorus of Westerly, "History of the Chorus" https://www.chorusofwesterly.org/history-of-the-chorus.

122. Ibid.

123. Ibid.

124. Ibid.

125. Ibid.

126. Ibid.

127. Ibid.

128. Ibid.

129. Ibid.

130. Lementowicz, Anthony Jr., "Labor's Eden: Worker Protest in Westerly Granite Quarries, 1870-1910" (1997).

131. Ibid.

132. The Babcock Smith House Museum, "The Granite Connection" Pamphlet; and Dale, T. Nelson, *The Commercial Granites of New England*, (Washington, D.C., 1923), pg. 408.

133. Ibid.

134. Lementowicz.

135. Brayley, Arthur Wellington, *History of the Granite Industry of New England*, (Boston, MA, 1913), pg. 165.

136. "The Granite Connection"

137. Lementowicz.

138. Ibid.

139. Mine and Quarry News Bureau, *The Mine, Quarry, and Metallurgical Record of the United States, Canada, and Mexico: Containing Carefully Prepared and Revised Lists of Companies and Individuals Engaged In and Information Regarding the Mining and Quarrying and Kindred and Dependent Industries of North America. Together with the Mining Codes of the United States, Canada and Mexico, and Digests of the Commercial, Corporation and Mining Laws of the States, Territories and Provinces of the United States and Canada*, (Chicago, IL, 1897).

140. Dale, T. Nelson, United States Geological Survey, "The Chief Commercial Granites of Massachusetts, New Hampshire, and Rhode Island" (1908), pg. 196-197.

141. "The Granite Connection"

142. Ibid.

143. Chaffee, Linda Smith and John B. Coduri and Ellen L. Madison, *Built from Stone: The Westerly Granite Story*, (Westerly, RI, 2011).

144. The Babcock Smith House Museum, "Westerly Granite at Antietam" Pamphlet.

145. Smith Chaffee, Coduri and Madison.

146. "The Granite Connection"

147. Smith Chaffee, Coduri and Madison.

148. United States Federal Census Data, Ancestry.com.

149. State of Rhode Island, "Rhode Island Population by City, Town, and County: 1790 – 2010" data for 1920, http://www.planning.ri.gov/documents/census/popcounts_est/pop_cities_towns_historic_1790-2010.pdf.

150. Acts and Resolves Passed at the Session of the General Assembly of the State of Rhode Island and Providence Plantations, 1917, pg. 600, and "Joseph T. Grills Chosen President: Italian Welfare Club Holds Annual Meeting" Westerly Sun, February 7, 1929.

151. "Fire" *Westerly Sun*, May 9, 1986, pg. 3.

152. "Calabrese Club observes 75th anniversary" *Westerly Sun*, May 21, 1993.

153. "Feast of Beato Angelo" Immaculate Conception Church, https://immcon.org/beato-angelo.

154. "Dante Fund Benefit Well Supported" *Westerly Sun*, December 13, 1934.

155. The Westerly-Pawcatuck Columbus Day Parade, http://columbusdayparade.net/.

156. Vanderkrogt.net, "Statues - Hither & Thither" Christopher Columbus, http://vanderkrogt.net/statues/object.php?webpage=ST&record=usri04.

157. "Westerly Observes Its 250th Birthday" *Providence Magazine*, Volume 31, June 1919, pg. 267.

158. Burkhardt, Roberta and Joanna M., "A Peninsular Paradise" in *Fair Westerly*, pg. 31.

159. McLoughlin, William G., *Rhode Island: A History*, (New York, NY, 1986), pg. 39-40.

160. *Records of the Colony of Rhode Island and Providence Plantations*, vol. I, pgs. 462-463.

161. Ibid, 469.

162. Ibid, 499.

163. Yale Law School, The Avalon Project, the Rhode Island Charter of 1663, http://avalon.law.yale.edu/17th_century/ri04.asp/.

164. Ibid.

165. McLoughlin, 40.

166. McLoughlin, 40, 56.

167. *The Hurricane: September 21, 1938: Westerly, Rhode Island and Vicinity Historical and Pictorial* (Westerly, RI, 1938).

168. "Misquamicut Scene of Desolation…" *Westerly Sun*, date unknown, appears in scrapbook in possession of the Westerly Historical Society.

169. Ibid.

170. *The Hurricane: September 21, 1938: Westerly, Rhode Island and Vicinity Historical and Pictorial*

171. "Powerful Search Lights Play on Wreckage of Former Summer Homes While Workers Search for Missing" *Westerly Sun*, date unknown, appears in scrapbook in possession of the Westerly Historical Society.

172. *The Hurricane: September 21, 1938: Westerly, Rhode Island and Vicinity Historical and Pictorial*

173. "Church Party, 10 Women, Perish at Misquamicut" *Westerly Sun*, date unknown, appears in scrapbook in possession of the Westerly Historical Society.

174. "Two Babies Are Carried Safely Across Pond" *Westerly Sun*, date unknown, appears in scrapbook in possession of the Westerly Historical Society.

175. "Powerful Search Lights Play on Wreckage of Former Summer Homes While Workers Search for Missing"

176. Rhode Island High School Sports, Football Thanksgiving Results, Westerly vs. Stonington, http://www.rihssports.com/Thanksgiving%20Football/Results/WES%20VS%20STON.htm.

177. Fulkerson, Vickie, "Bears vs. Bulldogs: High school football rivalry hits 100th year" *New London Day*, 24 November 2011.

178. Rhode Island High School Sports, Football Thanksgiving Results, Westerly vs. Stonington, http://www.rihssports.com/Thanksgiving%20Football/Results/WES%20VS%20STON.htm.

179. Ibid.

180. Cawley, Bill, "Second Period Safety Provides Bears With Slim Victory Margin" *Westerly Sun*, 26 November 1937, pg. 11.

181. Ibid.

182. "Bulldogs …6-6 Tie in Turkey Day Football Struggle" *Westerly Sun*, 25 November 1960, pg. 12.

183. "Two Thousand Five Hundred Fans See Gridiron Battle" *Westerly Sun*, 25 November 1927, pg. 8.

184. Sawyer, Edwin, "W.H.S. Ties Stonington" *The Senior*, December 1927, pg. 22.

185. Ibid.

186. "Bulldogs and Bears Will Contest for Jeff Moore Memorial Trophy; Kickoff at 10 a.m." *Westerly Sun*, 21 November 1962.

187. Kendzia, John, "Bulldogs are Better Mudders, Win 15-12" *Westerly Sun*, 23 November 1962, pg. 1, 13.

188. Ibid, 19-20.

189. Rhode Island High School Sports, Football Thanksgiving Results, Westerly vs. Stonington, http://www.rihssports.com/Thanksgiving%20Football/Results/WES%20VS%20STON.htm.

190. "Bulldogs In Iron-Men Roles In Scoring Over Stonington Rivals" *Westerly Sun*, 29 November 1940.

191. Cawley, Bill, "Joe Capalbo Carries Punt Back 72 Yards To Give Bulldogs Win" *Westerly Sun*, 29 November 1940.

192. Ibid.

193. Marr, Bob, "Bears Kept the Faith When The Going Was Its Toughest" *Westerly Sun*, 25 November 1988, pg. 15.

194. Ibid.

195.   Ibid.

196.   Kimberlin, Keith, "Thanksgiving Day Award Winners" *Westerly Sun*, 24 November 2000, pgs. 9, 12.

197.   Ibid.

198.   Kendzia, John, "Goodman, Weber Combine Talents to Pace Bears Past Stubborn Foes" *Westerly Sun*, 28 November 1969.

199.   "7200 Watch WHS Extend…" *Westerly Sun*, 27 November 1981.

200.   McLoughlin, 117.

201.   National Register of Historic Places Registration Form, Westerly, RI, North End Historic District, (2005), pg. 8-1 and Denison, 182.

202.   United States Patent Office, *List of Patents for Inventions and Designs Issued by the United States, from 1790 to 1847, with the Patent Laws and Notes of Decisions of the Courts of the United States for the Same Period*, (1847), pg. 88.

203.   "Westerly's Industrial March" A Paper Read before the Westerly Historical Society, pgs. 15-16.

204.   National Register of Historic Places Registration Form, Westerly, RI, North End Historic District, (2005), pg. 8-2 and Hall, Joseph Davis, *Biographical History of the Manufacturers and Business Men of Rhode Island, at the Opening of the Twentieth Century*, (1901), pg. 151.

205.   Ibid, 8-2.

206.   Ibid, 8-4.

207.   Ibid, 7-3.

208.   Ibid, 8-5.

209.   Ibid, 8-1.

210.   Ibid, 8-3.

211.   Ibid.

212.   Ibid.

213.   "Westerly's Industrial March," 15.

214.   *Textile World Journal*, Volume 54, 19 October 1918, pg. 69.

215.   Westerly Land Deeds, Book 45, pgs. 28-30.

216.   Westerly Land Deeds, Book 45, pgs. 139-141.

217.   National Register of Historic Places Registration Form, Westerly, RI, North End Historic District, (2005), pg. 8-3.

Chapter III

1. Town Council and Probate Records, 1699-1888, Westerly, Rhode Island, vol. 7, pgs. 474-475.

2. Ibid.

3. "The Centennial Fourth." *Narragansett Weekly*, 6 July 1876.

4. Zimmer, Ben, "Where did the Supreme Court get its 'parade of horribles'?" *Boston Globe*, 1 Jul 2012.

5. "Westerly." *Wood River Advertiser*, 23 July 1876 and "Celebrating the Fourth." *Narragansett Weekly*, 29 June 1876.

6. "The Centennial Fourth."

7. "Westerly."

8. "The Centennial Fourth."

9. "Westerly."

10. "The Centennial Fourth."

11. "The Glorious Fourth" *Westerly Sun*, 3 July 1900; and "Watch Hill: A Glorious But Hot Fourth" *Westerly Sun*, 4 July 1900.

12. "Fourth of July Boomings" *Westerly Sun*, 6 July 1900; and "St. Michael's Picnic" *Westerly Sun*, 4 July 1900; and "Watch Hill: A Glorious But Hot Fourth"; and "The Glorious Fourth"

13. "Christmas and the Sabbath Schools" *Narragansett Weekly*, 25 December 1873.

14. "Westerly." *Providence Evening Press*, 10 December 1873, pg. 3.

15. "Christmas and the Sabbath Schools" *Narragansett Weekly*, 25 December 1873.

16. "At the Churches Tonight." *Westerly Sun*, 17 December 1873.

17. Coy, Sallie E., "Christmas at the Turn of the Century" from *Westerly Memories*, pg. 31.

18. "Manger Scenes Are Featured in Christmas Decorations" *Westerly Sun*, 22 December 1949, pg. 6.

19. Bliven Opera House Collection, courtesy of the Westerly Historical Society.

20. Coy, 31.

21. Ibid, 36.

22. "Sing Carols Sunday Next" *Westerly Sun*, 16 December 1927.

23. Horton, John, "Christmas Dance" from the *Babcock Middle School Newspaper*, December 1959; and *Seaside Topics*, Winter 1999.

24. Advertisements, *Narragansett Weekly*, 25 December 1873.

25. Advertisements, *Westerly Sun*, 24 December 1892.

26. Coy, 32.

27. Ibid, pg. 31-36.

28. Advertisements, *Westerly Sun*, 20 December 1906.

29. "Moving Pictures." *Westerly Sun*, 23 December 1906.

30. "Gift Shoppers' Guide" *Westerly Sun*, 18 December 1927.

31. The P.H. Opie Company Advertisement, *Westerly Sun*, 16 December 1927.

32. "Over 100 Children Remembered at Christmas by Westerly PTA" *Westerly Sun*, 23 December 1949, pg. 2.

33. "New Year's Day" *Westerly Sun*, 1 January 1900.

34. "Happenings of the Year" *Westerly Sun*, 31 December 1899.

35. Advertisement for H.B. Gavitt Company, *Westerly Sun*, 27 December 1899 and Advertisement for P.H. Opie, *Westerly Sun*, 31 December 1899.

36. Ritchie, James Ewing, *The Religious Life of London*, (1870), pg. 223.

37. "Special Musical Program" *Westerly Sun*, 31 December 1899.

38. "Watch Meetings" Westerly Sun, 31 December 1899.

39. "Watch Meetings. Services Last Evening at the Various Churches" *Westerly Sun*, 1 January 1900.

40. "Small Talk of the Town" *Westerly Herald*, 1 January 1900.

41. "Small Talk of the Town"

42. "New Year's Day"

43. "Westerly says it's Y2K-OK" *Westerly Sun*, 28 December 1999.

44. Ibid.

45. Various advertisements, *Westerly Sun*, First Night Insert, 29 December 1999.

46. "Make First Night Westerly A Family Tradition" *Westerly Sun*, First Night Insert, 29 December 1999.

47. "Millennium Events Year 2000-2001" *Westerly Sun*, First Night Insert, 29 December 1999.

48. Ibid.

49. Ibid.

50. "Westerly Train Station on Venue Hit List This Year" *Westerly Sun*, First Night Insert, 29 December 1999.

51. "Westerly 2000 Events" *Westerly Sun*, First Night Insert, 29 December 1999.

52. Allik, Allana, "Tonight, have fun, stay safe" *Westerly Sun*, 31 December 1999.

53. Ibid.

54. TOTAL SOLAR ECLIPSE OF 1925 JANUARY 24, NASA Solar Eclipse Database, https://eclipse.gsfc.nasa.gov/SEsearch/SEsearchmap.php?Ecl=19250124.

55. "Eclipse Viewers Begin to Arrive" *Westerly Sun*, 23 January 1925.

56. "Appreciation Widely Shown" *Westerly Sun*, 25 January 1925.

57. "Business Suspended Till 10 A.M. Saturday for Eclipse" *Westerly Sun*, 22 January 1925.

58. "Eclipse Viewers Begin to Arrive"

59. "Business Suspended Till 10 A.M. Saturday for Eclipse"

60. "Eclipse Traffic Problem a Big One, But Well Solved" *Westerly Sun*, 25 January 1925.

61. Ibid.

62. "Business Suspended Till 10 A.M. Saturday for Eclipse"

63. "See Eclipse In Its Splendor" *Westerly Sun*, 25 January 1925.

64. "Eclipse Viewers Begin to Arrive"

65. "Edison's Son and Daughter Here; Inventor Gives Up Trip" *Westerly Sun*, 24 January 1925.

66. TOTAL SOLAR ECLIPSE OF 1925 JANUARY 24, NASA Solar Eclipse Database.

67. "Radio Tractor Here for Eclipse" *Westerly Sun*, 22 January 1925.

68. "Appreciation Widely Shown"

69. United States Department of Commerce, Natural Disaster Survey Report 78-1, Northeast Blizzard of '78, February 5-7, 1978: A Report to the Administrator, pg. 28.

70. "Weather Bureau Predicts Up to 16 Inches of Snow" *Westerly Sun*, 6 February 1978.

71. Ibid.

72. Coyle, Pat, "Officials to Seek Ways So Future Storms Won't Strand Pupils" *Westerly Sun*, 8 February 1978.

73. Natural Disaster Survey Report, 28.

74. "Officials to Seek Ways So Future Storms Won't Strand Pupils"

75. Ibid.

76. "Weather Bureau Predicts Up to 16 Inches of Snow"

77. "Area Paralyzed by Deadly Snow" *Westerly Sun*, 7 February 1978, pg. 1.

78. Most accounts state the total snowfall was 22 inches, however, some account suggest it was 20 and at least one indicated 24 inches.

79. "Area Paralyzed by Deadly Snow"

80. Rosati, Mark, "U.S. Troops Coming To Aid in Clean-Up" *Westerly Sun*, 8 February 1978, pg. 1.

81. "Area Paralyzed by Deadly Snow"

82. Ibid.

83. Ibid.

84. "General Store Fire" *Westerly Sun*, 8 February 1978.

85. "U.S. Troops Coming To Aid in Clean-Up"

86. "Westerly Slowly Returns to Normal" *Westerly Sun*, 8 February 1978, pg. 1.

87. "Westerly Slowly Returns to Normal"

88. Coyle, Pat, "Motorists Urged to Avoid Travel" Westerly Sun, 9 February 1978.

89. Ibid

90. "Motorists Urged to Avoid Travel"

91. "R.I. Schools Stay Closed Friday Conn. Expected to Hold Classes" *Westerly Sun*, 9 February 1978.

92. Hollis, Todd, "State Police Form I-95 Roadblock Halting Motorists Entering R.I." *Westerly Sun*, 10 February 1978.

93. Natural Disaster Survey Report 78-1, Northeast Blizzard of '78, 28.

94. "State Police Form I-95 Roadblock Halting Motorists Entering R.I."

95. Natural Disaster Survey Report 78-1, Northeast Blizzard of '78, Table 1.

96. Ibid, 1.

97. "1918 Flu (Spanish flu epidemic)" The Avian Bird Flu Survival Guide, https://web.archive.org/web/20080521071645/http://www.avian-bird-flu.info/spanishfluepidemic1918.html.

98. Barry, John M., *The Great Influenza: The Epic Story of the Deadliest Plague in History*, (New York, 2004), pg. 171.

99. Taubenberger, Jeffery K, and David M Morens, "1918 Influenza: The Mother of All Pandemics" *Emerging Infectious Diseases*, 2006 Jan; 12(1): 15–22.

100. "Westerly" *Norwich Bulletin*, 20 September 1918.

101. Deaths Registered in the Town of Westerly, R.I. for the Year ending December 31st, 1918, pg. 450, https://www.familysearch.org/ark:/61903/3:1:S3HY-6XWS-XT1?i=229&cat=698695.

102. Ibid, 450-452

103. "Westerly" *Norwich Bulletin*, 1 October 1918.

104. "Westerly" *Norwich Bulletin*, 27 September 1918.

105. Ibid.

106. "Westerly" *Norwich Bulletin*, 3 October 1918.

107. Ibid.

108. Ibid.

109. Ibid.

110. "Westerly" *Norwich Bulletin*, 8 October 1918.

111. Ibid.

112. Ibid.

113. Ibid.

114. Maxson, Jane Hoxsie, *Diaries of J. Irving Maxson, 1898-1923*, (2009), October 5, 1918 Entry.

115. "Local Laconics" *Norwich Bulletin*, 15 October 1918.

116. "Westerly" *Norwich Bulletin*, 18 October 1918.

117. Westerly Historical Society Meeting Records, pg. 105, November 1918 Meeting.

118. United States Federal Census Records, 1910 and 1920, Ancestry.com.

119. "Westerly" *Norwich Bulletin*, 5 November 1918.

120. "Local Laconics" *Norwich Bulletin*, 7 January 1919.

121. Deaths Registered in the Town of Westerly, R.I. for the Year ending December 31st, 1918, pg. 450-454.

122. "Westerly" *Norwich Bulletin*, 1 January 1919.

123. Deaths Registered in the Town of Westerly, R.I. for the Year ending December 31st, 1918, pg. 450-454.

124. "Local Laconics" *Norwich Bulletin*, 23 December 1918.

125. Spicer, Albert, *Momentous Events in Westerly, R.I., as Recalled by Dr. Spicer*, (2002), pg. 3.

126. Ibid.

127. "Westerly" *Norwich Bulletin*, 1 January 1919.

128. Ibid.

129. Ibid.

130. "Local Laconics" *Norwich Bulletin*, 7 January 1919.

131.   "Westerly" *Norwich Bulletin*, 4 February 1919.

132.   Clarke, Helen May, *An Account of My Life, 1915-1926, The Childhood Journals of Helen May Clarke of Mystic, Connecticut*, entry for July 1919.

133.   "Westerly" *Norwich Bulletin*, 4 November 1919.

134.   Deaths Registered in the Town of Westerly, R.I. for the Year ending December 31st, 1919, https://www.familysearch.org/ark:/61903/3:1:S3HY-6XWS-XT1?i=229&cat=698695.

135.   "Westerly" *Norwich Bulletin*, 3 February 1920.

136.   "Westerly" *Norwich Bulletin*, 19 February 1920.

137.   "Westerly" *Norwich Bulletin*, 6 April 1920.

Chapter IV

1.   "Former Slave First to Vote" *Westerly Sun*, 2 November 1920.

2.   Gravestone of Anna Thornton Williams, Rhode Island Historical Cemetery Commission, http://rihistoriccemeteries.org/newgravedetails.aspx?ID=371058.

3.   Some records, including newspaper accounts suggest her father's name was Shumake, however, her marriage record to George L. Williams gives his name as Benjamin.

   "Former Slave First to Vote" *Westerly Sun*, 2 November 1920 and "Mrs. Anna T. Williams Dies at State Hospital" *Westerly Sun*, 8 September 1936.

4.   Household of Anna Thornton, Cincinnati, Hamilton, Ohio, 1900 United States Census, Page: 2; Enumeration District: 0067; FHL microfilm: 1241275; and Household of George Williams, Westerly, Washington, Rhode Island, 1910 United States Census, Roll: T624_1445; Page: 18B; Enumeration District: 0310; FHL microfilm: 1375458; and Anna T. Williams, Westerly, Washington, Rhode Island, 1920 United States Census, Roll: T625_1681; Page: 13A; Enumeration District: 361.

5.   "Former Slave First to Vote" and War Department, The Adjutant General's Office, Colored Troops Division (05/22/1863–1888), Descriptive Lists of Colored Volunteer Army Soldiers 1864, Volumes 58–60, ARC: 1223643, Records of the Adjutant General's Office, 1762–1984/1780–1917, Record Group 94, (National Archives at Washington, D.C.).

6.   "Mrs. Anna T. Williams Dies at State Hospital" *Westerly Sun*, 8 September 1936; and "Perjury: Charge Against Walter Thornton by His Wife" *Cincinnati Post*, 10 March 1893.

7.   U.S. City Directories, 1822-1995, Cincinnati, 1877, pg. 976.

8.   Household of Walker Thornton, Miami, Clermont, Ohio, 1880 United States Census, Roll: 1000; Page: 116A; Enumeration District: 043.

9. Record of Births, Probate Court, Clermont County, Ohio, Record No. 466, Charles Thornton Jr.

10. "Perjury: Charge Against Walter Thornton by His Wife"

11. U.S. City Directories, 1822-1995, Cincinnati, 1894-1907.

12. "What a Woman Can Do." *The Colored American*, 17 November 1900, pg. 9.

13. Ibid.

14. "Cincinnati" *Cleveland Gazette*, 13 July 1895.

15. Obituary, *Norwich Bulletin*, 25 February 1920.

16. Marriage Record of Anna Thornton and George Lewis Williams, Rhode Island Vital Records.

17. U.S. City Directories, 1822-1995, Cincinnati, 1894-1907.

18. Westerly Town Land Deeds, Book No. 39, pgs. 90-91.

19. Household of George Williams, Westerly, Washington, Rhode Island, 1910 United States Census, Roll: T624_1445; Page: 18B; Enumeration District: 0310; FHL microfilm: 1375458.

20. Anna T. Williams, Westerly, Washington, Rhode Island, 1920 United States Census, Roll: T625_1681; Page: 13A; Enumeration District: 361.

21. "Westerly," *Norwich Daily Bulletin*, 19 November 1919.

22. Donation Card for the Lincoln Farm Association, Card No. 112708, Anna Thornton Williams, 17 April 1909.

23. *Annual Report of the President for the Tuskegee Institute*, 1915, pg. 103.

24. Anna T. Williams, Westerly, Washington, Rhode Island, 1920 United States Census, Roll: T625_1681; Page: 13A; Enumeration District: 361.

25. "Former Slave First to Vote"

26. Ibid.

27. "Westerly Stronger than Ever" *Westerly Sun*, 3 November 1920.

28. Anna Thornton Williams, Westerly, Washington, Rhode Island, 1925 Rhode Island State Census, Line Number: 26, Household number: 423, Volume Number: 17, Page Number: 50.

29. Rhode Island Public Health Commission, Certificate of Death, No. 36-571, Anna Williams.

30. Anna Williams, Cranston, Providence, Rhode Island, 1930 United States Census, Page: 12B; Enumeration District: 0197; FHL microfilm: 2341905; and Anna Williams, Cranston, Providence, Rhode Island, 1935 Rhode Island State Census, No. 464104, Tract 119.

31.   Rhode Island Public Health Commission, Certificate of Death, No. 36-571, Anna Williams.

32.   United States Census Records, 1790-1860, Ancestry.com.

33.   Obituary of Charles Perry, *Westerly Weekly*, 5 June 1890.

34.   Cole, J.R., *History of Washington and Kent Counties, Rhode Island*, (1889), pg. 352.

35.   Ibid.

36.   Obituary of Charles Perry.

37.   *Depositions Taken on Behalf of the Defendants in a Suit in Equity between Oliver Earle and Others, Complainants, and William Wood and Others, Defendants, in the Supreme Judicial Court of Massachusetts*, (Boston, MA, 1850), pg. 27.

38.   *History of Rhode Island, Biographical*, pg. 11, Charles Perry.

39.   Cole, 353.

40.   *History of Rhode Island, Biographical*, pg. 11.

41.   "Westerly." *Manufacturers' and Farmers' Journal*, 30 November 1868, pg. 1.

42.   Douglass, Frederick. "William the Silent" - Folder 1 of 7. Manuscript/Mixed Material. https://www.loc.gov/item/mfd.30005/.

43.   Snodgrass, Mary Ellen, *The Underground Railroad: An Encyclopedia of People, Places, and Operations*, (2015), pg. 409.

44.   DeSimone, Russell, "Narrative of an Ashaway Teenager's Role in the Underground Railroad Rediscovered" *Small State Big History*, 23 February 2019, http://smallstatebighistory.com/narrative-of-an-ashaway-teenagers-role-in-the-underground-railroad-rediscovered.

45.   Perry, Harvey, "Letter: Underground Railroad story has a family tie" *Westerly Sun*, 23 January 2019.

46.   Wilburites were viewed as conservative members of the Quaker faith who adhered to the tents laid out by John Wilbur, the grandfather of Charles' wife, Temperance.

47.   *Quakeriana Notes: Concerning Treasures New and Old in the Quaker Collections of Haverford College*, (Haverford, PA), pg. 5-8.

48.   Foster, Ethan, *The Conscript Quakers, Being a Narrative of the Distress and Relief of Four Young Men from the Draft for the War in 1863*, (1883).

49.   Cole, 354.

50.   Obituary of Charles Perry.

51.   Gravestone entry for Temperance Perry, RI Historic Cemetery Commission, http://rihistoriccemeteries.org/newgravedetails.aspx?ID=364508.

52.   Household of Charles Perry, Westerly, Washington, Rhode Island, 1850 United States Census, Roll: M432_847; Page: 396A; Image: 353.

53. Household of Charles Perry, Westerly, Washington, Rhode Island, 1870 United States Census, Roll: M593_1473; Page: 392B; Family History Library Film: 552972.

54. Gravestone entry for Temperance Perry.

55. "Obituaries: Dr. J. Gordon Anderson" *Westerly Sun*, 14 February 1982.

56. Household of John C. Anderson, Westerly, Washington, Rhode Island, 1910 United States Census, Roll: T624_1445; Page: 17B; Enumeration District: 0310; FHL microfilm: 1375458.

57. "Mrs. Anderson Is Dead at 90" *Westerly Sun*, 11 January 1951; and Household of John C. Anderson, Westerly, Washington, Rhode Island, 1910 United States Census, Roll: T624_1445; Page: 17B; Enumeration District: 0310; FHL microfilm: 1375458.

58. "Obituaries: Dr. J. Gordon Anderson"

59. University of Rhode Island, "The Grist 1917" (1917), https://digitalcommons.uri.edu/yearbooks/80.

60. Ibid.

61. "Obituaries: Dr. J. Gordon Anderson"

62. *Rhode Island Medical Journal*, Volume 4, February 1921, pg. 36.

63. "Westerly" *Norwich Bulletin*, 18 November 1922.

64. "Obituaries: Dr. J. Gordon Anderson"

65. "New Home of Margaret Edward Anderson Hospital Situated on Westerly-Watch Hill Road" *Providence Journal*, 25 December 1927.

66. Ibid.

67. Ibid.

68. Ibid.

69. "Obituaries: Dr. J. Gordon Anderson"

70. J. Gordon Anderson, "Autogenous Milk Vaccine Therapy" *American Journal of Surgery*, September 1934, Volume 25, Issue 3, Pages 521–524.

71. Deaths (1901-1943), Rhode Island, FamilySearch, FHL Film No. 1940953.

72. Ibid.

73. "Once on Hospital Staff" *Providence Journal*, 15 January 1950.

74. "Obituaries: Dr. J. Gordon Anderson"

75. Westerly Land Deeds, Book 92, pg. 488, 9 March 1968.

76. "Obituaries: Dr. J. Gordon Anderson"

77. "Master Marshall Brines Drew" *Encyclopedia Titanica*, biographical entry.

78. Verde, Tom, "James V. Drew- A Titanic Tale of Stone, Ice, and Flames" *Westerly Sun*, 6 May 2012.

79. "Master Marshall Brines Drew"

80. Ibid.

81. "Mr. Marshall Drew, 82" *Philadelphia Inquirer*, 10 June 1986.

82. "James V. Drew- A Titanic Tale of Stone, Ice, and Flames"

83. "Master Marshall Brines Drew"

84. Dziedzic , Shelley, "Journeys Through Time," Entry on Marshall Brines Drew, https://journeysintime.wordpress.com/marshall-brines-drew/.

85. "Some Whose Names Are Not on the List of the Saved" *Brooklyn Daily Times*, 17 April 1912.

86. Ibid.

87. "James V. Drew- A Titanic Tale of Stone, Ice, and Flames"

88. "James V. Drew- A Titanic Tale of Stone, Ice, and Flames"

89. Dziedzic.

90. "Master Marshall Brines Drew"

91. Ibid.

92. Westerly Land Deeds, Book 46, pgs. 516-517; and Westerly Land Deeds, Book 82, pgs. 250.

93. Dziedzic.

94. Ibid.

95. "Survivor of Titanic Marshall Drew Dies" *Westerly Sun*, June 1986.

96. "Titanic Memorabilia: Hat band Sells for $53,000 at Auction" *State Journal-Register*, 12 April 2003, pg. 2.

97. Gravestone of Marshall B. Drew, Rhode Island Historical Cemetery Commission, River Bend Cemetery, Westerly.

98. Household of Carrie L. Morris, Westerly, Washington, Rhode Island, 1930 United States Federal Census, Page: 22A; Enumeration District: 0022; FHL microfilm: 2341916.

99. Henry N. Morris, Westerly, Washington, Rhode Island, 1935 Rhode Island State Census, District 347.

100. "H.M. Morris Gets Medal For Heroism" *Westerly Sun*, 29 October 1939.

101. "Westerly Hurricane Hero Receives Carnegie Medal" *Westerly Sun*, 4 January 1940.

102. Various sources give the width of the breachway as 50, 75, and 112 feet.

103. "H.M. Morris Gets Medal For Heroism"

104. Buffum, Robert C., *The Weekapaug Inn: The Best of All Possible Worlds, 1899-1999*, (1999), pg. 85.

105. "H.M. Morris Gets Medal For Heroism" and undated *Westerly Sun* article from Henry M. Morris vertical file, courtesy of the Westerly Library.

106. Household of Henry Morris, Westerly, Washington, Rhode Island, 1940 United States Federal Census.

107. "Westerly Hurricane Hero Receives Carnegie Medal"

108. "Mission of the Carnegie Hero Fund Commission" from the Carnegie Fund Commission website, https://www.carnegiehero.org/about-the-fund/mission/.

109. Ibid.

110. Carnegie Fund Biographical Entry for Henry M. Morris, pg. 3119, Henry M. Morris vertical file, courtesy of the Westerly Library.

111. "Westerly Hurricane Hero Receives Carnegie Medal"

112. "H.M. Morris Gets Medal For Heroism"

113. "H.M. Morris Honored at C of C Dinner" *Westerly Sun*, January 9, 1940.

114. Ibid.

115. Ibid.

116. U.S., Department of Veterans Affairs BIRLS Death File, 1850-2010, Henry Morris, SSN: 036073800.

117. "OCS Has Color Girl Ceremony" *Newport Mercury*, December 25, 1964.

118. Advertisement for the Pine Lodge Motel in the Westerly High School Yearbook, 1960 and "Henry M. Morris" Providence Journal, November 6, 1960.

119. "Henry M. Morris" *Providence Journal*, November 6, 1960.

120. Kietzman, Susan B., "Lifeguard swam five trips across swollen breachway" from retrospective book regarding 1938 Hurricane.

121. "Dunn's Corners Fire Department, 1942-1992: 50th Anniversary" booklet published by DCFD, 1992.

122. Ibid.

123. U.S. Social Security Death Index, 1935-2014, Henry M. Morris, SSN: 036073800.

124. "Glorified the Turkey" *Norwich Bulletin*, 23 December 1913.

125. Rhode Island Births and Christenings, 1600-1914, Horace Vose, May 1840; and death record of Oscar Vose, 11 January 1927.

126. Household of Charles B. Vose, Westerly, Washington, Rhode Island, 1860 United States Census, Family No. 295; and Household of Horace Vose, Westerly,

Washington, Rhode Island, 1865 Rhode Island Census, Line Number: 28, Household number: 434, Volume Number: 3, Page Number: 127.

127. Household of Horace Vose, Westerly, Washington, Rhode Island, 1900 United States Census, Page: 29; Enumeration District: 0241; FHL microfilm: 1241513.

128. The Old Stone Bank, "The Rhode Island Turkey," (1931), pg. 7.

129. Palmer, Henry Robinson, "Where the President's Turkey Comes From" The Ladies' *Home Journal*, November 1901.

130. "The Rhode Island Turkey,"

131. "The Rhode Island Turkey,"

132. United States Senate, "Henry B. Anthony: A Featured Biography, https://www.senate.gov/artandhistory/history/common/generic/Featured_Bio_Ant hony.htm.

133. "The Rhode Island Turkey,"

134. Ibid.

135. Palmer.

136. "Has Furnished Turkey" *Dakota Farmers' Leader* (Canton, S.D.), 12 December 1902.

137. Westerly City Directories, 1873-1913, Ancestry.com.

138. *The Courier* (Waterloo, IA), 30 January 1878.

139. Palmer.

140. "A Land of Turkeys" *The Evening Star* (Washington, D.C.), 25 November 1893.

141. "Joint Sale of Trotting Stock" pamphlet, (Westerly, RI), 21 March 1893.

142. "Glorified the Turkey" *Norwich Bulletin*, 23 December 1913.

143. "Whence Come the Best Turkeys" *New York Herald*, 23 December 1894.

144. Ibid.

145. "The National Bird" *Evening Star* (Washington D.C.), 25 November 1896.

146. "Whence Come the Best Turkeys"

147. "Whence Come the Best Turkeys"

148. Palmer.

149. "The Rhode Island Turkey,"

150. Ibid.

151. Gravestone of Horace Vose, FindAGrave, Memorial No. 62611416.

152. "The Rhode Island Turkey"

153. Death record of Horace Vose, Rhode Island Vital Records.

154. *Norwich Bulletin*, 17 November 1916.

155. Benson, Brad, "Village of the Soul: The Life of a Jewish Community" (Westerly, RI, 2004).

156. Ibid.

157. Ibid.

158. Ibid.

159. Solovelitz, Ella, "A Study of the Jewish Population of the Town of Westerly, Rhode Island" *Rhode Island Jewish Historical Notes*, vol. 3, No. 1, pg. 141.

160. Benson.

161. Solovelitz.

162. Ibid, 146.

163. Ibid, 141.

164. Westerly Land Deeds, Book 44, pgs. 403,-404.

165. Solovelitz, 142.

166. "Local Synagogue to Raise Funds for Jewish Hospital" *Westerly Sun*, 29 April 1931; and "Open Local Campaign To Aid Jewish Refugees In Europe" *Westerly Sun*, 5 October 1937.

167. "Sharah Zedek Women to Organize Sisterhood" *Westerly Sun*, 5 May 1946.

168. "Tarzan Brown Enjoys First Trip on Sea" *Westerly Sun*, 14 July 1936.

169. Benson.

170. Ibid.

171. "21 In Sharah Zedek School" *Westerly Sun*, 14 September 1953.

172. *Westerly Sun*, 6 August 1968.

173. Ibid.

Chapter V

1. Information provided in unpublished research courtesy of Thomas A. O'Connell.

2. "The Gridiron Field." *Westerly Sun*, 22 October 1893.

3. All references to team records over extended periods were calculated by the author using a variety of sources.

4.   It should be noted that only two of their wins, 1899 and 1900, are true state-wide championships. The other fourteen championships were in the division in which Westerly played that season and they did not play the winners of other divisions.

5.   "The Gridiron Field."

6.   Westerly Sun football game accounts, 1893.

7.   "Football." Advertisement, *Westerly Sun*, November 1893.

8.   Westerly Sun football game accounts, 1895-1922. Westerly High School, The Senior, 1900-1922, courtesy of the Westerly Public Library.

9.   Westerly High School, *The Senior*, 18 December 1903, courtesy of the Westerly Public Library.

10. Westerly High School, *The Senior*, 1917, courtesy of the Westerly Public Library.

11. *Westerly Sun*, 22 November 1985, excerpts from *Westerly Sun*, 18 November 1917.

12. Westerly High School, *The Senior*, 1917, courtesy of the Westerly Public Library.

13. Westerly High School, Senior, Yearbook, 1945-1947.

14. Gentile, Donald L, *Goose Gentile's Scrapbook*, (2012).

15. Westerly High School, Senior, Yearbook, 1966-1967.

16. Westerly High School, Senior, Yearbook, 1974-1975.

17. RI High School Sports, 1973 Football Postseason Results, http://www.rihssports.com/POSTSEASON/RESULTS/PAST/BOYS/FOOTBAL L/1973%20Football%20Postseason%20Results.htm.

18. Westerly High School, Senior, Yearbook, 1974-1975.

19. RI High School Sports, 1974 Football Postseason Results, http://www.rihssports.com/POSTSEASON/RESULTS/PAST/BOYS/FOOTBAL L/1974%20Football%20Postseason%20Results.htm.

20. Advertisement, *Westerly Sun*, 15 September 1974, Fall Sports Preview, Radio Broadcast Advertisement.

21. Westerly High School, Senior, Yearbook, 1986.

22. Westerly High School, Senior, Yearbook, 1986.

23. RI High School Sports, 1985 Football Postseason Results, http://www.rihssports.com/POSTSEASON/RESULTS/PAST/BOYS/FOOTBAL L/1985%20Football%20Postseason%20Results.htm and RI High School Sports, Westerly vs. Stonington, http://www.rihssports.com/Thanksgiving%20Football/Results/WES%20VS%20ST ON.htm.

24. Kimberlin, Keith, "Bulldogs' Wrestling Foe All Too Familiar" *Westerly Sun*, 6 December 2002.

25. RI High School Sports, 2011 Football Postseason Results, http://www.rihssports.com/POSTSEASON/RESULTS/PAST/BOYS/FOOTBAL L/2011%20Football%20Postseason%20Results.html

26. MaxPreps, 2017 and 2018 Westerly High School Football Player Stats, https://www.maxpreps.com/high-schools/westerly-bulldogs-(westerly,ri)/football-fall-17/stats.htm and https://www.maxpreps.com/high-schools/westerly-bulldogs-(westerly,ri)/football-fall-18/stats.htm.

27. Donald M. Panciera, Westerly, Washington, Rhode Island, 1935 Rhode Island State Census, Record No. 532335; and Household of James L. Panciera, Westerly, Washington, Rhode Island, 1930 United States Federal Census, Enumeration District: 0022; FHL microfilm: 2341916.

28. Champion, Doug, "Don Panciera remembered as 'one of the greatest'" *Westerly Sun*, 11 March 2012.

29. Ibid.

30. Ibid.

31. Rhode Island High School Sports database, RI State Football Champions, http://www.rihssports.com/CHAMPIONS/BOYS/FOOTBALL/Football%20State %20Champions.htm.

32. "Don Panciera remembered as 'one of the greatest'"

33. Ibid and "Maroon Backs Outweigh H.C." *New Orleans Times-Picayune*, 19 December 1945.

34. "Holy Cross, La Salle Tied 6-6 in CYO Tilt" *Baton Rouge Advocate*, 24 December 1945; and "Catholic Clubs Play Tie at New Orleans" *The News and Observer* (Raleigh, NC), 24 December 1945, pg. 6.

35. "Don Panciera remembered as 'one of the greatest'"

36. "Late Tally Gives Boston College 13-7 Victory Over Crimson Tide" *The Stars and Stripes*, 25 November 1946.

37. MacCambridge, Michael, *ESPN College Football Encyclopedia*, (2005), pg. 173 and "Boston College Plucks Violets, 72-6" *Boston Globe*, 3 November 1946, pg. 25.

38. Boston College, 1947 Yearbook, NYU Game Summary.

39. Boston College, 1947 Yearbook, Georgetown Game Summary.

40. "Late Tally Gives Boston College 13-7 Victory Over Crimson Tide" and MacCambridge, 81.

41. Ibid, 173, 1205.

42. "Myers Hits 'Theft' of USF Star" *The Stars and Stripes*, 28 August 1947.

43. "Don Panciera remembered as 'one of the greatest'"

44. MacCambridge, 1208-1209 and 1947 San Francisco Dons Schedule and Results, Sports-Reference, College Football.

45. MacCambridge, 1213 and 1948 San Francisco Dons Schedule and Results, Sports-Reference, College Football.

46. "Don Panciera remembered as 'one of the greatest'"

47. Database-Football.com, 1949 NFL Player Draft, https://web.archive.org/web/20080327010859/http://www.databasefootball.com/draft/draftyear.htm?yr=1949&lg=NFL.

48. "Don Panciera remembered as 'one of the greatest'"

49. Database-Football.com, 1949 AAFC Season Scores, Schedules and Playoffs, https://web.archive.org/web/20070408203105/http://www.databasefootball.com/boxscores/scheduleyear.htm?lg=aafc&yr=1949.

50. "Don Panciera Married to Miss Gloria Bruno" *Providence Journal*, 3 January 1950.

51. All-America Football Conference Encyclopedia, Professional Football Researchers Association: AAFC Committee, 1950 Allocation Draft, pg. 7, https://web.archive.org/web/20140929212008/http://www.profootballresearchers.org/AAFC/Allocation_Draft.pdf.

52. "Panciera to Join Lion Eleven in Detroit" *Hartford Courant*, 7 November 1950.

53. Pro-Football-Reference, 1950 Detroit Lions, https://www.pro-football-reference.com/teams/det/1950.htm.

54. "Don Panciera Cut from Lions' Squad" *Providence Journal*, 12 August 1951.

55. "Don Panciera Signs with Chicago Cards" *Boston Traveler*, 18 July 1952.

56. Pro-Football-Reference, Don Panciera Page, https://www.pro-football-reference.com/players/P/PancDo20.htm.

57. "Chicago Cardinals Sign Two Quarterbacks" *Arkansas Democrat*, 9 July 1953; and "Toronto Contracts Passer Panciera" *The Stars and Stripes*, 16 August 1953.

58. "Argos Release Sub Quarter Panciera" *The Lethbridge Herald*, 22 September 1953.

59. "Notable Imports" *The Lethbridge Herald*, 14 July 1954.

60. "AIC Team Must Face Don Panciera's Passes" *Springfield Union*,

61. McHenry, Joe, "Don Panciera, Ex- La Salle Athlete, Named Dayton Backfield Coach" *Providence Journal*, 28 February 1956 and "Don Panciera Named B.C. Football Aide" *Providence Journal*, 2 February 1959.

62. "Don Panciera remembered as 'one of the greatest'"

63. Ibid.

64. Ibid.

65. Ibid.

66. Baseball Reference, Philadelphia Phillies Team Page, https://www.baseball-reference.com/teams/PHI/.

67. Eddie Sawyer Biography, SABR, https://sabr.org/bioproj/person/a54376db.

68. SABR Biography.

69. "The Senior" Westerly High School Yearbook, 1927, pg. 33.

70. SABR Biography.

71. "Sawyer Upsets Durocher Theory That 'Nice Guys Finish Last'" *Westerly Sun*, 27 September 1950.

72. SABR Biography and Ithaca College, "The Cayugan 1935" (1935). The Cayugan 1926-1939. 12, https://digitalcommons.ithaca.edu/cayugan_1926-1939/12.

73. Ibid.

74. "Sawyer Upsets Durocher Theory That 'Nice Guys Finish Last'"

75. "I'm Glad We're Out of Baseball" *Philadelphia Inquirer Magazine*, 6 June 1954, pg. 10.

76. SABR Biography.

77. Ibid.

78. Ibid.

79. "Eddie Sawyer, 87, Manager of Phillies' 'Whiz Kids' in 1950" *Philadelphia Inquirer*, 23 September 1997.

80. "Sawyer Upsets Durocher Theory That 'Nice Guys Finish Last'"

81. SABR Biography.

82. Ibid.

83. Ibid.

84. Ibid.

85. "Sawyer Upsets Durocher Theory That 'Nice Guys Finish Last'"

86. SABR Biography.

87. Baseball Reference, Philadelphia Phillies 1950 Team Page.

88. SABR Biography.

89. Ibid.

90. SABR Biography.

91. "Eddie Sawyer, Phillie Pilot, Is Named '50 Manager of the Year" *Westerly Sun*, 9 November 1950.

92. "Sawyer to Get Trophy" *Westerly Sun*, 8 February 1951.

93.   "Sawyer's Achievement Is Hailed In Resolution of Town Council" *Westerly Sun*, 3 October 1950.

94.   "Home Town Key" *Westerly Sun*, 15 December 1950.

95.   "Eddie Sawyer Honored by Home Town" *Westerly Sun*, 9 January 1951.

96.   SABR Biography.

97.   Ibid.

98.   Ibid.

99.   Ibid.

100. "Eddie Sawyer, 87, Manager of Phillies' 'Whiz Kids' in 1950"

101. Baseball Reference, 1969 MLB Season Standings, https://www.baseball-reference.com/leagues/MLB/1969-standings.shtml.

102. SABR Biography.

103. "Eddie Sawyer, 87, Manager of Phillies' 'Whiz Kids' in 1950"

104. SABR Biography.

105. "Little League Chronology" Little League Online, https://web.archive.org/web/20070514082522/http://www.littleleague.org/about/chronology.asp.

106. Ibid.

107. "Rhode Island teams at the Little League World Series" *NBC10 News*, 12 August 2014.

108. "Four Pint-Sized Westerly Teams Battle for Pennant in State's Only Little League" *Westerly Sun*, 27 July 1950.

109. "Small Fry Baseball" *Providence Sunday Journal*, 12 August 1951.

110. "Four Pint-Sized Westerly Teams Battle for Pennant in State's Only Little League"

111. "Little League Deal" *Westerly Sun*, 21 June 1950.

112. "Four Pint-Sized Westerly Teams Battle for Pennant in State's Only Little League"

113. "Westerly Little League Members Feted" *Providence Evening Bulletin*, 31 August 1950.

114. "Four Pint-Sized Westerly Teams Battle for Pennant in State's Only Little League"

115. "Little League Donations Amount to $1,537.81" *Westerly Sun*, 3 August 1950.

116. "Local Little Leaguers Win" *Westerly Sun*, 6 August 1950.

117. "Locals Qualify for Regionals at Schenectady, NY Next Weekend" *Westerly Sun*, 13 August 1950.

118. Ibid.

119. "Westerly Defeats Pittsfield To Win Little League Tourney" *Berkshire Eagle*, 4 August 1950.

120. "Locals Qualify for Regionals at Schenectady, NY Next Weekend"

121. "Westerly Defeats Pittsfield To Win Little League Tourney"

122. "Port Chester Termed Polio Epidemic Area" *Poughkeepsie Journal*, 16 August 1950.

123. "Garafolo, Bailey, Sposato, Lead Locals to Victory at Schenectady" *Westerly Sun*, 20 August 1950.

124. Ibid.

125. "Local Nine Qualifies for Little World Series in Williamsport" *Westerly Sun*, 21 August 1950.

126. "Westerly All-Stars Victims of No-Hitter in Loss to Houston" *Westerly Sun*, 25 August 1950.

127. Ibid.

128. 1950 Little League World Series Bracket, http://www.littleleague.org/series/history/year/1950.htm.

129. "Westerly Little League Members Feted"

130. "Westerly Pockets Little League Title, 1-0, Over Bristol" *Providence Evening Bulletin*, 13 August 1950.

131. "Westerly Lad Makes Big Bid for Spot in Braves' Lineup" *Westerly Sun*, 4 May 1960.

132. "John Garofalo" [sic] Baseball Reference, https://www.baseball-reference.com/register/player.fcgi?id=garofa001joh.

133. Mrs. John Garafolo Jr." *Westerly Sun*, Marriage Announcement; and "Awarded Grant" *Westerly Sun*.

134. 1996 Little League World Series Recap, https://web.archive.org/web/20170930051209/http://www.littleleague.org/series/history/year/1996.htm.

135. David Stenhouse, 1935 Rhode Island State Census, No. 343545.

136. "Mike Stenhouse" *Springfield Union* (MA), 14 December 1985, pg. 8.

137. "Dave Stenhouse Gets Plaque at Providence Event" *New London Day*, 25 January 1952.

138. "Dave Stenhouse Signs Pact with National League Cubs" *Westerly Sun*, 29 June 1955; and 1953-54 Rhode Island Rams Roster and Stats, https://www.sports-reference.com/cbb/schools/rhode-island/1954.html.

139. Ibid.

140. Ibid and "Stenhouse Will Return to Demons"

141. Ibid.

142. Ibid.

143. Scouting Report, Dave Stenhouse, 25 June 1955, Branch Rickey Collection, Library of Congress.

144. "Dave Stenhouse Minor League Statistics and History". Baseball-Reference.com.

145. Ibid.

146. Ibid and "Fires 7-Hitter—Raps 2 Vital Blows Himself"

147. "Hurls No Hitter" *Billings Gazette* (MT), 22 June 1958, pg. 18.

148. Transactions, Associated Press, 3 December 1958.

149. "Left DeMars Makes Western Loop All-Stars" *Hartford Courant*, 15 September 1958, pg. 15.

150. "Minor League Draft Moves Five Pioneer Loop Players" *Great Falls Tribune* (MT), 3 December 1958, pg. 19.

151. "Dave Stenhouse Minor League Statistics and History"

152. Ibid.

153. "Dave Stenhouse is Recipient of Look Award" *Westerly Sun*, 8 October 1961.

154. "Mets Obtain Neal" *Bridgeport Post* (CT), 17 December 1961, pg. 87.

155. "Dave Stenhouse Major League Statistics and History," "1962 Washington Senators" Baseball-Reference.com; and "Stenhouse No Rookie On Hill" *Baltimore Sun*, 12 May 1962, pg. 10; and "Senators Find Ace Hurler In Rookie Dave Stenhouse" *The Daily Mail* (Hagerstown, MD), 17 May 1962, pg. 41; and "Hurler Dave Stenhouse sometimes does 'kooky' things off diamond" *Honolulu Star-Bulletin*, 24 March 1966, pg. 50.

156. "'The Happiest Day of My Baseball Life'" *Westerly Sun*, 6 August 1962.

157. Ibid.

158. "Rookie Dave Stenhouse R.I. Athlete Of Year" *Newport Daily News*, 15 January 1963, pg. 10; and "1962 Washington Senators" Baseball-Reference.com.

159. "Dave Stenhouse Major League Statistics and History"

160. Ibid.

161. Ibid.

162. "Baseball Coach" *Honolulu Star Bulletin*, 5 December 1968, pg. 58.

163. "Transactions" Associated Press, 9 March 1990.

164. Excerpt from Martha Mitchell's *Encyclopedia Brunoniana*, entry for 'Baseball.'

165. "R.I. Nine Boasts High Averages" *Newport Daily News*, 2 July 1974, pg. 11.

166. Toobin, Jeffery R., "Mike Stenhouse Meets Charles O. Finley" *Harvard Crimson*, 6 November 1979.

167. Baseball Almanac Entry, Mike Stenhouse, http://www.baseball-almanac.com/players/player.php?p=stenhmi01.

168. "Mike Stenhouse Minor League Statistics and History". Baseball-Reference.com.

169. Baseball Almanac Entry, Mike Stenhouse, http://www.baseball-almanac.com/players/player.php?p=stenhmi01.

170. Perrault, Denise,"Mike Stenhouse: Too much taxing, regulation making state uncompetitive". *Providence Business News*, 8 January 2011.

171. Baseball Reference, Dave Stenhouse Jr., Bullpen, https://www.baseball-reference.com/bullpen/Dave_Stenhouse,_Jr.

172. Ibid.

173. Ibid.

174. "Westerly Slasher Held" *Norwich Evening Bulletin*, 4 January 1913.

175. "Local Laconics" *Norwich Evening Bulletin*, 18 January 1909.

176. *Norwich Evening Bulletin*, 9 April 1909.

177. "Collins Meets Abe Again." *Norwich Evening Bulletin*, 2 March 1909.

178. "McGrath Too Rough for Westerly" *Norwich Evening Bulletin*, 24 March 1909.

179. "McGrath Gets Two on Chief Fighting Bear" *Norwich Evening Bulletin*, 27 December 1909.

180. "Collins Signs With Clayton" *Norwich Evening Bulletin*, 17 February 1910.

181. "Features in Wrestling and Boxing" *Norwich Evening Bulletin*, 4 March 1910; and "Boxing for Bill Collins" *Norwich Bulletin*, 19 August 1910; and "To Settle Which is the Better Man" *Norwich Evening Bulletin*, 3 May 1910.

182. "Bill Collins Back into the Wrestling Game" *Norwich Evening Bulletin*, 25 August 1911.

183. "Bill Collins Had Successful Wrestling Tour" *Norwich Evening Bulletin*, 2 February 1912; and "Stage Show." *Norwich Evening Bulletin*, 15 September 1911.

184. *Norwich Evening Bulletin*, 25 January 1912.

185. "Wants to Meet Collins" *Norwich Evening Bulletin*, 7 November 1911.

186. "Collins Turned Tables on Charlie Rogers" *Norwich Evening Bulletin*, 2 January 1912.

187. Ibid.

188. "Parker Took Two Falls" *Norwich Evening Bulletin*, 16 February 1912.

189. "Westerly Wrestling a Fizzle" *Norwich Evening Bulletin*, 23 March 1912.

190. Ibid.

191. "Where Doc Roller Was" *Norwich Evening Bulletin*, 28 March 1912.

192. "Collins Not in Court at Westerly" *Norwich Evening Bulletin*, 28 December 1912.

193. "Prison for Westerly Stabber" *Norwich Evening Bulletin*, 18 February 1913.

194. "Two Decisions by Judge Reed" *Norwich Evening Bulletin*, 27 February 1914; and "Bill Collins Meets Young Dementhral" *Norwich Evening Bulletin*, 25 December 1913.

195. *Norwich Evening Bulletin*, 3 September 1917; and *Norwich Evening Bulletin*, 18 September 1919, pg. 10; and *Norwich Evening Bulletin*, 12 June 1922, pg. 6.

196. Ellison Brown, 1936 Rhode Island Census, Card No. 371025, Tract 340, 1915 Rhode Island Census, Enumeration District 444, Family No. 46; and 1920 United States Census, Enumeration District 360, Family No. 118, 1925 Rhode Island Census, Enumeration District 380, Family No. 86; and 1930 United States Census, Enumeration District 5-5, Family No. 485; and birth record of Ellison Myers Brown, Westerly, Rhode Island.

197. Census Records, See No. 1.

198. "Injuries Fatal to Olympian Tarzan Brown" *Westerly Sun*, 24 August 1975.

199. "Westerly Boy Becomes National Hero of Sporting World Over Night" *Westerly Sun*, 21 April 1936.

200. "'Tarzan' to Have His Night Tonight" *Providence Evening Bulletin*, 8 November 1974.

201. "Tarzan is Fed Up on Chicken He Says But Likes Plenty of Clams" *Westerly Sun*, 21 May 1939.

202. Szostak, Mike, "Rhode Island's Tarzan: The Legend Remains" *Providence Journal-Bulletin*, 14 April 1979.

203. "Ellison Brown is Ready for Boston Marathon Friday" *Westerly Sun*, 18 April 1935.

204. "Tarzan Brown is Reinstated" *Westerly Sun*, 8 September 1935, pg. 2.

205. Ellison Brown, 1936 Rhode Island Census, Card No. 371025, Tract 340.

206. "Westerly Boy Wins Boston Marathon Defeating Field of 183 Expert Runners" *Westerly Sun*, 20 April 1936.

207. "Rhode Island's Tarzan: The Legend Remains"

208. "Westerly Boy Wins Boston Marathon Defeating Field of 183 Expert Runners"

209. King, Bill, "Brown Heads Selections for Olympics" *Westerly Sun*, 21 April 1936.

210. Vega, Michael, "At Heartbreak Hill, a Salute to a Marathoner for the Ages" *Boston Globe*, 19 April 1993.

211. "Westerly Boy Becomes National Hero of Sporting World Over Night" *Westerly Sun*, 21 April 1936.

212. "State Assembly Joins in Acclaiming Victory of Westerly Indian Runner" *Westerly Sun*, 21 April 1936.

213. "Westerly Boy Becomes National Hero of Sporting World Over Night"

214. "Tarzan Brown Enjoys First Trip on Sea" *Westerly Sun*, 14 July 1936.

215. "KiteiSon Wins Japan's First Major Race" *Westerly Sun*, 9 August 1936.

216. "Brown Drops Out At End of 17th Mile" *Westerly Sun*, 10 August 1936.

217. "Tarzan Brown to Defend His Marathon Title" *Westerly Sun*, 8 April 1937.

218. Ibid.

219. "Stomach Pains Put Tarzan in Background" *Westerly Sun*, 20 April 1937.

220. Ward, Michael, *Ellison Tarzan" Brown: The Narragansett Indian Who Twice Won the Boston Marathon*, (2006), pg. 163.

221. Ibid.

222. "Tarzan Brown is Winner of Boston Marathon; Sets New Record By 3 Minutes" *Westerly Sun*, 19 April 1939.

223. "World's Champion Tells Own Story" *Westerly Sun*, 19 April 1939.

224. "Brown Wins Ten Mile Road Contest Here" *Westerly Sun*, 21 May 1939.

225. Ibid.

226. "Rhode Island's Tarzan: The Legend Remains"

227. Ward, 369.

228. "Denies Damaging Cell" *Providence Journal*, 25 May 1950; and "Charlestown Man Fined" *Providence Journal*, 12 September 1950; and "Denies Assault Count" *Providence Journal*, 19 November 1950; and "Fined for Speeding" *Providence Journal*, 10 February 1951; and "Former Marathon Ace Haled for Breach of Peace" *Providence Journal*, 23 August 1954; and "Tarzan Brown Arrested" *Providence Journal*, 23 August 1954; and "Court Fines 'Tarzan' Brown $40 for Driving Recklessly" *Providence Journal*, 21 June 1955; and "'Tarzan' Brown Displays His Power, Lands in Court" *Providence Journal*, 28 July 1955; and "2 Face Charges in Westerly" *Providence Journal*, 9 June 1958; and "Conviction, Failed to Report an Accident" *Providence Journal*, 5 September 1959.

229. "Tarzan Brown Runs Again" *Providence Journal*, 17 April 1955.

230. "Injuries Fatal to Olympian Tarzan Brown" *Westerly Sun*, 24 August 1975.

Chapter VI

1. Rhode Island General Laws Sect. 11-22-11, http://webserver.rilin.state.ri.us/Statutes/TITLE11/11-22/11-22-11.HTM.

2. McDermott, Jennifer, "That R.I. law against dueling — still used, lawmaker learns" *Providence Journal*, 11 July 2018.

3.   Rhode Island General Laws Chapter 11-12,
      http://webserver.rilin.state.ri.us/Statutes/TITLE11/11-12/INDEX.HTM.

4.   "That R.I. law against dueling — still used, lawmaker learns"

5.   Rhode Island General Laws Sect. 11-12-
      6, http://webserver.rilin.state.ri.us/Statutes/TITLE11/11-12/11-12-6.HTM.

6.   Rhode Island General Laws Sect. 45-16-1,
      http://webserver.rilin.state.ri.us/Statutes/TITLE45/45-16/45-16-1.HTM.

7.   Ibid.

8.   Rhode Island General Laws Sect. 15-1-2,
      http://webserver.rilin.state.ri.us/Statutes/TITLE15/15-1/15-1-2.HTM

9.   Rhode Island General Laws Sect. 15-1-4,
      http://webserver.rilin.state.ri.us/Statutes/TITLE15/15-1/15-1-4.HTM

10.   Rhode Island General Laws Sect. 5-2-9,
      http://webserver.rilin.state.ri.us/Statutes/TITLE5/5-2/5-2-9.HTM

11.   Rhode Island General Laws Sect. 41-6-6,
      http://webserver.rilin.state.ri.us/Statutes/TITLE41/41-6/41-6-6.HTM

12.   Rhode Island General Laws Sect. 9-6-9,
      http://webserver.rilin.state.ri.us/Statutes/TITLE9/9-6/9-6-9.HTM

13.   "Rhode Island Defamation Laws and Standards" R.M. Warner Law Firm,
      https://kellywarnerlaw.com/rhode-island-defamation-laws/.

14.   Rhode Island General Laws Sect. 44-18-30,
      http://webserver.rilin.state.ri.us/Statutes/TITLE44/44-18/44-18-30.HTM.

15.   Fazendeiro, Rory Zack, Sarah K. Heaslip, Melissa Coulombe Beauchesne, and
      Heather M. Spellman, "1999 Survey of Rhode Island Law: Cases: Constitutional Law"
      Roger Williams University Law Review, vol. 5, no. 2, pg. 642.

16.   Ibid.

17.   *The National Cyclopedia of American Biography*, vol. 13, (1906), pg. 333.

18.   *The Sabbath Recorder*, 27 July 1854, vol. 1, no. 7.

19.   *George Herbert Utter Memorial Addresses Delivered in the House of Representatives and the
      Senate of the United States*, (Washington, D.C., 1914), pg. 39.

20.   Ibid, 9.

21.   *The First One Hundred Years: Pawcatuck Seventh Day Baptist Church*, (Westerly, RI, 1940),
      pg. 114.

22.   *George Herbert Utter Memorial Addresses Delivered in the House of Representatives and the
      Senate of the United States*, 9.

23.   Amherst College, *Olio 1877*, pg. 26.

24. Household of George B. Utter, Westerly, Washington, Rhode Island, 1880 United States Census, Roll: 1211; Page: 487C; Enumeration District: 162.

25. Utter Scrapbook, Courtesy of the Westerly Historical Society, Certificate of Appointment as Aide-de-Camp to the Commander in Chief, 29 May 1883.

26. *Representative Men and Old Families of Rhode Island: Genealogical Records and Historical Sketches of Prominent and Representative Citizens and of Many of the Old Families*, (1908), pg. 146.

27. *George Herbert Utter Memorial Addresses Delivered in the House of Representatives and the Senate of the United States*, 39.

28. Ibid, 40.

29. Ibid, 24.

30. Minkins, John C., "There Were Giants in Those Days: George H. Utter" *Providence Daily Evening News*.

31. Utter Scrapbook, Courtesy of the Westerly Historical Society, Letter from Charles R. Brayton to George H. Utter, 3 November 1906.

32. *George Herbert Utter Memorial Addresses Delivered in the House of Representatives and the Senate of the United States*, 40.

33. Memorial & Library Association of Westerly, *Westerly Library and Wilcox Park: Celebrating 125 Years*, (2018), pg. 40.

34. *The First One Hundred Years: Pawcatuck Seventh Day Baptist Church*, 114.

35. Ibid, 135.

36. Utter Scrapbook, Courtesy of the Westerly Historical Society, Letter to George H. Utter from Charles Perry, 11 January 1910.

37. *George Herbert Utter Memorial Addresses Delivered in the House of Representatives and the Senate of the United States*, 40.

38. "1904 Rhode Island Gubernatorial Election" https://en.wikipedia.org/wiki/1904_Rhode_Island_gubernatorial_election

39. "1905 Rhode Island Gubernatorial Election" https://en.wikipedia.org/wiki/1905_Rhode_Island_gubernatorial_election

40. *George Herbert Utter Memorial Addresses Delivered in the House of Representatives and the Senate of the United States*, 10.

41. *New Haven Journal and Courier*, 1 April 1905, pg. 4.

42. "1906 Rhode Island Gubernatorial Election" htts://en.wikipedia.org/wiki/1906_Rhode_Island_gubernatorial_election

43. "1907 Rhode Island Gubernatorial Election" https://en.wikipedia.org/wiki/1907_Rhode_Island_gubernatorial_election

44. "List of United States Representatives from Rhode Island" https://en.wikipedia.org/wiki/List_of_United_States_Representatives_from_Rhode _Island

45. Carlisle Indian School, *The Red Man*, Vol. 4, No. 9, May 1912. http://carlisleindian.dickinson.edu/publications/red-man-vol-4-no-9

46. *The Sabbath Recorder*, 11 November 1912, vol. 73, No. 20, pg. 609.

47. *George Herbert Utter Memorial Addresses Delivered in the House of Representatives and the Senate of the United States*, 15.

48. Ibid, 43.

49. Counting The Votes, Election of 1920, http://www.countingthevotes.com/1920/.

50. Counting The Votes, Election of 1912, http://www.countingthevotes.com/1912/ and Counting The Votes, Election of 1916, http://www.countingthevotes.com/1916/.

51. 1920 Presidential General Election Results – Rhode Island, https://uselectionatlas.org/RESULTS/state.php?year=1920&fips=44&f=1&off=0& elect=0.

52. "Proclamation That Suffrage Has Been Ratified Is Signed by Secretary Colby" *Westerly Sun*, 26 August 1920.

53. "Poll Tax for the Year of 1920" *Westerly Sun*, 25 October 1920.

54. "Things Voters Ought to Know" *Westerly Sun*, 26 October 1920.

55. "Council to Canvas the Voting List" *Westerly Sun*, 26 October 1920.

56. "Republican Candidate for Congress" *Westerly Sun*, 27 October 1920.

57. "Westerly Voters to Hear Issues" *Westerly Sun*, 25 October 1920.

58. Ibid.

59. Ibid.

60. "Sweeping Republican Victory Is Predicted at Rally Here" *Westerly Sun*, 28 October 1920.

61. Ibid.

62. "Westerly" *Norwich Bulletin*, 30 October 1920.

63. "Westerly Women to See Ballot" *Westerly Sun*, 31 October 1920.

64. Advertisement, *Westerly Sun*, 31 October 1920.

65. Ibid.

66. "Former Slave First to Vote" *Westerly Sun*, 2 November 1920.

67. "Sun Plans for Election Results" *Westerly Sun*, 1 November 1920.

68. "Election Results by Radio Telephone" *Westerly Sun*, 2 November 1920.

69. "Westerly Strong for Harding" *Westerly Sun*, 3 November 1920.

70. 1920 Presidential General Election Results – Rhode Island.

71. 1920 Presidential General Election Results.

72. "Westerly Leads State in Ratios" *Westerly Sun*, 3 November 1920.

73. "Westerly Sends These Men to the Legislature" *Westerly Sun*, 3 November 1920.

74. "Westerly Leads State in Ratios"

75. 1924 Presidential General Election Results – Rhode Island, https://uselectionatlas.org/RESULTS/state.php?year=1924&fips=44&f=0&off=0&elect=0&minper=0.

76. "Westerly" *Norwich Bulletin*, 9 November 1920.

77. Maine, Birth Records, 1715-1922, Pre 1892 Delayed Returns; Roll Number: 4, Charles E. Bailey.

78. Household of Elbridge G. Bailey, Parkman, Piscataquis, Maine, 1870 United States Census, Roll: M593_556; Page: 152B; Family History Library Film: 552055.

79. Household of Elbridge G. Bailey, Parkman, Piscataquis, Maine, 1870 United States Census, Roll: M593_556; Page: 152B; Family History Library Film: 552055; and Household of Elbridge G. Bailey, Parkman, Piscataquis, Maine, 1880 United States Census, Roll: 487; Page: 17C; Enumeration District: 059.

80. "Westerly" *Norwich Bulletin*, 10 November 1920.

81. "Charles Bailey of Westerly Guilty of Manslaughter" *Norwich Bulletin*, 1 December 1920.

82. U.S. City Directories, 1822-1995, Westerly, Rhode Island, 1919, pg. 38.

83. "Westerly" *Norwich Bulletin*, 10 November 1920.

84. Household of Julia Bailey, Westerly, Washington, Rhode Island, Roll: T625_1681; Page: 12A; Enumeration District: 363.

85. "Westerly" *Norwich Bulletin*, 10 November 1920.

86. "Westerly" *Norwich Bulletin*, 22 November 1920.

87. "Charles Bailey of Westerly Guilty of Manslaughter" *Norwich Bulletin*, 1 December 1920.

88. "Westerly" *Norwich Bulletin*, 25 November 1920.

89. Medical Examiner's Report, "Case of Death of Edgar A. Bailey of the Town of Westerly, R.I., October 26, 1920," pg. 199.

90. Ibid.

91. "Westerly" *Norwich Bulletin*, 25 November 1920.

92. "Charles Bailey of Westerly Guilty of Manslaughter" *Norwich Bulletin*, 1 December 1920.

93. "Westerly" *Norwich Bulletin*, 10 November 1920.

94. "Westerly" *Norwich Bulletin*, 9 November 1920.

95. Ibid.

96. Ibid.

97. "Westerly" *Norwich Bulletin*, 28 October 1920.

98. "Westerly" *Norwich Bulletin*, 9 November 1920.

99. "Westerly" *Norwich Bulletin*, 10 November 1920.

100. Ibid.

101. "Westerly" *Norwich Bulletin*, 9 November 1920.

102. "Westerly" *Norwich Bulletin*, 10 November 1920.

103. "Westerly" *Norwich Bulletin*, 17 November 1920.

104. Ibid.

105. "Westerly" *Norwich Bulletin*, 22 November 1920.

106. "Charles Bailey of Westerly Guilty of Manslaughter" *Norwich Bulletin*, 1 December 1920.

107. Ibid.

108. "Charles Bailey of Westerly Guilty of Manslaughter" *Norwich Bulletin*, 1 December 1920.

109. Ibid.

110. Ibid.

111. Ibid.

112. Ibid.

113. Ibid.

114. Ibid.

115. Ibid.

116. "Westerly" *Norwich Bulletin*, 6 December 1920.

117. "Westerly" *Norwich Bulletin*, 30 November 1920.

118. "New England News in Tabloid Form" *Oxford Democrat*, 3 May 1921.

119. Rhode Island State Prison, Cranston, Providence, Rhode Island, 1925 Rhode Island Census, Enumeration District 96, pg. 20.

120. Rhode Island State Prison Records, Rhode Island State Archives, Charles Bailey, No. 24703; and U.S. City Directories, 1822-1995, Westerly, Rhode Island, 1939, pg. 109.

121. Household of Arthur C. Maine, Westerly, Washington, Rhode Island, 1940 United States Census, Roll: m-t0627-03772; Page: 8B; Enumeration District: 5-31.

122. Rhode Island Department of Public Health, Certificate of Death, Charles Bailey, City No. 42-14, State File No. 12.

123. Acri, Calabria, Atto di Nascita, Num. d'ordine 373, Folio 187, 11 December 1864.

124. Naturalization, Supreme Court of Washington County, Rhode Island, 14 July 1902.

125. Rhode Island Public Health Commission, Certificate of Death, No. 78, Christina Bonvenuto, June 9, 1941 and

126. Customs List of Passengers, District of the City of New York, RMS Campania, 8 December 1894.

127. "Not Santa Claus" *Westerly Sun*, December 1908.

128. "There was beer flowing down the gutters…." *Norwich Bulletin*, 15 January 1909.

129. "Natale Benvenuti attempted the Adam and Eve act…" *Norwich Bulletin*, 16 January 1909.

130. "There is certainly a muddle over the status…." *Norwich Bulletin*, 25 March 1911.

131. "The disputed ownership…" *Norwich Bulletin*, 13 February 1912.

132. Ibid.

133. Ibid.

134. "There was a special meeting of the Westerly town council" *Norwich Bulletin*, 15 February 1912.

135. "Local Laconics" *Norwich Bulletin*, 7 April 1913.

136. "Kerosene in Westerly Saloon" *Norwich Bulletin*, 18 April 1913.

137. "The Little Wooden Building" *Norwich Bulletin*, 14 August 1913; and "Wrecked at Last" *Westerly Sun*, August 1913.

138. "The Little Wooden Building" *Norwich Bulletin*, 14 August 1913.

139. "The dynamiters who have made…" *Norwich Bulletin*, 3 November 1913.

140. "In the Superior Court…." *Norwich Bulletin*, 21 April 1914.

141. *Norwich Bulletin*, 12 February 1914.

142. "What is Interesting in Westerly" *Norwich Bulletin*, 10 June 1914.

143. "Cases in Westerly Superior Court" *Norwich Bulletin*, 18 May 1915.

144. "Current Topics in Westerly" *Norwich Bulletin*, 18 May 1915.

145. *Norwich Bulletin*, 16 November 1915.

146.   "Last Tuesday…" *Westerly Sun*, 14 November 1916.

147.   1917 Westerly Directory.

148.   Return of a Death, State of Rhode Island, Natale Bonvenuto, 7 January 1927.

Chapter VII

1.   "Local Laconics" *Norwich Morning Bulletin*, 29 September 1917, pg. 7.

2.   "First in the Nation; Westerly Ambulance Corps is Planning to Celebrate Its 75th Birthday" *Westerly Sun*, 30 August 1992.

3.   "Local Laconics" *Norwich Morning Bulletin*, 10 December 1917, pg. 7; and "Local Laconics" *Norwich Morning Bulletin*, 11 March 1918, pg. 7.

4.   Westerly Ambulance Corps, About Us, History, http://www.westerlyambulance.org/content/history/.

5.   "Local Laconics" *Norwich Morning Bulletin*, 16 May 1918, pg. 7.

6.   Westerly Ambulance Corps, About Us, History, http://www.westerlyambulance.org/content/history/.

7.   "Westerly" *Norwich Morning Bulletin*, 20 October 1919, pg. 7.

8.   "First in the Nation; Westerly Ambulance Corps is Planning to Celebrate Its 75th Birthday" *Westerly Sun*, 30 August 1992.

9.   "Westerly Sanitary Corps Planning to Erect New Building" *Westerly Sun*, 10 February 1920.

10.   "Westerly" *Norwich Morning Bulletin*, 20 November 1920, pg. 9.

11.   Westerly Land Deeds, vol. 49, pg. pg. 69-70.

12.   Westerly Land Deeds, vol. 62, pg. 415-416.

13.   "Testimonial to Dr. F.I. Payne" *Westerly Sun*, 8 January 1926.

14.   "$2.50 Membership in Sanitary Corps Saves Local Family $307." *Westerly Sun*, 31 December 1931.

15.   "First in the Nation; Westerly Ambulance Corps is Planning to Celebrate Its 75th Birthday"

16.   "Sanitary Corps to Open New Rooms This Evening" *Westerly Sun*, 14 December 1934.

17.   "Sanitary Corps Rendered Heroic Service at Time of Hurricane" *Westerly Sun*, 10 October 1938.

18.   Ibid.

19. "The Sanitary Corps" *Westerly Sun*, 1 March 1940.

20. Westerly Land Deeds, vol. 69, pg. 37-38.

21. Westerly Land Deeds, vol. 69, pg. 37-38.

22. Westerly Land Deeds, vol. 69, pg. 190.

23. Westerly Ambulance Corps, About Us, History, http://www.westerlyambulance.org/content/history/.

24. "New Name is Adopted by Local Unit" *Westerly Sun*, 15 January 1956.

25. "Rolling Equipment" *Westerly Sun*, 16 November 1960, pg. 11.

26. "Ambulance Corps Notes 50th Anniversary" *Westerly Sun*, 23 August 1967.

27. "First in the Nation; Westerly Ambulance Corps is Planning to Celebrate Its 75th Birthday"

28. Westerly Ambulance Corps, About Us, History, http://www.westerlyambulance.org/content/history/.

29. Ibid.

30. "The YMCA, 1928-1978: A History of a Half Century of Service of the YMCA in Westerly and Vicinity" (1978), pg. 3.

31. Ibid, 13.

32. "Y.M.C.A. Organized" *Westerly Sun*, 8 April 1894.

33. Ibid.

34. "Y.M.C.A. Disbanded" *Westerly Sun*, 7 September 1894.

35. "The YMCA, 1928-1978: A History of a Half Century of Service of the YMCA in Westerly and Vicinity" 13.

36. Ibid, 14.

37. Ibid.

38. Ibid, 15.

39. Ibid, 16.

40. Ibid, 23.

41. Ibid, 17.

42. Ibid.

43. Ibid, 19.

44. Ibid.

45. Obituary of Grace Panciera, *Westerly Sun*, 7 March 2001.

46. "The YMCA, 1928-1978: A History of a Half Century of Service of the YMCA in Westerly and Vicinity," 20.

47. Advertisements, *Hartford Courant*, 26 May 1988, 4 April 1972, and 14 June 2000.

48. Lavin, Nancy, "Renovated YMCA is 'bright and new'" *Westerly Sun*, 7 September 2013.

49. "The YMCA, 1928-1978: A History of a Half Century of Service of the YMCA in Westerly and Vicinity," 11.

50. Nilsson, Casey, "New Bookstore Alert: Savoy Bookshop Opens in Westerly" *Rhode Island Monthly*, 29 March 2016.

51. National Register of Historic Places Inventory-Nomination Form, Westerly Downtown Historic District, 1978, pg. 6.

52. Westerly Land Deeds, Book 25, pgs. 90-91.

53. Westerly Land Deeds, Book 21, pgs. 143-144.

54. Parsekian, Penny, "Owners glimpse into landmark's past: The Savoy is for sale" *Westerly Sun: Places in the Sun*, 19 February 1993, pg. 1.

55. *Westerly Weekly*, 26 September 1889, "The Martin House"

56. Westerly City Director, 1892, Martin House advertisement.

57. "Hotel Martin Landmark For 50 Years Closes Doors Tonight" *Westerly Sun*, 20 October 1939; and National Register of Historic Places Inventory-Nomination Form, Westerly Downtown Historic District, 1978, pg. 6.

58. *Sixth Annual Report of the State Board of Soldiers' Relief*, (Providence, RI, 1895), pg. 10.

59. Foster House advertisement, source unknown, courtesy of Westerly Library Local History Collection.

60. Westerly City Director, 1896, Foster House advertisement.

61. Westerly City Director, 1896, Foster House advertisement.

62. Westerly City Director, 1896, Foster House advertisement.

63. "Hotel Bars Raided" *Waterbury Democrat* (CT), 3 May 1897, pg. 2.

64. "Raided Fellow Councilman" *Boston Globe*, 3 May 1897, pg. 2.

65. "Councilman F.B. Cook Resigned" *Boston Globe*, 4 May 1897, pg. 7.

66. "Change in Landlords" *Westerly Sun*, 15 October 1897.

67. "Granite City Hotel Closed" *Westerly Sun*, 13 August 1899.

68. "Hotel to Reopen" *Westerly Sun*, 3 September 1899.

69. "The Granite City Hotel" *Westerly Sun*, 2 October 1899.

70. *Fibre and Fabric*, No. 702, Vol. XXVII, 13 August 1898, pg. 303.

71. *Norwich Morning Bulletin*, 8 May 1911, pg. 7.

72. "Hotel Westerly Guests Flee Fire" *Providence Journal*, 1 August 1951, pg. 2.

73. "Hotel Martin Landmark For 50 Years Closes Doors Tonight" *Westerly Sun*, 20 October 1939.

74. "Hotel Martin Landmark For 50 Years Closes Doors Tonight" *Westerly Sun*, 20 October 1939.

75. "Martin House Deed Filed" *Westerly Sun*, 22 January 1943.

76. "Several Held in Raid on Delman Hotel" *Westerly Sun*, 1 June 1943.

77. Ibid.

78. Ibid.

79. "Several Held in Raid on Delman Hotel" *Westerly Sun*, 1 June 1943.

80. "Delman Hotel Property Sold" *Westerly Sun*, date unknown; and Westerly Land Deeds, vol. 63, pg. 23.

81. "Hotel Named for Westerly" *Westerly Sun*, 2 July 1945.

82. "Owners glimpse into landmark's past: The Savoy is for sale"

83. Westerly City Director, 1954, Hotel Westerly advertisement.

84. "Canal Street Hotel to Be Known as 'Savoy'" *Westerly Sun*, 16 May 1955.

85. Ibid and "Owners glimpse into landmark's past: The Savoy is for sale"

86. "Canal Street Hotel to Be Known as 'Savoy'" *Westerly Sun*, 16 May 1955

87. "Owners glimpse into landmark's past: The Savoy is for sale"

88. Russell, Gloria, "A New Day for the Old Savoy" *Westerly Sun*, 14 July 2007.

89. Westerly Land Deeds, vol. 2013, pg. 11945.

90. "Business College" *Westerly Sun*, 21 January 1898.

91. "Westerly Business College: A Change in Its Management, Mr. Wales, Its Founder, Retiring." *Westerly Sun*, 22 August 1902.

92. "Business College Card" *Westerly Sun*, 23 January 1898.

93. "Westerly Business College: A Change in Its Management, Mr. Wales, Its Founder, Retiring."

94. "Believers in Expansion: The Westerly Business College to Add Another Room to Its Quarters in the Wells Block" *Westerly Sun*, 9 July 1899.

95. "The First Anniversary" *Westerly Sun*, 16 February 1899.

96. "Westerly Business College: A Change in Its Management, Mr. Wales, Its Founder, Retiring."

97. "Westerly Business College" *Pitman's Journal: Devoted to Shorthand, Typewriting and Commercial*, Vol. 4, pg. 338.

98. Ibid.

99. Ibid.

100. Ibid.

101. "New Literary Society Formed" *Westerly Sun*, 20 February 1908.

102. "Stonington: Railroad and Highway Improvements—Local Students Do Good Work in Typewriting Test" *Norwich Bulletin*, 14 March 1910.

103. "Stonington" *Norwich Bulletin*, 8 September 1910.

104. "Showed Their Speed Here." *Norwich Bulletin*, 17 June 1911.

105. "Westerly" *Norwich Bulletin*, 4 October 1912.

106. "To Play Westerly." *Norwich Bulletin*, 6 June 1914.

107. "Principal Canfield Attending Big Meeting of Educators" *Norwich Bulletin*, 27 May 1916.

108. Myers, Harry J., *College and Private School Directory of the United States and Canada*, Volume 13 (1922), pg. 237.

109. Best, 150.

110. Emerson, Margaret, "The Development of the Secondary School in Westerly" (1950), pg. 1; and Best, 146.

111. Carroll, Charles, *Public Education in Rhode Island*, (Providence, RI, 1918), pg. 72; and Addeman, Joshua, *Index to the Printed Acts and Resolves of, and of the Reports to the General Assembly of the State of Rhode Island and Providence Plantations, from the Year 1863 to 1873*, (Providence, RI, 1875), pg. xxxv.

112. Untitled Manuscript, Westerly Historical Society, pg. 2.

113. Addeman, xxxv; and Emerson, 1.

114. Stockwell, Thomas B., *A History of Public Education in Rhode Island from 1636 to 1876*, (Providence, RI, 1876), pg. 19.

115. Emerson, 1.

116. *Westerly Daily Tribune*, "The Old Pawcatuck Academy Building" Engraving, c. 1894.

117. Emerson, 1.

118. Untitled Manuscript, Westerly Historical Society, pg. 1.

119. Stockwell, 50.

120. Emerson, 3.

121. Stockwell, 49.

122. Emerson, 2.

123. *Narragansett Weekly*, 16 September 1858, Engraving of the Westerly Institute.

124. Denison.

125. "The Old Pawcatuck Academy Building" Engraving, c. 1894.

126. Barnard, Henry, *Report and Documents Relating to the Public Schools of Rhode Island for 1848*, (Providence, RI, 1849), pg. 284.

127. *Catalogue of the Officers and Students of the Westerly High School, 1857-1858*, (Westerly, RI, 1859), pg. 7-8.

128. Best, 156.

129. Program, "Rhode Island Teachers' Institute at Westerly, R.I., October 5-7, 1870; and Report of the Dedication of the Elm Street School, Westerly Library Special Collections.

130. Stockwell, 94 and 96.

131. Best, 159.

132. Westerly High School website.

133. "The Washington Trust Company of Westerly, Rhode Island" *The Banker's Magazine*, vol. LXXXIII, 1911, pg. 248.

134. Rhode Island Currency, Timeline of Rhode Island Banking, https://www.ricurrency.com/timeline-of-rhode-island-banking/.

135. Washington Trust, Celebrating 200 Years of Service, *Westerly Sun* Insert, 20 August 2000.

136. The Washington Trust Company, *One Hundred Years of Banking in Westerly*, (Westerly, RI, 1908).

137. Washington Trust, Celebrating 200 Years of Service

138. "Interesting Notes about Interesting Notes" *Paper Money*, vol. XX, No. 5, 252.

139. Washington Trust, Celebrating 200 Years of Service

140. *One Hundred Years of Banking in Westerly*; and Rhode Island Historic Cemetery Commission, Gravestone of Rowse Babcock, http://rihistoriccemeteries.org/newgravedetails.aspx?ID=361513.

141. *One Hundred Years of Banking in Westerly*

142. Cooney, Ralph Bolton, *Westerly's Oldest Witness: How Westerly and the Washington Trust Company Have Progressed Together for 150 Years*, (1950), pg. 62.

143. Ibid, 16.

144. "The Washington Trust Company of Westerly, Rhode Island," 249.

145. Cooney, 80.

146. Chalk, Sandra Kersten, *Washington Trust: Two Hundred Years Along the Pawcatuck*, (2000), pg. 62.

147. George Thurston and Sons Records, Rhode Island Historical Society, Mss 733 Scope.

148. Biographical Directory of the United States Congress, Nathan Fellows Dixon, https://bioguideretro.congress.gov/Home/MemberDetails?memIndex=D000376.

149. Cooney, 81.

150. Biographical Directory of the United States Congress, Nathan Fellows Dixon

151. Cooney, 38.

152. Ibid, 30.

153. "The Washington Trust Company of Westerly, Rhode Island," 249-250, and Cooney, 55.

154. Chalk, 55.

155. "Shocking Affair in Westerly" *Providence Evening Bulletin*, 28 December 1870.

156. "New England News" *Fall River Daily Evening News*, 22 February 1871.

157. "Rewards." *New York Daily Herald*, 19 January 1871.

158. "Will Take Over Bank" *Providence Evening Bulletin*, 25 February 1904.

159. "The Washington Trust Company of Westerly, Rhode Island" 248.

160. Cooney, 81.

161. "The Washington Trust Company of Westerly, Rhode Island," 250.

162. Cooney, 53.

163. Cooney.

164. "Providence Trust Concerns Were Bidders, but the Washington National Bank Was the Highest Bidder for the National Phenix Bank of Westerly" *Providence Evening Bulletin*, 31 May 1901.

165. "The Washington Trust Company of Westerly, Rhode Island," 250.

166. "A Full Century" *Providence Evening Bulletin*, 29 January 1906.

167. "The Washington Trust Company of Westerly, Rhode Island," 250.

168. Cooney, 57.

169. "The Washington Trust Company of Westerly, Rhode Island" The Banker's Magazine, vol. LXXXIII, 1911, pg. 248.

170. "The First National Bank of Hopkinton" Norwich Morning Bulletin, 20 March 1914.

171. Cooney, 59.

172. Washington Trust, Celebrating 200 Years of Service.

173. Cooney, 65.

174. "Westerly." *Providence Evening Bulletin*, 19 March 1920.

175. "Westerly." *Norwich Morning Bulletin*, 3 November 1922.

176. Washington Trust, Celebrating 200 Years of Service.

177. Cooney, 68.

178. Washington Trust, Celebrating 200 Years of Service.

179. Cooney, 72.

180. 200 Washington Trust, Celebrating 200 Years of Service.

181. Cooney, 76.

182. Chalk, 89.

183. Ibid, 93.

184. Ibid, 96.

185. Washington Trust, Celebrating 200 Years of Service.

186. Chalk, 98.

187. Ibid, 103.

188. Washington Trust, Celebrating 200 Years of Service.

189. Ibid.

190. Garceau, Zachary, "Charles Perry: Westerly's Most Ardent Abolitionist" WesterlyLife, https://westerlylife.com/charles-perry-westerlys-most-ardent-abolitionist/.

191. *The Literary Echo*, vol. 1, No. 2, April 10, 1851.

192. *The Literary Echo and Pawcatuck Advertiser*, vol. 1, No. 22, August 23, 1851.

193. *Monthly Bulletin*, Westerly Public Library, Vol. 4, No. 2, December 1898, pg. 6.

194. *Narragansett Weekly*

195. Introduction, Microfilm collection of Narragansett Weekly, courtesy of the Westerly Public Library.

196. Introduction, Microfilm collection of The News and Stillman's Idea, courtesy of the Westerly Public Library.

197. Introduction, Microfilm collection of The News and Stillman's Idea, courtesy of the Westerly Public Library; and entry for Stillman's Idea from the Library of Congress, Chronicling America, https://www.loc.gov/item/sn92064233/.

198. Introduction, Microfilm collection of Westerly Daily Tribune, courtesy of the Westerly Public Library.

199. *Westerly Daily Tribune*, Vol. 20, No. 31, 12 April 1898.

200. *Westerly Daily Tribune*, 29 September 1896.

201. Introduction, Microfilm collection of Westerly Daily Tribune, courtesy of the Westerly Public Library.

202. *Westerly Daily Tribune*

203. *Westerly Daily Tribune*, 27 June 1890.

204. *Westerly Daily Tribune*, 16 February 1889; and *Westerly Daily Tribune*, 27 June 1890.

205. *Westerly Daily Tribune*, 29 September 1896.

206. Introduction, Microfilm collection of Westerly Daily Tribune, courtesy of the Westerly Public Library.

207. Introduction, Microfilm collection of Watch Hill Surf, courtesy of the Westerly Public Library.

208. *Watch Hill Life*, 12 July 1894.

209. *Watch Hill Life*, 12 July 1894.

210. Watch Hill Life entry, Library of Congress, https://chroniclingamerica.loc.gov/lccn/sn92064020/; and Household of John C. Kebabian, New Haven, New Haven, Connecticut, 1900 United States Census, Page: 6; Enumeration District: 0341; FHL microfilm: 1240144.

211. Watch Hill Topics entry, Library of Congress, https://chroniclingamerica.loc.gov/lccn/sn92064240/ and Seaside Topics entry, Library of Congress, https://chroniclingamerica.loc.gov/lccn/sn92064021/.

212. *The Westerly Times*

213. *The Westerly Times*

214. *The Westerly News*, 24 January 1919.

215. Entry for Westerly News from the Library of Congress, Chronicling America, https://www.loc.gov/item/sn92064015/.

216. "Tri-State Agency to Study Proposed Long Island Span" *Westerly Sun*, 16 August 1963.

217. New York Department of Transportation, "Long Island Sound Crossing Feasibility Study" December 2017, pg. 7.

218. Ibid.

219. Utter, Charles W., "Orient Point to Rhode Island Bridge Creating Local Concern" *Westerly Sun*, 13 November 1963.

220. "Long Island Sound Crossing Feasibility Study", pg. 7.

221. "Orient Point to Rhode Island Bridge Creating Local Concern"

222. "Tri-State Agency to Study Proposed Long Island Span"

223. "Orient Point to Rhode Island Bridge Creating Local Concern"

224. "Bridge Project Ends Here" *Westerly Sun*, 9 October 1963.

225. "Orient Point to Rhode Island Bridge Creating Local Concern"

226. "L. I. BRIDGE STUDY STARTED AFRESH; Earlier Plans for 23.4-Mile Span Across the Sound Are Called 'Superficial'; A WIDER REPORT SOUGHT; Committee Governor Named Holds First Meeting on Long-Sought Project" *New York Times*, 23 May 1964.

227. "Tri-State Agency to Study Proposed Long Island Span"

228. "Orient Point to Rhode Island Bridge Creating Local Concern"

229. "Tri-State Agency to Study Proposed Long Island Span"

230. "Orient Point to Rhode Island Bridge Creating Local Concern"

231. Ibid.

232. "Directors Firmly Opposed" *Westerly Sun*, 9 October 1963.

233. "Orient Point to Rhode Island Bridge Creating Local Concern"

234. Ibid.

235. "Long Island Sound Crossing Feasibility Study", pg. 7.

236. "Bridge Project Ends Here"

237. "Orient Point to Rhode Island Bridge Creating Local Concern"

238. "Westbrook, Conn., Proposed Terminus" *Westerly Sun*, 3 February 1964.

239. "A Tunnel Instead of Span" *Westerly Sun*, 3 February 1964.

240. "L. I. BRIDGE STUDY STARTED AFRESH; Earlier Plans for 23.4-Mile Span Across the Sound Are Called 'Superficial'; A WIDER REPORT SOUGHT; Committee Governor Named Holds First Meeting on Long-Sought Project"

241. "Full Survey of L.I. Span Plan Backed" *Westerly Sun*, 23 June 1964.

242. Ibid.

243. "Rhode Island Committee Traces Course" *Westerly Sun*, 19 August 1964.

244. "N.Y. Awards Contracts for Studies" *Westerly Sun*, 29 December 1964.

245. New York Department of Transportation, "Long Island Sound Crossing Feasibility Study", pg. 8.

246. Coyle, Pat,"RI-LI Bridge Unlikely" *Westerly Sun*, 28 June 1979.

247. Coyle, Pat, "Watch Hill-Orient Point Bridge Seen Unfavorable," *Westerly Sun*, 21 September 1979.

248. Finn, Lisa, "New Ferry Added to Cross Sound Ferry Fleet" Patch.com, 3 September 2016.

249. "Second Anniversary of the People's Mission" *Westerly Sun*, 19 March 1907.

250. People's Mission Constitution, Westerly Historical Society Records, Article II

251. People's Mission Constitution, Westerly Historical Society Records, Article III

252. "Second Anniversary of the People's Mission"

253. Ibid.

254. "Interesting Service Held" *Westerly Sun*.

255. "Second Anniversary of the People's Mission"

256. Ibid.

257. "Annual Reports Made on Sunday" *Westerly Sun*, 19 March 1907.

258. "The Work in India Explained" *Westerly Sun*, 9 April 1908.

259. Records of the People's Mission, Westerly Historical Society, 8 April 1908.

260. "Needy Cared For" *Westerly Sun*.

261. Ibid.

262. Ibid.

263. "To Leave Westerly" *Westerly Sun*, 7 October 1909.

264. "Mrs. Dagmar Smith is Dead" *Westerly Sun*, 18 January 1965.

265. "To Leave Westerly"

266. Records of the People's Mission, Westerly Historical Society, 1915-1935.

267. Records of the People's Mission, Westerly Historical Society, 1915-1935.

268. Records of the People's Mission, 43.

269. Records of the People's Mission, Westerly Historical Society, 1915-1935.

270. Records of the People's Mission, Westerly Historical Society, 1915-1935.

271. Records of the People's Mission, Westerly Historical Society, Ledger.

Chapter VIII

1. Driscoll, Robin, "Watch Hill in the Gay Nineties" *Tidings*, July 1983.

2. Ibid.

3. National Register of Historic Places Inventory Nomination Form, Watch Hill Historic District, 1978.

4.   Driscoll.

5.   "Advertisement, *Watch Hill Life*, 12 July 1894.

6.   Driscoll.

7.   Ibid.

8.   Ibid.

9.   "The Bicycle Fete" *Watch Hill Life*, date unknown, in the "Cragie Brae Guestbook" courtesy of the Westerly Historical Society.

10.   Invitation for a Bicycle Meet, Saturday, August 29, 1896, in the "Cragie Brae Guestbook" courtesy of the Westerly Historical Society.

11.   "The 'Martha' of Westerly" *Watch Hill Life*; and "The Steamer Block Island," *Watch Hill Life*, both from the "Cragie Brae Guestbook" courtesy of the Westerly Historical Society, and Stonington and Watch Hill Ferry Advertisement, *Watch Hill Life*, 12 July 1894.

12.   N.Y.N.H & H.R.R. Advertisement, *Watch Hill Life*, 12 July 1894.

13.   Invitation for a Hop, Saturday, July 25, 1895, in the "Cragie Brae Guestbook" courtesy of the Westerly Historical Society.

14.   Invitation for the Red Golf Coat Hop, Saturday, July 22, 1899, in the "Cragie Brae Guestbook" courtesy of the Westerly Historical Society.

15.   "First Annual Ball" Watch Hill Life in the "Cragie Brae Guestbook" courtesy of the Westerly Historical Society.

16.   Ibid.

17.   Account of the Larkin House Minstrel Company Concert, *Watch Hill Life* in the "Cragie Brae Guestbook" courtesy of the Westerly Historical Society.

18.   Invitation for the Opening of the Misquamicut Golf Club, Thursday, July 4, 1895, in the "Cragie Brae Guestbook" courtesy of the Westerly Historical Society.

19.   "Tennis at Watch Hill" *Watch Hill Life*, 23 July 1894.

20.   "A Challenge Game" *Watch Hill Life*, 15 July 1896, and "Monday's Ball Game" *Watch Hill Life*, 22 July 1896.

21.   "The Bicycle Fete"

22.   Ibid.

23.   Ibid.

24.   Ibid.

25.   Account from *Watch Hill Life*, in the "Cragie Brae Guestbook" courtesy of the Westerly Historical Society; and Cripps, Aaron, "Women on the Move: Cycling and the Rational Dress Movement" Cycling History,

https://cyclehistory.wordpress.com/2015/01/30/women-on-the-move-cycling-and-the-rational-dress-movement/.

26. *Representative Men and Old Families of Rhode Island: Genealogical Records and Historical Sketches of Prominent and Representative Citizens and of Many of the Old Families*, vol. III, (Chicago, IL, 1908), pg. 1627.

27. "Fire Wipes Out Opera House, Two Tenement Buildings Lost, Four Families Are Homeless," *Westerly Sun*, 4 January 1925.

28. Bliven Opera House Collection, Westerly Historical Society.

29. Ibid.

30. Ibid.

31. "Fire Wipes Out Opera House, Two Tenement Buildings Lost, Four Families Are Homeless," *Westerly Sun*, 4 January 1925.

32. O'Connell, Tom A., *Westerly's Gold*, pg. 34.

33. "Memorial Service in Honor of Hon. George H. Utter" *The Sabbath Recorder*, Volume 73, pg. 809.

34. O'Connell, Tom A., *In and About Westerly*, pg. 142.

35. Ibid, 148.

36. "Fire Wipes Out Opera House, Two Tenement Buildings Lost, Four Families Are Homeless,"

37. Ibid.

38. Ibid.

39. Ibid.

40. Ibid.

41. U.S. City Directories, 1822-1995, Westerly, Rhode Island, 1962, pg. 11.

42. Buicks.net, 1962, https://www.buicks.net/years/62.php

43. *The Jewelers' Circular*, Vol. 87, Issue 2, 1923, pg. 96.

44. Correspondence from Carol Itteilag, September 2020.

45. U.S. City Directories, 1822-1995, Westerly, Rhode Island, 1962, pg. 11.

46. Howell, Sarah Rees, *Ringo's Gift*, 2008, pg. 188.

47. Westerly Land Deeds, Book 66, pg. 372, 11 June 1948.

48. Vintage Dancer, 1960s Shoes: 8 Popular Shoe Styles, https://vintagedancer.com/1960s/1960s-shoes-8-popular-shoe-styles/.

49. U.S. City Directories, 1822-1995, Westerly, Rhode Island, 1962, pg. 32.

50. Advertisement, Westerly High School Yearbook, 1962.

51. Correspondence from Carol Itteilag, September 2020.

52. Correspondence from P.C. Wilson, September 2020.

53. U.S. City Directories, 1822-1995, Westerly, Rhode Island, 1962, Advertisement.

54. Obituary, Kaliope "Kay" (Lanides) Tsouris, https://www.buckler-johnston.com/tributes/Kaliope-Tsouris.

55. Correspondence from Richard Yost, September 2020.

56. U.S. City Directories, 1822-1995, Westerly, Rhode Island, 1962, pg. 32.

57. Fall River Historical Society, Marita Frances (Vokes) Harnett Photo Gallery, https://lizzieborden.org/WomenatWork/marita-harnett-photo-gallery/.

58. Advertisement, Westerly High School, *The Barker*, 1962.

59. Rhode Island Radio, "Radio Sales and Service" http://www.61thriftpower.com/riradio/stores.shtml.

60. Advertisement, Westerly High School, *The Barker*, 1962.

61. U.S. City Directories, 1822-1995, Westerly, Rhode Island, 1962, Advertisement.

62. U.S. City Directories, 1822-1995, Westerly, Rhode Island, 1956.

63. Bata Bullets Advertisement, *Boston Globe*, 24 June 1965; and U.S. Keds Booster Advertisement, *Providence Journal*, 1 May 1955.

64. Correspondence from P.C. Wilson, September 2020.

65. Correspondence from Carol Itteilag, September 2020.

66. Correspondence from Ellen Madison, September 2020.

67. U.S. City Directories, 1822-1995, Westerly, Rhode Island, 1962, pg. 15.

68. "Art Deco Commercial Architecture: Montgomery Ward's Mid-Size Department Stores and Child's Restaurant Exhibit" Tiles in New York, 1 June 2017, https://tilesinnewyork.blogspot.com/2017/06/art-deco-commercial-architecture.html.

69. Bartlett, Richard A., *The World of Ham Radio, 1901-1950: A Social History*, (2015), pg. 198.

70. U.S. City Directories, 1822-1995, Westerly, Rhode Island, 1962, pg. 15

71. Advertisement for Knickerbocker, *Westerly Sun*, 21 November 1979.

72. Concert Page, Rhode Island Rocks, http://www.rirocks.net/Band%20Articles/Stevie%20Ray%20Vaughan%201979%2011.22%20-%20Roadhouse.htm.

73. Huey, Steve, "Review for 'The Sky is Crying'" AllMusic, https://www.allmusic.com/album/the-sky-is-crying-mw0000598616.

74. Correspondence from Greg Piccolo, 7 October 2017.

75.   Entry for We Are Double Trouble! From Discogs.com, Dandelion 008/009/0010/0011/0012, https://www.discogs.com/Stevie-Ray-Vaughan-We-Are-Called-Double-Trouble/release/8494447.

76.   Patoski, Joe Nick; Crawford, Bill, *Stevie Ray Vaughan: Caught in the Crossfire*, (Little, Brown and Company, 1993), pg. 152.

77.   Associated Press, "Vaughan Just Peaking, Stunned Colleagues Say" *Westerly Sun*, 28 August 1990.

78.   Ibid.

79.   Gregory, Hugh, *Roadhouse Blues: Stevie Ray Vaughan and Texas R&B*, (2003), pg. 72.

INDEX

C

D

H

I

J

K

L

N

O

P

Y

Made in United States
Orlando, FL
12 March 2022

15716696R00217